Reform and Intellectual Debate
in Victorian England

WORLD AND WORD SERIES
Edited by Professor Isobel Armstrong,
University of Southampton

REFORM AND INTELLECTUAL DEBATE IN VICTORIAN ENGLAND

Edited by
Barbara Dennis and David Skilton

CROOM HELM
London • New York • Sydney

© 1987 Barbara Dennis and David Skilton
Croom Helm Ltd, Provident House,
Burrell Row, Beckenham, Kent BR3 1AT

Croom Helm Australia, 44 – 50 Waterloo Road,
North Ryde, 2113, New South Wales

Published in the USA by
Croom Helm
in association with Methuen, Inc.
29 West 35th Street,
New York, NY 10001

British Library Cataloguing in Publication Data

Reform and intellectual debate in Victorian England
   1. England—Social Conditions—19th century—
Sources
   I. Dennis, Barbara   II. Skilton, David
   III. Word for word series
   942.081   HN385

   ISBN 0 – 7099 – 2375 – 9
   ISBN 0 – 7099 – 5428 – X (Pbk.)

Library of Congress Cataloging-in-Publication Data

Reform and intellectual debate in Victorian England / edited by
   Barbara Dennis and David Skilton.
      p.   cm. — (World and word series)
   Bibliography: p.
   Includes index.
   ISBN 0-7099-2375-9. ISBN 0-7099-5428-X (pbk.)
   1. Great Britain — History — Victoria, 1837-1901 — Sources. 2. Great
Britain — Intellectual life — 19th century — Sources. I. Dennis,
Barbara, 1942-   II. Skilton, David. III. Series.
DA550.R43   1987
941.082 — dc 19   87-21726

Photocomposition by Pat and Anne Murphy,
Highcliffe-on-Sea, Dorset

Printed and bound in Great Britain by
Biddles Ltd, Guildford and King's Lynn

Contents

General Editor's Preface

The *World and Word* series, as its title implies, is based on the assumption that literary texts cannot be studied in isolation. The series presents to students, mainly of English literature, documents and materials which will enable them to have first-hand experience of some of the writing which forms the context of the literature they read. The aim is to put students in possession of material to which they cannot normally gain access so that they may arrive at an independent understanding of the inter-relationships of literary texts with other writing.

There are to be twelve volumes, covering topics from the Middle Ages to the twentieth century. Each volume concentrates on a specific area of thought in a particular period, selecting from religious, philosophical or scientific works, literary theory or political or social material, according to its chosen topic. The extracts included are substantial in order to enable students themselves to arrive at an understanding of the significance of the material they read and to make responsible historical connections with some precision and independence. The task of compilation itself, of course, predetermines to a great extent the kind of connections and relationships which can be made in a particular period. We all bring our own categories to the work of interpretation. However, each compiler makes clear the grounds on which the choice of material is made, and thus the series encourages the valuable understanding that there can be no single, authoritative account of the relationships between word and world.

Each volume is annotated and indexed and includes a short bibliography and suggestions for further reading. The *World and Word* series can be used in different teaching contexts, in the student's independent work, in seminar discussion, and on lecture courses.

ISOBEL ARMSTRONG
University of Southampton

Acknowledgements

The editors acknowledge with appreciation the help, in various forms, of the Librarian and staff of St Deiniol's Library, Harwarden and of Shirley Foster, B. A. Humfrey, L. H. Dennis and especially Elsie Davies.

Introduction

Barbara Dennis

G. M. Young declared that the world has witnessed two great ages
of the human intellect — one the age of Pericles, the other the age of
Victoria. It would follow that to aim for a comprehensive commentary on all that was achieved by the human intellect, in all fields of
reform, in the years between 1830 and 1880 would be unthinkable,
and this anthology has not attempted it. The possible areas of
debate which might be represented are almost unlimited, and any
selection will seem arbitrary, when every human activity, physical
and mental, it seemed, arrived at a significant or even critical stage
during these years. The sections into which the book is divided,
therefore, simply represent seven unquestionably major topics in
any examination of Victorian society, and many other areas,
arguably as important, are unmentioned. Even the areas selected
frequently and inevitably overlap, and this has been acknowledged
and indicated with cross-references.

The editors have deliberately selected passages from less accessible sources, and have avoided, on the whole, the big names
readily available elsewhere to which students are presumably
directed in other contexts. Discussions of important new contribu-
tions to learning and opinion have generally been preferred to
extracts from the key books themselves, because an assemblage of
articles, reviews and pamphlets better indicates the quality and
form of the debate before the educated public than would a succession of different and separate pieces from the masters themselves.
So the sources of which the editors have made use represent a cross-
section of discussions on some of the burning topics of the day in the
forms in which it was generally available — in periodicals, newspapers, lectures, popular books, pamphlets, and so on.

Of these forms newspapers, until the last years of the century,
were of comparatively minor importance, and quite the most
significant vehicle of communication was the literary periodical,
the most widely represented form in the anthology. This was the
golden age of periodical writing, when the literary periodical was
pre-eminently the common voice of the literate. The weeklies,
monthlies and quarterlies poured out information, commentary
and opinion on every topic to come before the public, gave first

publication to a great many of the significant books of the age, fiction and non-fiction, and acted as a general forum of discussion and debate for the educated public. In 1859 alone, for example, 115 new periodicals appeared in London, and when the *Cornhill* started in 1860, it sold 110,000 copies of the first issue.

The form of the literary periodical was in itself of some import, for an individual number might contain four or five different, closely argued articles, each of 20,000 words. The editors have chosen, as far as possible, to preserve this format in the selections they have made; they have tried to retain at least the outline of the argument in each extract, rather than presenting simply a paragraph from the original, which might do no more than announce the subject. In this way they hope to have preserved the flavour of the contemporary debate. They also intend that each extract should stand by itself as a document for discussion when the book is being used as source material by students of English literature, or Victorian studies, or related disciplines.

Key themes emerge from a selection of documents relating to this section of Victorian society, the educated middle class. They concern the nature of that society, both as it appeared to those living in it, and as it appears to those who view it with hindsight. These themes recur frequently in the extracts selected here, sometimes implicitly, sometimes in the articulate voices of the time, nearly always in a variety of contexts.

The Victorians, after all, could scarcely fail to be aware of the remarkableness and fluidity of their age. When the queen acceded to the throne in 1837, her subjects numbered 17 million, and when she died not much more than sixty years later, she governed 37 ½ million. The pace of life had accelerated at a proportional rate. The Industrial Revolution, already well under way in 1830, had gathered speed at the impulse of the middle classes, and in the course of the next half-century had transformed Britain from a nation of agricultural yeomen to a nation of factory hands. They toiled in the 'Workshop of the World' in the new smoke-blackened towns, and had made Britain the acknowledged leader of world industry. Their daily lives, too, had been transformed at a stroke, not only by industrial advances, but by the technology of travel — the railway arrived during the 1830s, and by the 1840s every part of the realm, for the first time in history, was accessible to all.

Social mobility

The immediate beneficiaries of the nation's prosperity were not, of course, the factory hands, but the middle classes. As their personal wealth and power increased, these masters of industry even became the new nobility, for the ranks of the peerage were swelled with new creations drawn not, as always in the past, from traditional landowners, but from the moguls of trade and textiles and engineering. (Already their mansions and palaces covered London and the North of England. See 'The Gentleman's House', in *The Gentleman*.) The class question is one of the most pervasive themes in all Victorian society. The social mobility and the aspirations of the new leaders of society are the most frequently articulated theme, as solutions to their rapidly multiplying needs were advanced, dissected and resolved. It is a theme, in one form or another, in almost all the chapters of this book. The topic of 'The Gentleman' was, of course, of quite absorbing interest as the term moved through every shade of meaning and one definition after another was challenged or expanded. The Great Reform Bill of 1832 had seen the simultaneous extension of the franchise and the middle class, and both were expanded again in 1867 with the Second Reform Bill. (See 'Mr. Bright and Democracy', in *Politics and Administration*.) The new class must be educated, and the ancient public schools and universities, traditional spawning grounds of the gentleman, were inadequate for the task: both were reformed or re-founded with the new requirements in mind. (See 'Thoughts of an Outsider: Public Schools' and 'The University of London and Middle-Class Education', in *Education*.) The professions, previously safely limited in number, now, in the wake of the Industrial Revolution and the reforms of all the institutions in society, multiplied bewilderingly: guidance was needed. (See 'Professions and Professional Classes', in *The Gentleman*.) One important one, the civil service, was thrown open for the first time to competitive examination. (See Sir Charles Trevelyan's 'Evidence to the Playfair Commission', in *Politics and Administration*.) Nor was the spiritual life of the nation untouched by the class question. The Reform Bills, particularly the Second, had enfranchised a large body of Dissenters — and by every old definition a Dissenter could not be a gentleman. (See 'Conformity a Sin, because Unjust to Nonconformists', in *The Religious Debate*.) Indeed, definitions of the whole concept were pursued obsessively. (see 'The Grand Old Name of Gentleman' and 'Character — the

True Gentleman', in *The Gentleman*.)

The unprecedented surge in empire building too had its own part to play in the class question. British colonialism during Victoria's reign expanded to the point where Britain ruled one-tenth of the earth's surface, and the stimulus to this growth was trade, the hallmark of the middle class. The empire was largely won, governed and administered by the younger sons of England who, as a matter of course, went out to seek the unlimited opportunities in colonial trade, colonial administration, colonial education, the colonial armed services, and so on, and often stayed on to found fresh dynasties. And the British middle class recruited fresh generations of their number from those foreign fields that were for ever England. (See 'Mr. Gladstone and Our Empire', in *Politics and Administration*.)

Meanwhile it was the shifting, growing, powerful middle class at home who largely controlled most dimensions of Victorian society, and engaged in the intellectual debate and commentary which marked it, and the middle class which examined its own identity unremittingly. The professions were reorganised and redefined and expanded as science and technology redrew the old social boundaries, and the phrase 'a professional man' took on complete new layers of meaning. The new organisations, the new institutions, in which Parliament was restructuring society, required management. Parliament itself, of course, was and went on being the exclusive preserve of the well-to-do middle class, for until long after our period the payment of MPs was unthought of, and mere representation implied a private income — as much for the expenses of an election (see 'The Ballot', in *Politics and Administration*) as for the maintaining of an appropriate position afterwards. But the innovations and reforms — in education, in the armed services, in local government, in the church — all pointed to the need for a trained middle class, and added fresh impetus to the questions society was beginning to ask about the traditional hierarchy. These questions permeate and inform — however implicitly — nearly all the sections into which the book is divided. The popular voice, which was first heard in Britain at this time with the Chartists in the 1830s, never became the organised movement which galvanised Europe, but nevertheless was a threatening growl in middle-class ears throughout the period. The question of class is obsessive, and is a key theme in nearly every section.

Religion

So too is religion. While it might raise eyebrows to call this age the most religious ever, it is unquestionably true that this age took religion more seriously, was more interested in theological questions and problems, than any time previous or to come. Every Victorian topic, in fact, has its theological dimension, and this is obvious in the extracts here, as we see the religious response to the intellectual, technical and scientific developments of the day. (See 'The Attitude of the Clergy towards Science', in *The Religious Debate*, for example; or 'Convocation and Dr. Colenso', in *The Scientific Approach*.) Education, of course, had long been the preserve of the church, and the wrangling and bitterness provoked as it gradually passed to the control of the state led to some notable exchanges. But until the appearance of the new universities, in London and the industrial North, and government insistence on elementary schooling for all, few had questioned that religion was a prime function of education at all levels. (See 'An Inquiry into the State of Girls' Fashionable Schools', in *Education*.) And the role in society assigned by men to women, of course, was a quasi-religious one. (See "The Angel in the House", in *The "Woman Question"*.)

The church itself, both Established and Free, passed through significant stages in its history during this period. It is, perhaps, no coincidence that the age should produce, on the one side, such exhilarating and intoxicating advances in material progress, and on the other, disillusionment with materialism and a nostalgia for the past and the immutable values of religion. All round was change, novelty, 'progress': the human mind in reaction turned instinctively to the unchanging, and sought the safety of the traditional in the most ancient institution of the western world.

The Church of England was markedly conscious of the stir. The Anglicans, responding to the challenge of the state's attempted interference in its domain (the suppression of two bishoprics in Ireland), denounced this 'direct disavowal of the sovereignty of God', and erupted with the Oxford Movement, the Tracts for the Times, which claimed its precedents in history. The English Church, it reminded its members, was a branch of the original Church Catholic, no less Catholic than the Roman branch, but reformed. The writers of the Tracts set about re-Catholicising the Church of England — a movement which has lasted to the present day. To many bewildered Victorians, confused and disorientated by the flux of society, the appeal to history was heady, and they turned in relief to an institution unaffected, in essentials, by change. And others — a frightening number, it seemed, to Protestant England — reacted still further, to embrace a yet more unchanging church, the Roman, where no uncertainties threatened.

One other possible explanation for the Catholic revival of the English Church was political. An earlier revival in the church, late in the eighteenth century and in the early decades of the nineteenth, had been evangelical, and had led to the fragmentation of the church in the breakaway congregations of Methodists who had joined the earlier Dissenters, the Baptists, Independents and Unitarians. Their nonconformity had been a handicap to them in the past, but by 1830 they were largely free of former legal restriction. They had prospered, and now made up a sizeable proportion of the middle class. The Reform Bill of 1832 had enfranchised many, and Anglican clergy feared a backlash of anti-Establishment measures in Parliament, unless they attempted a more dominant role in their own affairs.

Suspicion and distrust between the different churches and parties, however, were hushed when they became conscious of another frighteningly powerful voice in the debate, that of unbelief. Doubt was no new thing, of course, but this period saw, for the first time, attacks on religion from every area and class in society, including, it seemed, from the church itself as old certainties were examined afresh by some of the clergy. (See 'The Causes of Unbelief', 'The Clergyman Who Subscribes for Colenso' and 'Atheism', in *The Religious Debate*.) The causes of unbelief were varied: some new discoveries and hypotheses of science worked powerfully against traditional religious beliefs — Darwin's were merely the most notorious — and the whole direction of science was materialistic and rational. Even before the later impact of science, in the 1830s religious faith seemed to be challenged by the geologists whose researches questioned the literal truth of the Bible; and textual scholars were taking these conclusions further when they demonstrated the wild inconsistencies of the Bible, and the inaccuracy of its dating.

The field of Biblical scholarship was dominated by Germany. In the 1830s it was the school of Tübingen in particular which was making the very word 'German' synonymous with all that was menacing to believers; and D. F. Strauss was perhaps the most notorious in the school. The question of miracles was the vital issue to the German critics, and in Strauss's *Life of Jesus* it is axiomatic that 'miracles do not happen': in calm, reasonable tones he demolished all that was supernatural in Christianity, and demonstrated that contemporary belief in the miracles was to be explained in terms of self-fulfilling prophecies and the Messianic expectation of the Jews. The translation of this sinister work was undertaken by George Eliot, then still Marian Evans, and the 'sewage of unbelief' flowed unchecked into England.

The prevailing modes of philosophic thought, too, were distinctly anti-spiritual in their bent. Utilitarianism and Positivism were enormously influential, and markedly secular in their implications (see 'Utilitarianism and the *Summum Bonum*' in *The Scientific Approach*): Newman at Oxford, till 1845, had celebrated theology as the Queen of the Sciences, but a generation later it was a view challenged in the new universities.

All these questions of faith, and the implications of scepticism, were largely of more concern to the middle class than to the proletariat, and the middle class was conscious of it. Now the swollen masses, for the first time urban-dwellers, and a new force in the land, represented a threat to the Establishment, of which the Establishment was uneasily aware. The Bible had directed the masters' proper attitude of compassion to the poor, but the poor themselves, it seemed, cared little if at all for religion. The awful warning of what the godless poor might wreak when they gained control was only just across the Channel — the spectre of the 1789 Revolution haunted the British middle class throughout the century. (In 1851 a commentator was deploring 'the separation between rich and poor — the dissympathy of classes, and that mutual disgust which appears to threaten some sort of violent revolution in society at no very distant future': and worse was to come.) Genuine middle-class concern for the social welfare of the poor, exploited as they were by the industrial society, is expressed in 'The Poor Law and Charity' (*Politics and Administration*); and the prudence of such concern is implied. As for the attitude of the church to the proletariat, however, the church was only too conscious that its influence over the working class as a whole was minimal. The churches and chapels, built all over the land to accommodate the expanding population in the towns, were attended, on the whole, not by coalminers, steelworkers and factory hands, but by the masters. The attempts of the Anglican Church to come to terms with the situation as the century wore on were most obviously in the hands of the Anglo-Catholic party in the church. The richness and grandeur of the ritual (though no part of early Tractarian practice) attracted packed congregations in the slums of the cities, and missions manned by worker-priests flourished. The Broad Church party, led by Kingsley and Maurice, urged Christian Socialism; and among their own ranks the poor found a leader in William Booth, and their own church in the Salvation Army. But increasingly the church was fighting a losing battle. As time went by the proletariat, with this world rather than the next in mind, was turning more and more to the new socialist movement, and had little energy to spare for organised religion.

'Scientific' thought

The fifty years with which we are most concerned cover a period of most obvious and general concern with religion. Not all contemporaries viewed religion as the key theme of the age, however. Writing near the end of the century T. H. Huxley declared:

> I conceive that the leading characteristic of the nineteenth century has been the rapid growth of the scientific spirit, the consequent application of scientific methods of investigation to all the problems with which the human mind is occupied, and the correlative rejection of traditional beliefs which have proved their incompetence to bear such investigation. . . . The activity of the scientific spirit has been manifested in every region of speculation and of practice.

It was also an Age of Science, in fact, in every sense of that word, and science is a theme to be found in nearly every section of this anthology. In *The Gentleman* science was still making its way as a socially acceptable profession in one form or another for the middle classes (see 'Professions and Professional Classes', in *The Gentleman*), though the very term 'scientist' was not coined until 1840, and the different branches of science are sharply distinguished in social terms. In *Education* the commentators are on surer ground, and there are no two minds about the urgent necessity for the teaching of science at school level ('Technical Education a National Want') or in the universities (see 'Universities of England — Oxford'). And the new universities were founded primarily as bases for scientific research.

But it is in the section on *The Religious Debate* that science figures most prominently, of course, for its emphases, on the whole, were anti-religious. It is a position which Huxley certainly helped to form for all his most significant and most popular work stresses that religion is debased by dogma and must be purged by science to a creed that was exclusively of ethics. It was Huxley who, as 'Darwin's bulldog', was the chief populariser of the theory of evolution, the scientific hypothesis which, among all the threats from science, most dramatically fluttered the dovecotes of traditional religion.

It was a popular misconception of *The Origin of Species* that Darwin there contradicts the Biblical account of Creation, denies the existence of the soul, and defines the Creator as an impersonal force, as heedless of species as of individuals. Darwin makes no such assumptions anywhere, of course, but it was the myth of Darwinism which flourished, and a significant section of the religious debate is taken up with the anguish of the church in the face of this menace. (See 'The Tendencies of Science' and 'The Attitude of the Clergy towards Science', in *The Religious Debate*.) The Bishop of Gloucester and Bristol deplored the doubt provoked by science of all kinds, but particularly by the theory of natural selection (see 'The Causes of Unbelief', in *The Religious Debate*) — and the clergy concurred.

In the 1860s it was the biological sciences which posed the gravest threat, but before this time it was sciences like geology and palaeontology, rationalised by the church as 'natural theology', which, to the conservative faithful, had been a potential hazard to faith. To the conservative believer the discoveries of men like Robert Chambers (*Vestiges of Creation*, 1844), and Charles Lyell (*Principles of Geology*, 1830) seemed to question the Biblical account of the Creation. A science which provoked more real alarm, though, was the historical criticism of Scripture, which demonstrated, by supplying scientific criteria, the inaccuracy of dating and the confusion of authorship in the Bible. They concluded that the New Testament was by and about ordinary men writing in specific historical circumstances, and not, after all, the inspired and literal word of God. The Germans were first in this branch of science. (George Eliot's translation of Strauss's *Life of Jesus*, 1846, was a notable landmark.) But Renan's *Life of Jesus* (1863) and J. R. Seeley's *Ecce Homo* (1865) were both notorious debunkers.

Huxley had pinpointed 'the growth of the scientific spirit' as the prime characteristic of the age; he was referring to the way science had affected the nature of so many fields of cultural life which had

previously been uncharted. These now began to identify themselves as professional disciplines in their own right, and invite
scholarly research and systematic investigation. So theology,
literature, history, modern foreign languages, and so on, began to
emerge as topics to be organised systematically, and, as the
century wore on, located and studied in the universities. (See 'The
Study of History' and 'On the Scientific Study of Poetry', in *The
Scientific Approach*.) Moreover, the traditional fields of science —
chemistry, physics, engineering — were joined by new sciences
like sociology, psychology, philology and political science and,
briefly, by such pseudo-sciences as phrenology and physiognomy.
(See 'On Physiognomy', in *The Scientific Approach*.)

Science, in fact, was in everybody's mind. British achievement
in the connected fields of science and industry had been triumph-
antly displayed to the world at the Great Exhibition of 1851 in the
Crystal Palace, headed by Prince Albert. The profits from the
Great Exhibition went towards a Museum of Science in South
Kensington, and in due course towards the foundation of the
Royal College of Science. The Paris Exhibition of 1867 (an imitation of the London version) led indirectly to the appointment of a
Royal Commission, the Devonshire Commission, to investigate
the provisions for scientific advancement. (See 'Technical Education a National Want', in *Education*.) And the new universities in
the North of England had, of course, been established primarily in
the cause of science. Owens College — soon to be the University of
Manchester — was founded in 1851 and almost at once took an
international lead in chemistry under Henry Roscoe, and the
university colleges established in surrounding cities frequently
reflected the dominant local industrial science.

The Benthamite philosophy

The establishment of the new universities admirably illustrates the
overlap of the themes that run through this representation of
Victorian intellectual debate: the system of thought of which this
burgeoning of the scientific spirit is part is largely the political and
economic philosophy of Jeremy Bentham, and this too is a key
theme in the anthology.

Jeremy Bentham's influence far outlasted his lifetime. When he
died in 1832, the effects of his thinking were scarcely apparent in
society, but at the other end of our period, nearly fifty years

later, a commentator could observe:

> His system is even an important element of our current
> political thought; hardly a decade . . . has elapsed since it
> might almost have been called a predominant element . . .
> [Bentham's] name still carries with it an audible demand that
> we should reckon with his system, and explain to ourselves
> why and how far we agree or disagree with his opinions.
> ('Bentham and Benthamism in Politics and Ethics', *The
> Fortnightly Review*, 1877)

It was his principle to test all the institutions of social life by the
criterion of their usefulness. The steady stream of reform in the
Victorian period — parliamentary, legal, municipal, academic,
ecclesiastical, economic — originated in the spirit of his perpetual
question, 'What is the use of it?'. It is this political and ethical
theory of 'utility' for which he is principally remembered. He took
the ultimate good to be the greatest happiness of the greatest
number, and defined the rightness of actions in terms of their contribution to the general happiness. Benthamite philosophy can be
found at work in nearly all branches of Victorian activity as one
institution after another was reformed, clearing the path for democratic individualism. Its insistence on freedom of action for all
individuals and its firm support for unrestrained competition led
to a system of free enterprise, both of which promoted the
spectacular success of the middle class. (See *The Gentleman*.)

Benthamism, ('Utilitarianism' was the name given to the
system by its most famous, if qualified, exponent, John Stuart
Mill), in more obvious ways or less, informs many of the sections
here. It is most obvious, perhaps, in the section which includes
parliamentary and social reform (*Politics and Administration*). The
very idea of efficiency and reform in government belonged to the
Benthamites, and they were responsible initially for the first moves
towards the suppression of the rotten boroughs and the extension
of the franchise in the Reform Bill of 1832. It was the thin end of
the wedge, and parliamentary reform continued throughout the
period. (See 'The Ballot' and 'Corrupt Practices at Parliamentary
Elections'.) Social reform, too, began in a serious way with the
Benthamite measures of Grey's government of 1830–35, which
passed the New Poor Law, brought in the first effective Factory
Act, made the first government grant for education, and abolished
slavery. Conscience, once roused, kept the social concern of the

nation alert (see 'The Poor Law and Charity'), and by the end of the period legislation was in effect to reform many other branches of society — education, the administration, the armed services, and so on. The constant and informed agitation of the Utilitarians influenced the programmes of both major parties, and was behind most of the reforms on the statute book.

One outcome of industrial reform was the Ten Hours Bill of 1847, which gave some factory hands the novel experience of leisure. It was a reform prompted as much by Benthamite economic considerations as by humanitarian. As Macaulay was quick to point out, the man who has some relaxation each day and at the weekend, 'returns to his labours on the Monday with clearer intellect, with livelier spirits, with renewed corporeal vigour'. Among the rival Germans, on the other hand, who often worked 17 hours out of 24, 'there is not one who grows to such stature that he can be admitted into the army!' (and see 'Sundays and Festivals', in *Leisure and the Arts*).

Education is probably the other area most obviously affected by the Utilitarian system of thought. University reform, and the establishment of the new universities, were a direct result of the Utilitarian ethic. Oxford and Cambridge, before 1830, were still offering the largely medieval curriculum of classics, or mathematics, and the Scriptures, and were virtually a branch of the Established Church. It was no part of their function, as they saw it, to act as centres of academic excellence, and research was no part of their activity. 'The object of a University', Pusey had said rather loftily, 'is not simply or mainly to cultivate the intellect. . . . [It is], with and through the disciplines of the intellect, as far as may be, to discipline and train the whole moral and intelligent being. . . . It would be a perversion of our institutions to turn the University into a forcing-house for intellect.' Nor did the faculty of the university regard themselves as professional teachers: a college fellowship was almost invariably a means to an end, and from it the young clerical don looked forward to a country curacy and a college living. Some, no doubt, fulfilled Pusey's moral ideal as they trained the intelligent being, but such results were on the whole incidental.

In the 1830s the reforming spirit of the Utilitarians deplored such inefficiency. They saw the influence of the Anglican Church as a stranglehold, choking the potential usefulness of the university to business and industry, and social and political progress in general. They deplored the narrowness of the curriculum and the unprofessionalism of the teaching, and during the next forty years revolutionised both. (See 'Universities of England — Oxford', in *Education*.) Royal Commissions at Oxford and Cambridge over the years transformed the ideal of a university from the recruiting ground for the clergy to a secular, professional institution offering a multiplicity of disciplines and acting as a centre of academic research.

The new universities were founded with just these ideals in view. 'London University', almost in itself a definition of Utilitarianism (Bentham's skeleton is preserved at University College to this day), opened its doors in Gower Street in 1828, not in rivalry with Oxford and Cambridge, but to offer to Dissenters, Jews and atheists a useful education denied them elsewhere. The University of London (incorporated in 1836) based both teaching and organisation rather on Scottish and European models than on the old universities (see 'The University of London and Middle-Class Education'): the new civic universities which followed were on the same Utilitarian pattern, opening education to a wider public, specialising in science, and having direct links with local industry.

Education at other levels was in a similar process of reform. The Great Exhibition of 1851 and the other international exhibitions which followed it had brought home to Benthamite observers what Britain's position would be in the industrial world as the gap narrowed between the developing nations. Britain's lead, they declared, was diminishing daily, and the rest of Europe was feverishly educating its rising generations as successors in technical supremacy. (See 'Technical Education a National Want', in *Education*.) Vocational training, a wholly new concept in English thinking, appeared as a result of Benthamite ideas, and by the end of the period most middle-class occupations and professions had their own preparatory institutions — teacher training colleges, agricultural colleges, theological colleges, and so on.

In the same vein, University Extension lectures offered instruction to the middle class at large, and elsewhere in society this new enthusiasm for education was expressed in the Mechanics' Institutes. Founded in 1823, they were deliberately organised by Utilitarian thinking to offer some elementary education to the working class, particularly in the fields of science. Most important of all from a Utilitarian point of view, however, was the government's recognition of the need for national popular education. The state had made half-hearted gestures towards a national education system from 1833 onwards, when a grant towards first school buildings, and then a system of inspection, was made. But the mass of English children were quite neglected until 1870 and the passing of the Education Bill. This, late though it was, finally gave England a system where education was within the reach of all; and by 1880 primary education was made compulsory and free.

The 'Woman Question'

Every element in society, in fact, bore the impress of this reforming zeal in education, from the ambitious young freethinker in the Oxford common-room, to the guttersnipe in the slums. Even women, the most underprivileged section of all, began to feel the effects of the combined ideals of usefulness and the felicific principle, as their role in the community began to be redefined. (See 'The Practice of Medicine by Women' and 'College Education for Women', in *The 'Woman Question'*.) The 'Woman Question' is another theme to pervade middle-class thinking in these fifty years, as throughout the period the whole question of the identity and the position of women was more and more pressingly raised and discussed. Serious commentators and reformers confirmed the importance of the topic in their analyses: Barbara Leigh Smith's *Women and Work*, 1857; Josephine Butler's *Women's Work and Women's Culture*, 1861; Frances Cobbe's *Essays on the Pursuits of Women*, 1863, for instance — or particularly J. S. Mill's *On the Subjection of Women*, 1869. It was a favourite and persistent topic in many forms in the periodical press too. In periodicals that reflected every shade of ideology and opinion article after article — exhortatory, reflective, decisive — was devoted to explorations of woman's role in society, her education, her enfranchisement, her function and status, her position as wife, or mother, or spinster, or employee, and so on, from the solemn pages of the *Westminster* and the *Edinburgh* to the anti-feminist sallies of *Punch*.

A single unexpected periodical, selected at random, demonstrates the pervasiveness of the topic. When Charlotte Yonge's demurely conservative *Monthly Packet*, founded on High Church principles and hardly a predictable expositor of the 'Woman Question', first appeared in 1854, to the day she retired from the editorship in 1891, scarcely a number appeared without an article on women — women's opportunities ('Women's Work in London'), callings ('Female Recruits for the Church'), duties ('Work of Women at Home'), responsibilities ('What Can Be

Done for Our Young Servants?') or on 'Womankind' in all its aspects (a series which ran from 1874 to 1877).

Public opinion, in fact, at the impulse of Benthamite thinking, was moving all the time towards justice for women. There were, of course, many voices eager to take the other side in the debate, who saw the inferiority of women as ordained by God (Charlotte Yonge was one!), to interfere with which would be impiety; and there were those who were quick to point out that the Lord knew very well what He was about. (See the Rev F. O. Morris's 'The Rights and Wrongs of Women', in *The 'Woman Question'*.) But the most famous Victorian attitude to women substitutes reverence for equality, and makes of woman an object that was scarcely mortal. 'Woman Worship' is the view which elevated a woman conveniently above the world of men, and assured her that her role was to inspire rather than to perform: her function was spiritual, and the highest glory of womanhood was to preserve and quicken the moral idealism of her husband. The view finds classic expression in Tennyson's *The Princess*, Ruskin's *Sesame and Lilies*, and Coventry Patmore's *The Angel in the House* (see ' "The Angel in the House" ', in *The 'Woman Question'*); and Mrs Sarah Stickney Ellis had written standard manuals on *The Daughters of England, The Wives of England* and *The Women of England* to advance the theory.

Voices on the other side were insistent, however, and grew louder. The political rights of women were a long way off; but the question of female suffrage was raised in the *Westminster* in 1851 by J. S. Mill's friend and later wife, Harriet Taylor. (See 'Female Suffrage and Married Life' and 'Criminals, Idiots, Women, and Minors: Is the Classification Sound?', in *The 'Woman Question'*.) Mill himself, the most forceful exponent of their cause, introduced the first Bill for the enfranchisement of women in 1866, and though it was defeated by 196 votes to 73, he ensured that the 'Woman Question' was always before the House. The statute book demonstrates the outcome of persistent agitation in the House in these middle decades of the century.

Social thought and custom were already on the move, and now a series of crucial Bills materially altered the legal position of women in society. The outrageously unjust divorce laws began a course of reform in 1857, for example, and the Matrimonial Causes Acts were passed in 1857, 1867 and 1870. The insistent voices of women like Josephine Butler and Frances Cobbe were behind similar reforms in the law: during the 1870s Parliament repealed the degrading Contagious Diseases Acts (see 'Male and Female

Morality', in *The 'Woman Question'*) and the Married Women's Property Acts, which gave the 3,200,000 working women the right to their own earnings, which before belonged to their husbands, were passed in 1870 and 1882.

In the field of education the 'Woman Question' had been raised vociferously. At the beginning of the period girls' education at any level was very scanty indeed, and any form of higher education was unthought of. Now, in the wake of Benthamite thinking, female education became a serious principle. 'It cannot be denied', declared the Royal Commission of 1864, 'that the picture brought before us of the state of Middle-Class Female Education is, on the whole, unfavourable. Want of thoroughness and foundation . . . inattention to rudiments . . . and those not taught intelligently or in any scientific manner, . . . these indicate the character of the complaints we have received'. (See 'An Inquiry into the State of Girl's Fashionable Schools' in *The 'Woman Question'*.) In the hands of notable pioneers like Dorothea Beale and Frances Mary Buss, schools grew up through the period, next to the reformed schools for boys or independent of them, and educational corporations like the Girls' Public Day School Trust (founded 1872) and the Church Schools Company flourished.

Concern spread through all levels of education. The reforms of the universities included the admission of women — reluctantly on the part of first Cambridge and then Oxford, who finally, in the 1870s, made a tentative beginning towards including women in the lecture rooms, though not to membership of the university; while the University of London, anticipating the older universities by decades, admitted women to degrees on the same terms as men in 1878. (See 'College Education for Women', in *Education*.)

Impatient at the delay in the universities, ambitious women had, by the 1850s, set up their own institutions for vocational training, particularly in the field of medicine, and were demanding recognition and acceptance by the professions. In 1849 Elizabeth Blackwell had qualified as the first woman doctor in the United States, and ten years later returned to her native England, which was still vigorously resisting the idea. (Dr Elizabeth Garrett, after qualifying in Paris, became the first British woman doctor, in 1876.) But in 1864 came the Female Medical Society; and Florence Nightingale opened the first training school for nurses at St Thomas's Hospital, when she returned from the Crimea in 1856. (See 'The Practice of Medicine by Women', in *The 'Woman Question'*.) The Society for the Employment of Women had been founded in 1860, and other professions were beginning to yield to the pressures from society. Queen's College had opened in 1848 primarily for the training of governesses; teacher training colleges were founded to staff the National Schools and then the new Council Schools; and in 1854 the new Electric Telegraph Company was training bands of women for employment as clerks.

It took a world war to demonstrate conclusively the value of trained and educated women; but the seven decades before that had prepared the way.

Leisure

Finally one other theme that runs through the age (more often implied than spoken, perhaps) is that of leisure. What it was, what purpose it served, what were the solutions to the problems it posed, were the inevitable questions that followed the twin explosions in technology and population. The Benthamite thinking of the Philosophical Radicals provided one set of answers, the unreflecting manufacturing class another. In an age when the gospel of work provided an appendix to religion, and sages like Carlyle elevated labour as a sanctified end in itself, the very concept of its opposite was one to be examined by a thoughtful society. The common-sense Whig, Thomas Macaulay, declared sturdily to the House of Commons in 1846, in a debate on the Ten Hours Bill:

> A day of rest recurring in every week, two or three hours of leisure, exercise, innocent amusement or useful study, recurring every day, must improve the whole man, physically, morally, intellectually; and the improvement of the man will improve all that the man produces. . . . Never will I believe that what makes a population stronger, and healthier, and wiser, and better, can ultimately make it poorer.

Arguing from a less obviously Benthamite platform, the Positivist thinker, Frederic Harrison, declared that the British had failed dismally to answer the questions posed by the prevailing 'work ethic'. (See 'Sundays and Festivals', in *Leisure and the Arts*.) He deplored the Demon of Overwork, exclaiming: 'For the sake of a livelihood we are throwing away the very objects of life.' The Protestant Sunday of England, grim, joyless and oppressive, had become a symbol to him of the negative English attitude to leisure; Merrie

17

England had mistaken the means for the end, and denied leisure its positive function.

Other commentators viewed the leisure question from a different angle. It was one which was very often a question of class — leisure demarked a gentleman, and one sign that distinguished the proletarian was the scantness of time he could call his own. The gentleman called attention to his class by the modes with which he chose to occupy his leisure — in his choice of sport, for example: fox-hunting was the traditional pursuit of the gentleman. (See 'A Sportsman's Apology', in *Leisure and the Arts*.) This period also saw the beginnings of the cult of organised sport — it takes in, for instance, the start of Test Matches (1876), the invention of rugby, we are told (1829), the foundation of the Football Association (1863), and all these sports were taken up enthusiastically by the public schools. Leslie Stephen points with irony to the pre-eminence of sport as an ingredient in the public school myth, which fostered the notion of sport as an arbiter of what was gentlemanly. (See 'Thoughts of an Outsider: Public Schools', in *Education*.) A gentleman, in fact, can be identified by his attitude to leisure and his skill at team games.

The leisure of the lower classes, however, as the gentleman saw it, served quite a different purpose. As expressed by the author of 'The Manufacturing Poor: Education' (see *Education*) one intention of the Ten Hours Act of 1847 was to give the working man the opportunity for self-improvement, and rudimentary education at night school — though another observer commented ruefully that the current degraded state of the theatre was due largely to the taste of the rabble who flocked there nightly! (See 'A Word About Our Theatres', in *Leisure and the Arts*.)

The Ten Hours Bill (and other industrial legislation) had given the working-class man some idea of the concept of leisure; but the working-class woman was largely unaffected by it: the vast majority of working women were employed not in the factories but as servants, and for most women employed in, for example, the cotton mills of Lancashire, the hours of freedom from the factory scarcely amounted to leisure. For their wealthy sisters, of course, the problem had always been, ironically, the reverse. With most professions and social rights and all higher education closed to them, the enforced leisure of the wealthier class of women, from adolescence on, is a problem expressed repeatedly. (See throughout in *The 'Woman Question'*.) Now, however, the reforming conscience of the public, stirred by the Utilitarians, began to recognise the futility of so many women's lives, and the frustrations of unwanted leisure expressed by intelligent and ambitious women (seen here in Sophia Jex-Blake, Frances Cobbe, and Emily Shirreff, in *The 'Woman Question'*) finally began to be acknowledged by society.

As for the arts, represented here by painting and the novel, they too bear the imprint of Utilitarian thought, for by the mid-century, Victorian society was largely conditioned by Benthamism, and Benthamism led them to view art as the occupation of leisure. The taste of many average Victorians in these moments was, to a large extent, that of Mr Podsnap:

> Literature; large print, respectively descriptive of getting up at eight, shaving close at a quarter-past, breakfasting at nine, going to the City at ten, coming home at half-past five, and dining at seven. Painting and Sculpture; models and portraits representing Professors of getting up at eight, shaving close at a quarter-past, breakfasting at nine, going to the City at ten, coming home at half-past five, and dining at seven . . . (*Our Mutual Friend*, Book 1, Ch. XI)

'Realism' was a criterion that was reflected in every kind of mid-Victorian art. George Eliot had called for novels that were 'to paint the life of the People' — 'our social novels profess to represent people as they are', she said (Review of *The Natural History of German Life*, 1856); and in her own *Adam Bede* she had warmly commended novelists who were 'ready to give the loving pains of a life to the faithful representing of commonplace things' (Ch. 17). And the Pre-Raphaelites, encouraged by Ruskin, were determined to paint the natural world with the minutest regard for detail. So here Wilkie Collins is tilting at the prevailing convention which dictates the techniques of the novel ('A Petition to the Novel-Writers', in *Leisure and the Arts*); and George Richmond is extolling the laws established by the Pre-Raphaelite Brotherhood ('Pictures and Picture-Criticism').

Finally, science, the most obvious demonstration of Utilitarianism, seemed, with the new craze for photography, to have joined art in the quest for 'realism' as the hobby of the middle class. The possible threat to art expressed by the enthusiast in 'The Present State of Photography' (in *Leisure and the Arts*) is a panic reaction, as he points out — and the Pre-Raphaelite Brotherhood, far from rejecting technology nervously, were very glad to make use of it as an aid to established techniques.

1

Politics and Administration

The whole arena of politics and administration was in a hum of debate and reform from the beginning of the period to the end. Parliamentary and electoral reforms, all the machinery of government, national and local, were earnest questions of the day to a degree never seen before in Britain as, in a space of two or three generations, the country changed from a predominantly agrarian society of 15 million in 1831, which retained many old feudal forms, to an industrialised urban society of 30 million in 1880. The process had begun fifty years before Victoria became queen in 1837, but the pace accelerated dramatically from the turn of the century.

The five years before her accession saw a series of critically important Acts of Parliament, from which great movements were to spring. The Great Reform Bill of 1832 was first, followed by the Municipal Corporations Act (1835), both reforming the machinery of government; the legalisation of trade unions had begun in 1823, and led to Robert Owen's Grand National Trades Union in 1833. The beginnings of social reform were made with Lord Althorp's Factory Act in the same year. And the notorious New Poor Law was passed in 1835.

Two results of this political activity recur frequently enough to stamp themselves as signs of the times. One is the emergence of government control as the state began to assume more and more responsibility in the different areas of society. The factories, the coalmines, the steelworks, health, sanitation, education, were increasingly subjected to state inspection and regulation and, as time went on, to the local authorities. The organisation of society, in fact, was passing from the individual philanthropist or entrepreneur to the public sector. The second result of the early legislation could be seen as the increasing democratisation of society, as inherited wealth and position began to give way to new wealth and the self-made man: during the period successive Acts of Parliament threw open the civil service to competitive examination, abolished the purchase of commissions in the armed services, and opened the universities, till now the prerogative of wealthy Anglicans only, to all. At the other end of the educational scale, elementary schooling, long wrangled over by Church and Dissent, and a problem no prudent administration would touch, was made compulsory for all by the Act of 1870, and popular education became largely the concern of the state.

Meanwhile abroad Britain controlled an ever-expanding colonial empire. To the Dominions of Canada, Australia, South Africa and India had been added the fruits of victory in the Napoleonic Wars, and in the long years of peace in Europe which followed this, British trade and industry had developed at a speed which was quite unprecedented. The government deliberately, in fact, kept out of wars between the time of Waterloo and the First South African War at the end of the century, preferring diplomacy to aggression when successive crises arose. The one exception was the Crimean War (1854–56) and some local troubles in the colonies. (One 'colonial problem' more insistent than all the others was Ireland, as it had been since at least the twelfth century. Seven hundred years later, in the Victorian age, prime minister after prime minister, most notably Gladstone, wrestled unavailingly with the problem.)

The general movements of nationalism and liberalism had erupted in revolution, violence or brutal repression in Italy, France, the Austro-Hungarian Empire and elsewhere. But in spite of the potential threat of Chartism, or the uneasy rise of the Trade Union and Co-operative Movements, or the fears of mob violence in the 1860s, British institutions had been unshaken by the turbulence in Europe in the years that followed 1848 — Matthew Arnold's *Culture and Anarchy* (1867) is more a comment on attitudes than a warning of impending misrule. The peace brought to Britain (or to some of the British) the prosperity which gave observers like Macaulay their feelings of complacent well-being, epitomised for many by the Great Exhibition of 1851.

1.1   Politics of the present, foreign and domestic

From Macmillan's Magazine, *Vol. 1, November 1859 — the first number. The Editor of* Macmillan's, *David Masson, gives an overall view of the current political situation. He is most concerned with foreign affairs and Britain's position in Europe. The Crimean War, against Russia and her ambitions in the Balkans where the Turks hold sway, has just been fought. Now the traditional threat of France recurs, in the person of Napoleon III, nephew of the Emperor, who in the last years has alarmed all Europe with his designs. His intentions over Italian Liberation, which Britain supports, are viewed here with great misgiving. At home parliamentary reform is most pressing, superseding (with education) even the problems of our colonial empire.*

It is eleven years[1] since the Peace established by Waterloo was broken, and the irritability which had been pretty well pent up during the preceding thirty-three years within the separate bodies-politic of Europe again broke forth in insurrections and wars. This fact, that we are now in the twelfth year of a new period of war and commotion, succeeding a period of comparative peace, ought to be distinctly borne in mind. Eleven years of the period have passed; but, according to all probability, many more years will have to elapse before the period shall have reached its historical close.

What meant such an epidemic of political irritability throughout Europe eleven years ago but that certain wrongs or mal-arrangements, of which the nations had been complaining since the so-called general adjustment of 1815, were now felt in such accumulated degree as no longer to be endurable? The wrongs openly complained of were of two kinds — wrong as between certain peoples and their own proper governments; and wrong as respected the way in which certain peoples were parcelled out among governments not their own. Of the feeling of one or other of these kinds of wrong, or of the two united, the well-remembered events of 1848–9 were an emphatic proclamation. . . . [T]he only result on which the popular eye could rest as the positive and tangible issue of so much turmoil was the unexpected appearance in the centre of European affairs of one most extraordinary man, long vagrant in the outer spaces of the world as a fragment of the old Napoleon, but now restored to his uncle's place,[2] with his Napoleonian ideas all within him, and with a system of ethics such as belongs only to exiles that have been purple-born.

Say what we will, the appearance in the centre of affairs of this one man — whom some eccentric persons persist in regarding as stupid, but whom others have uniformly praised, since his success, as wise and profound, — is the most pregnant fact in recent European history. How it modifies, for one thing, the notion with which some philosophers have been recently entertaining us, that the importance of the individual in society is necessarily becoming less and less! . . . Twice or thrice, Great Britain, incapable of penetrating his meaning, but knowing that he is not a man of the old calculable kind, has fancied that the immense forces he was accumulating in France, and which must have some outlet, were destined for her shores. Among the continental nations round France there has been the trepidation of a like uncertainty. Twice, relieving this general anxiety as to the direction his will might take, he *has* acted, and acted characteristically. It is in the East of Europe, where national masses have not yet been formed, as in the West, but where Austria and Turkey hold between them provisionally a medley of races, tugged at by the huge Slavonic power of Russia, and otherwise agitated by instincts of their own — it is there that the question of nationality is both most rife and most difficult. Into this region the genius of Napoleon III took its first aggressive walk. . . . The scene now is Italy — that country whose unhappy pre-eminence it is to have offered for so long the spectacle at once of native despotism and bad government in their worst conceivable forms and of the bitterest agony under foreign rule. Undertaking, after an ominous pause, one part of the Italian problem, the French Emperor threw his armies into the Austrian portion of the peninsula. Russia, it is understood, having her own views on Austria, acquiesced. But, within a few weeks, the enterprise was bursting the bounds that its promoters had hoped to set to it. Accordingly through Europe flew the news that the war was stopped. . . . Since then the Italians have been doing their best to wind up the unfinished business as satisfactorily for themselves as the state of the case will permit. . . .

Such has been the course of European events during the last eleven years; on the fringe of such a continental state of things as the attained result, does Great Britain now stand. The important consideration, we repeat, is that all is not yet over — and this not in the ordinary sense which implies that there never is rest in human affairs, but in a sense more special. Nothing is in a state which, even by a figure of speech, can be called permanent; all is glaringly out of equilibrium. The man who has done so much already is still in his cabinet in Paris, inscrutable as ever, twirling his moustache, and thinking what he shall do next. . . . Populations that made a start for constitutional government eleven years ago, and failed, are ready, on opportunity, to start again. The principle of nationality, laughed at as pedantry by some in our part of Europe, beats in the very blood and brain of other parts, so that armies are required to watch its pulsations. Italy may be patched, and patched; but all the patching that Congresses can devise will not smother, it seems, her passion for unity. It is not in the nature of things that the East of Europe can long remain as it is, an amorphous mass of struggling religions and races — one set leashed together by a Germanic knot and called Austria; another held more loosely in the clutches of the degenerate Turk; the whole with a bit of independent Greece for its Mediterranean tip, and a huge yellow Russia for its northern butt-end. The theory already in possession of the field for the organization of this chaos is that theory of Panslavism of which we have lately heard so much, which our practical little men of the West are also accustomed to deride, but which will awaken them some day with a vengeance . . .

Britain must make *herself* safe. That is the first duty. There must be a navy sufficient to ride round and round her, to keep the silver seas clear between her and the rest of the world, and to maintain her guard over her scattered dependencies. Her coasts must have the means of ample defence. Her population must be inferior to no other nation in the best and most approved gymnastic of arms. . . . [S]urely there is no greater infatuation than that which would oppose the universal desire of the country to see itself insured to the utmost amount of contemporary risk, and which, not hesitating to call Wellington[3] a dotard for having given it sorrowfully as his dying opinion that an invasion of this island was a military possibility, or to call Lyndhurst[4] foolish for accepting that opinion, or to make fun of past panics of invasion because it is eight centuries since an invasion actually succeeded, reserves all its denunciations of the war-spirit for our own modest and healthy efforts at defensive soldiering in our own field, and proposes as a better safeguard the habit of speaking soft of the very men abroad who practise this iniquity on the largest scale, and walk in war and bloodshed.

But Britain cannot lie like a log on the waters, contented to be secure herself, and regardless of what happens on all the earth besides. . . . At all times and in every emergency as it rises, there is one duty which Britain may systematically perform, whether active interference seems desirable or not — the duty of vigilant observation, and of honest and open criticism. At the present time especially the world is entitled to look at Great Britain for the efficient performance of this kind of service. Chaucer, in one of his poems, fancies a definite place, or focal point in the universe, called the House of Fame, where all the sounds from all the regions of the world meet and commingle, and where Fame, enthroned amid the roar of rumours, listens judicially to all, and blows back in response her blasts of praise or blame. England is at present this House of Fame for Europe — the one land where all reports may meet and none needs be stifled, where all facts and characters can be discussed in all ways, and where the trumpets of praise and blame can be freely blown. England may perform an inestimable service to the other nations by realizing this obvious fact about herself, and by maintaining, through her Press, a steady and courageous play of English public opinion upon European potentates and their acts. It is difficult to limit the good that may be done, or that has been done already, by this fulmination from our land of our independent insular verdicts on what passes abroad.

But we are not restricted to this kind of service, powerful as it may be . . . England is a powerful nation, a member of the commonwealth of nations, represented everywhere by ambassadors and ministers, and actually, through them, at every moment contributing for better or worse her advices on European emergencies as they successively arise. Every week there go despatches from our Foreign Office, committing us as a nation to some opinion on some international question, and to some course of policy affecting the interests of myriads of fellow-men whom our eyes shall never behold. Here then is a second form of international service which we actually do perform, through our Diplomacy, and which we may perform well or ill. Lastly, beyond this, and as a service of the last resort, not to be used except in great and rare exigencies — but the abnegation of which altogether would be to render all else without effect and to announce ourselves to the world as a passive crowd of insular lecturers — there is the exertion of our power to enforce our views. To decide the moment when this final mode of service shall be resorted to is the extreme responsibility of statesmanship, a question of combined principle and prudence so terrible and so complex, that perhaps it is well that we should have among us men whose eternal argument it is that it need never be resorted to at all. . . . Of all conceivable cases in which self-defence to the last extremity might be considered lawful, that one is least to be questioned in which the instinct of self-defence would coincide with the determination to preserve for England her right to be still an open House of Rumours wherein shall be performed for Europe, if no other service, at least the faithful service of free discussion. A blow at the appendages of our Empire were nothing so fatal as a blow at this liberty of our heart. . . . There is far less likelihood, despite the precedent of the Russian war, of a positive exertion of our strength in a cause not obviously and immediately our own. There may possibly, however, be occasions of this kind — occasions when either in a general conflict between organized Despotism and Liberty we should see ourselves compelled to take a part, or when some intolerable outrage of the fundamental principles of human society should bring us armed to the spot of the wrong. Were there a massacre of Christians in any Mohammedan part of the earth, we should make short work of the principle of non-interference. . . .

Whatever good Britain can do must be done by being true to herself — to her own principles, her own acquired convictions, even to what she and the world may regard as her peculiarities. Now, were an Englishman himself, or were a foreigner for him, to try to express generally in a few terms the distinctive characteristics of England, what else could he say but something to this effect — that England is a country of free institutions, Protestant in respect of religion, and mainly of the Anglo-Saxon branch of the Gothic race? Her compacted system of civil liberty, her Protestantism, and her Gothic descent and affinities — these are at least three facts or elements in her history and constitution. To a great extent, they are identical. It is in the Protestant nations that civil liberty has been realized in fullest degree; Protestantism, rightly understood, is but a name for the spirit of liberty; and the only nations in which Protestantism has succeeded have been those of the Gothic group — which nations, indeed, always had been, in a manner, Protestant. . . . Free herself Britain is bound to extend her sympathies to every manifestation in other lands of the spirit of liberty, to make liberty the object of her search, her anxiety, her reverence. Save for the presence among us of a few perverse spirits, who blaspheme our Liberty while they are eating its bread, and are clothed by its purchases, and protected in their very gabble by its shelter — a few passionless souls who sneer at that in the present which comes nearest, in aim and in promise, to what we all venerate in our own past — we have been true perhaps, within merely sentimental limits, to our own traditions of freedom in our judgments of recent continental events. We have not been so true to our Protestantism. Had we been so, then surelý, regarding it as one of our greatest advantages to have emancipated ourselves and all our concerns long ago from the notion of any duty of allegiance to a pontiff stationed in central Italy, and professing to be the one authorized button connecting earth and heaven, we should have welcomed, as supremely interesting, any spontaneous sign of a tendency, in still Papal parts of the earth, to follow our example, or (which might be equivalent) any efforts in those parts to reduce the Papacy to a purely spiritual power dependent thenceforth on its own merits. . . .

Within the limits of our own British islands, and much more within the limits of our varied and ocean-dislocated Empire, there are perpetually rising new difficulties and wants, craving the attention of whatever wisdom or authority may be nearest the spots where they rise, and also, in the last resort, of the collective wisdom and authority concentrated in Westminster. The application of social wisdom and ingenuity, through whatever organ, to the needs and uses of the community as they successively arise — this constitutes our Home Politics. Under this name, however, are usually comprehended only those questions which, from their nature, do not admit of being locally settled, but must be directly or indirectly referred to head-quarters.

It is said, indeed, that such questions are becoming rarer and rarer, and that ultimately the sole office of a central government will be that of a police preventing injustice between man and man, and so allowing free scope to individual action and to joint-stock enterprise; but even those who maintained that such a time is coming, do not say that it has come yet, but allow that there still remains for Government much deliberative business, if only in studying how to remove the restrictions, in the shape of past laws and institutions, by which individual action and the right of co-operation are still clogged. Others go farther, and maintain that even should a society ever reach the prophesied period when all shall be done by absolutely free individual action, coagulating into Joint-stock enterprise, Government would still emerge again in a positive form as the systematized Art of Joint-stock Enterprise; and so that even now, in this time of preliminary confusion, Government, besides its negative service of protection and the removal of restrictions, may assume the positive service of directing the co-operative tendency, indicating objects for it, and even provisionally doing some of its work. The difference may seem one of speculation; but it pervades our practical politics through and through, giving rise to discussions concerning Centralization and Local Government, and obviously distinguishing our statesmen into two classes — those who regard Government chiefly as a machinery for making new laws and institutions, and those who regard it rather as a machinery for removing old ones. For many years our most powerful and popular, perhaps also our most useful, politicians, have been of the latter class, destructive rather than constructive.

Whichever notion is entertained as to the true business of Government, there is no substantial difference anywhere among us as to the method by which the business must be performed. Ours is and has been for centuries a Government on the system of Representation. The greatness of Britain, its very existence, is identified with its representative or Parliamentary Constitution. True, in our House of Peers we have a part of our Constitution nominally not representative — a traditional and undissolved fragment of that older system in which a certain number of individuals in the community claimed the right of government as inhering in their own persons by their birth and position. True also there are different degrees of affection among us for that system of Representation of which we boast as our national possession, and different estimates of its sufficiency for all the work that is now or may soon be required of it . . . Nay, . . . all parties are at the present moment agreed that the basis of our representative system as established in 1832[5] is no longer adequate for our national purposes, and that a new measure is necessary which, besides other changes in our electoral arrangements, shall sound depths in our national being that have not yet been reached, and admit a far larger proportion of our population to the franchise of full citizenship. . . .

While Parliamentary reform, and its related questions of Ballot, Payment of Members, and the like, are the questions of home politics now most conspicuous on the board, other classes of questions are likewise presenting themselves. In Colonial administration, properly so called, nothing of much interest is at present under discussion; our compelled assent to the principle of colonial self-government having rid us of such questions of this class as might otherwise have been continually recurring. There is, however, the imperial question of India[6] — a question likely to task all

28

our ingenuity and all our energies for many a day to come. Nor must we forget, among our immediate home-questions, an important class of which we are likely to hear more and more, as stock political questions of Parliamentary Reform, &c. are disposed of and laid to sleep — those questions, we mean, of which the recent strikes have been at once an illustration and an announcement. Political Economy is the particular science of those social phenomena which relate to the acquisition of wealth; Politics is the general and more comprehensive science of social exigencies; and there is no order of questions more really pressing than those, little regarded at present, which lie athwart these two sciences, and will have to be settled between them.

Ever at the end of the list, as still unsettled and far from any probability of settlement, comes the question of the means of National Education[7] . . . Of all franchises that can be conferred on the working-man, the greatest is the franchise of books. Teach a man thoroughly to read and write; and he has the means of being almost anything he chooses to be, intellectually. Might it not be well, then, if we were to consider it as the primary function of a national school system — other things, of course, being reserved — to impart to all the children in a community, the full use of this franchise; in other words, if we were to be content, in the first place, with such a scheme of national education as would render it impossible for any boy or girl born on British ground to grow up untaught to read and write.

Notes

1. *eleven years*: 1848 was the 'year of revolutions' when a number of European countries under repressive and foreign governments, largely established by the Congress of Vienna in 1815, broke out in anti-despotic movements. The Second French republic was formed, the Italian and German princes, with the King of Prussia and even the Austrian Emperor, were compelled to accede to popular demands. By 1859 the most threatening centres of conflict were in 'the East of Europe' in the Austrian Empire where the revolts of Hungary and Italy had been put down with extreme brutality, and in south-eastern Europe, where the plight of the subject nations threatened to invite Russian interventions. Italy, meanwhile, struggled to be united and free of the oppressor Austria, and the threat of France.

2. *his uncle's place*: Napoleon III, nephew of Bonaparte, had been declared emperor in 1852. He had returned to France from exile in England, after the 1848 revolution had toppled Louis Philippe, 'The Citizen King'.

3. *Wellington*: The Duke of Wellington was Prime Minister, 1828–30.
4. *Lord Lyndhurst* was Lord Chancellor.
5. *1832*: The Great Reform Bill.
6. *India*: Masson is writing two years after the Indian Mutiny, after which the British government had officially replaced the East India Company as administrators.
7. *National Education*: See *Education*, below.

1.2 Mr. Bright and democracy

From a pamphlet, a reprint of a letter to the Scotsman, *dated 20 January 1866, from Edinburgh University, where John Blackie was Professor of Greek. Blackie writes, in his own phrase, as 'a tried friend of the working-classes', but who none the less opposed this extension of the franchise, for the reasons given in his letter. There had been growing pressure for parliamentary reform, which came to a climax in the Reform Riots in Hyde Park in 1866.*

If there be any supporters of the present measure who imagine that the bill now contemplated is in any sense to be accepted as a final settlement of a great organic question, they are among the most short-sighted of mortals. The present lowering of the franchise will in due season descend to household and manhood suffrage, just as certainly as a heavy vehicle, once launched from a hill top, without a drag, down a steep incline, will find the bottom. . . .

That the present measure[1] . . . has its real origin in John Bright[2] — is, in fact, a part of his scheme to remodel our political organisation after the type of America — no well-informed person can doubt. Some years ago . . . after having been assaulted by repeated demonstrations of democratic sentiment from him for more than two hours, against every one of which I stoutly rebelled, I put the question — What do you mean by democracy, Mr. Bright? — do you really mean to say that, with regard to all public questions, a statesman has nothing to do but call the masses of the people together, and follow the verdict of the majority? 'Yes,' he said, 'unquestionably this is my creed — *the majority is always right.'* . . . This sentence, in fact, is the foundation-stone of all democracy; and whether confessed or not, lies as the postulate of all the arguments generally advanced by those who support what I think may fairly be termed American in contra-distinction to British views on this important subject. . . . [H]e told me . . .

that, in order to arrive at a correct appreciation of the subject, I should study — what do you imagine? — de Tocqueville's[3] famous work! I never felt more astonished. I told him that this was the very book from which, chiefly, I had derived my ideas about the action of democracy in America . . .; and from the perusal of this very book I had risen with the conviction that democracy is one of the worst of all forms of government; and, wherever it gets free scope, acts as a moral and social poison, which, like strong liquor, degrades the people whom it inspires. . . . I have, and have all along, been as decidedly in favour of a representation of the working classes as I am set against any further importation of American ideas into this country. That labour specially, as labour, was not represented in the Reform Bill of 1832, I consider a great misfortune, and no small defect; but that number, and number alone, should be made the determining element in all political struggles certainly never entered into the thoughts of the wise men who introduced that measure, as the absence of such a gross absurdity certainly never can be accounted one of its defects which it was left to the superior wisdom of the present generation to supply. Whatever principle the Reform Bill did assert, it did not assert this. My opinion is, that it asserted no principle at all; that it merely threw in, more or less at random, a strong popular element, as a make-weight against the aristocratic element in the Constitution, which had hitherto been too highly favoured. . . . [I]t meant to say, practically at least, if not in a scientific formula, that the monarchy of the middle classes is best. But what we are now told is, that the monarchy of the middle classes is bad, and that the only effective way for the country to advance in a healthy political life, is to introduce the sub-middle and the lower classes on an equal footing with the middle and upper classes as rulers of the country in the last resort; the effect of which, of course, will be, by a mere trick of elementary arithmetic, to outvote all the other classes — practically disfranchise all who do not believe in the superior wisdom and discernment of these new leaders of public thought. Such a radical change is as much contrary to sound reason as to the whole habits and traditions of our mixed government in this country. . . . The classes of society lie above one another in the main, exactly as the strata do in a geological series. Each layer of rocks has its own characteristic fossils; and so each social formation, so to speak, has characteristic opinions, interests, tendencies, prejudices, and passions. I hold it quite certain, therefore, that if Edinburgh had twenty thousand voters to-morrow, the great majority of the new electors . . . would hold together, and the monarchy of the lower classes would be established. . . . Those, therefore, who advocate the proposed changes must be fully convinced in their own mind that the working classes are the most trustworthy portion of the community — that in political matters we can have no safer guides — and that it is right and proper that the influence of the upper and middle classes of society — with all the intelligence, virtue, property, character, and position which belong to them — should be surrendered to the one determining element of number in the lower classes. For let this be distinctly noted, it is by this element of number alone that the working classes can assert any superiority to the middle classes. . . . About their intelligence a great deal has been said by their advocates in this movement. I do not in the slightest degree doubt it. I have met many most sensible, well-informed, and sometimes even scientific-minded men in that class. But that, taken as a class, they are equally intelligent with the classes above them, I do not believe — nay, more, I am convinced they never can be. But be this as it may, what is to be represented, according to my view, in their case is labour, not intelligence; and what I protest against, in the democratic movement now made in their name, is not their lack of intelligence . . . but simply and sheerly their numbers. I object to being ruled by a mere indiscriminate accumulation of human units. . . . One great object of all good government, I conceive, was to protect the weak against the strong — to save minorities from the natural tendency of all the majorities to domineer, and overbear, and overwhelm. But now, according to the democratic doctrine, in the first and most important act of all government — the choosing of the men who are to determine our social happiness or misery — we are to fling overboard all considerations but that of mere arithmetical preponderance. What is this, as history in a thousand forms teaches, but to deliver ourselves bound hand and foot into the power of men elected under the swell of some popular excitement, not because they are themselves the wisest men of the community, or because they who elect them are so, but merely because the contagion of some plausible idea has seized on the majority, and the representative is the man who has been most largely infected with the poison? . . . I do not go to mobs for the collective wisdom of the community: I select — I sift — I distribute, and, if I cannot do better, I balance one class against another, and, by a composition of forces, strive to get a middle result, by which, at all events, reason may hold its own for a season between the antagonistic struggles of parties more anxious for victory than for justice. But from the political dominance of mere numbers I can look only for a reign of unreason, and the subjection of all virtues, excellences, and dignities in the State, to that element in society which makes a congregation of human beings most like to a troop of sheep or a battalion of bears.

Notes

1. *the present measure*: The Second Reform Bill (1867), as finally passed, practically doubled the electorate. It granted complete male household suffrage, giving the vote in addition to £10 lodgers and £12 leaseholders. It gave the vote to many of the middle class, and effectively enfranchised the Nonconformists. Forty-five new seats were also created for the big towns.

2. *John Bright*: MP for Birmingham and famous orator. Led a reform campaign in 1866 for the enfranchisement of town artisans and the lower middle class.

3. *de Tocqueville*: Alexis de Tocqueville (1805–59), French writer, author of *Democracy in America* (1845).

1.3   The ballot

From a pamphlet written by S. C. Kell in answer to J. S. Mill's remarks opposing the 1867 ballot in his Considerations on Representative Government. *The Ballot Act was passed in Gladstone's first administration, 1868–74, in 1872.*

As the time approaches when large numbers of the working classes of our fellow-countrymen are to be invested with the exercise of the electoral franchise, it becomes more and more important to discuss whether the votes with which they are to be entrusted shall be given with or without the protection of the ballot. My own opinion is most strongly in favour of the protection of secret voting, as the only mode by which the real conscientious opinion of the voter can be obtained. Where the voter has no conscience, or no opinion, of course neither the ballot nor open voting can give the public the benefit of a good vote; but the ballot would at least prevent the rogue from selling his vote, and some equally unprincipled candidate from buying it, thereby lessening by so much the influence of money and knavery at elections.

That the minds of a vast proportion of the present constituency and the present House of Commons have been debauched by the system of open voting, there can be little doubt. All parties have so often witnessed, experienced, or exercised some form of degree of the corrupting influence, from the pressure of a little 'cold shoulder' at the church or chapel, club, or other clique, up to the shameless bribery at Lancaster and Totnes,[1] that electors and elected have come to regard the offence of unconscientious voting with the most disgusting leniency. Here is a crime at least equal, in moral turpitude, to embezzlement with breach of trust, or to perjury; and yet if it were proposed in the House to visit both briber and bribed with the same punishment as is awarded to these crimes, the proposition would certainly not be sanctioned either by the House or by the public opinion of our present constituent body.

[I] will now shortly notice [some] objections to secret voting which have been advanced.

1st. That it is un-English. This argument I hold to be entirely *in its favour*. What takes place at every contested election under the 'English' system, ought to make the ears of every Englishman tingle with shame. . . .

2nd. That it induces lying. Well, there certainly would, *at first*, be some false promises made, which broken promises might well be called *white* lying, and be put on about the same footing as a promise to a highwayman, which he extorted with a pistol at your head, that you would send him £50 next evening to a certain place, and which promise you kept by sending a set of policemen to take him into custody. Both these classes of promises are those *which it is every man's bounden duty to break* . . .

3rd. It is asked, If the ballot be good for choosing a Member of Parliament, why not for the voting in the House of Commons? The positions are essentially different. The elector, it is allowed on all hands, has to give his vote according to his own individual opinion of the public good; he is an integer of that body, 'The people, the only legitimate source of political power' (as the old Whig toast had it), and there is no ultimate authority you can make him responsible to greater than his own; you cannot go farther back. The Member of Parliament, on the other hand, is elected to represent the opinions of the constituency who choose him, and it is only by his votes they can know he really does so; therefore while the electors have a right to know how the member votes, no one has a right to know how they vote, they being the ultimate political power.

4th. It is stated the ballot will not be necessary for the new enlarged constituency of working men about to be admitted to the franchise, because by means of their trades unions and other associations they will be able to defend themselves against the arts of the tempter. But suppose a good proportion of them should *like* being tempted, as we find to be actually the case with the same class of voters in the municipal elections? I have been told by those who must know that in very many cases success in the election of town councilman will go with whoever will spend the most money in drink and cabs. Trades unions cannot hinder votes from being bought and sold for liquor; nothing but the secret vote which puts a wall of separation between the buyer and seller, can stop this traffic. . . .

5th. That the ballot tends to make men cowardly sneaks, seeing that a man should go up to the poll and declare his opinion by his vote in the eyes of all the world, not caring for any one's smile or frown. But suppose a man's bread and that of his wife and children depend on some one's smile or frown? the present system, working through his holiest affections, makes a sneak of him, for you cannot expect a man to plunge all he loves best into misery for the sake of voting right. With the ballot he would simply do his duty, none daring to make him afraid. . . .

6th. It is said that bribery and undue influence may be put down by severe penal enactments. I deny that any laws would, or could, bring into court and prove one in a million of the cases that occur. In the first place, only bribery, the actual purchase and sale of the vote for money is tangible enough to be laid hold of legally at all, and how seldom can a case of bribery be proved! The only witnesses of the act are generally the two culprits, the buyer and the seller themselves, both equally interested in concealing it. But direct bribery does not form a thousandth part of the cases of undue influence. Consider the innumerable ties of quasi-dependence that exist throughout society, between its richer and poorer portions, between landlord and tenant, customer and tradesman, employer and employed, the dispensers of all sorts of social favours and the candidates for the same. All these countless leverages, great and small, numerous as the sands of the sea, are brought to to bear at elections, and the law cannot touch a single case of them all. A landlord makes it known that he expects his tenants to vote for a certain candidate, and experience has shown that tenants who on former occasions have voted against the wish of that landlord, have always been evicted from their houses or farms. The magnates near a country town rule the electors of that town through a tacit understanding regarding their custom. Employés get to know without ever being told so, that the security of their situations depend[s] on their being compliant. The law can touch none of these cases. . . .

7th. It has been said that a House of Commons elected by ballot would not have passed the Reform Bill[2] accepted by the present House. If it would not, it would have been compelled, *as the present House has been, against its will*, by pressure from without to pass it. But no one, I should think, can doubt that on the whole, *very far more* of the foul influences have always been exercised by toryism upon radicalism, than by radicalism upon toryism, so that the want of the ballot has always on the whole worked *against* the liberals. A constituency chosen by ballot would probably have given us a better Reform Bill than the present one long ago.

Notes

1. *shameless bribery at Lancaster and Totness*: See article 1.4 below by Lewis Emanuel on 'Corrupt Practices at Parliamentary Elections', which records that these two boroughs were disenfranchised in 1867.
2. *Reform Bill*: The Second Reform Bill was actually before the House for several years. Gladstone had introduced a small measure of working-class enfranchisement in the Bill before Russell's Liberal government of 1865–66, which had been defeated. It was passed in modified form by Disraeli's government in 1867.

1.4 Corrupt practices at parliamentary elections

From an address delivered at Lewisham, 1881. The author, Lewis Emanuel, a lawyer, reflects ruefully that in spite of fifty years of electoral reform, the 'Augean stable' remains!

Fifty-six . . . close boroughs were swept away by the Reform Bill of 1832, and the seats thus set free were allotted to large, populous, and wealthy communities. No Act of Parliament can make a nation virtuous. The legislator cannot alter the habits of a people by a stroke of the pen; and it is to be feared that this measure, bold and decisive as it was, failed to cleanse the Augean stable. There is a corrupt element in almost every constituency. In the larger ones it is comparatively harmless; it is counteracted by the influence of the pure and respectable electors; but, in small constituencies, it is otherwise; in these close and stagnant bodies there is nothing to leaven the old habits and traditions, to resist or to correct corrupt tendencies. In such places, the recollection of the high price which had formerly been given for a vote is so dearly cherished that nothing but radical measures will ever remove the existing abuses. To deprive the voters, in these small boroughs, of the price of their vote would be, in their estimation, to deprive political life of its great, its only charm.

The evils of the old system not having been entirely removed by the Reform Bill, it has been found necessary, from time to time, to repeat the purging process introduced by that Bill, whenever very flagrant cases of electoral corruption have been brought to light.

Thus, in 1852, Sudbury and St. Albans were disfranchised by Act of Parliament. Under the Representation of the People's Act of 1867, Yarmouth, Lancaster, Totnes, and Reigate forfeited their seats; and Bridgewater, Beverley, Sligo, and Cashel were dealt with in like manner in 1870. It is important to observe that these condemned boroughs were all small and comparatively unimportant places. In others, the extreme penalty of the law was not imposed, but the constituency was warned by the suspension of the issue of a fresh writ.

The second Report of the Commissioners, appointed in 1869, to inquire into the existence of corrupt practices at Bridgewater, is a painfully interesting document. No honest-minded Englishman can read it without a blush. Bridgewater was a borough so thoroughly steeped in corruption that, according to the Report, not a single pure election had been held there within the present century; three-fourths of the voters were found to have been guilty of bribery: so entirely had electoral corruption become a habit that the bribes were often claimed as of right.

After the last general election (1880) forty-two petitions were presented, impeaching the validity of the returns in as many constituencies. If we read the names of these forty-two suspected constituencies we shall find that certain characteristics distinguish nearly all the boroughs. It will be seen, 1st, that (with the solitary exception of Macclesfield) they are old constituencies, *i.e.*, they existed prior to the Reform Bill; 2nd, that the number of registered electors is comparatively small, ranging from 288 at Dungarven to 7,611 at Chester; 3rd, they are places which in population, wealth, and importance, are not progressive. . . . In nine of the forty-two cases in which petitions were presented, the judges reported that corrupt practices had extensively prevailed. . . .

The effect of such a report is, that the House of Commons advises Her Majesty to issue a Royal Commission to inquire into the allegations of bribery. The Commissioners, who are always members of the Bar, are charged with the investigation of the electoral practices in the constituency, not only on the last occasion, but at previous times also. The Commissioners are invested with ample powers for compelling the attendance of witnesses, examining them on oath, calling for the production of documents, and committing for contempt. A witness who tells all he knows receives a certificate which indemnifies him, and protects him from all penal consequences. Those, on the other hand, who fail to make a full disclosure do not receive a certificate, and, if they have been guilty of electoral offences, expose themselves to the risk of prosecution. It should be stated that if a person who has been guilty of corrupt practices can be proved to be an authorised agent of a candidate, the latter loses his seat; but, unless he be personally implicated, he suffers no other penalty; the actual offender is always liable to fine and imprisonment, and to forfeiture of his political rights, unless he obtain a certificate of indemnity from the Commissioners. Practically he always does obtain one by giving evidence. . . .

Every Englishman who loves his country, and whether he be Liberal or Conservative, should desire to see the political system purged of these impurities. It has been said that the last General Election cost two millions, — double the amount of any previous contest. How was all that money spent? The greater portion of it went to enrich the agents, the publicans, and the sinners of the electoral body. The amount of the bribe ranged from a few shillings to £30 or £40, according to the rank of the elector and the severity of the fight. In many instances the electors made no disguise in selling their votes; very often they regarded it (as under the old rotten borough system) as their right and privilege, and bargained for as high a price as they could get. Instances, and not a few, are recorded, in which an elector received a bribe from both parties; in some cases he was bribed by one party, and voted for the other; electors more than once received a bribe, and did not vote at all. Over and over again, money intrusted to an inferior agent for distribution was appropriated by the agent to his own use, thus adding embezzlement to the minor offence. Sometimes, the bribery was open, and undisguised, at others, cunning and mysterious contrivances were resorted to in order to avoid detection. . . . We find magistrates, mayors, aldermen, and councillors, professional men, merchants, and manufacturers grovelling together in this mire of corruption. It is a sickening picture, a sad parody on representative government! The theory is that England is governed by the people. The fact is beginning to force itself upon our conviction that England is ruled by money. . . . The practice disgraces us as a nation; it is, perhaps, more conspicuous in us than it would be in any other people, inasmuch as the British Constitution is studied, as a model, by every country that is desirous of organising a Constitutional Government.

1.5   Evidence to the Playfair Commission

Sir Charles Trevelyan, co-author with Sir Stafford Northcote of a previous report in 1853 on the civil service, is submitting evidence to the Civil Service Inquiry Commissioners, chaired by Lyon Playfair, 19 March 1875.

I wish briefly to explain the circumstances which led up to the report of Sir Stafford Northcote and myself on the organization of the permanent Civil Service. The revolutionary period of 1848 gave us a shake, and created a disposition to put our house in order, and one of the consequences was a remarkable series of investigations into public offices, which lasted for five years. . . . We inquired into a large number of public establishments, some of them, as for instance the Post Office and the Office of Works, more than once, and we found, as we went on, the same evils, and circumstances pointing to the same remedies, with reference to every department . . .

   The general purport of the report was to indicate a great evil and an effective remedy. The evil is what is generally known under the

head of 'patronage'. The then state of the public service with
reference to it is described as page 336 . . . It is as follows:—

It would be natural to expect that so important a profession
would attract into its ranks the ablest and the most ambitious
of the youth of the country; that the keenest emulation would
prevail among those who had entered it; and that such as were
endowed with superior qualifications would rapidly rise to
distinction and public eminence. Such, however, is by no
means the case. Admission into the Civil Service is indeed
eagerly sought after, but it is for the unambitious and the
indolent or incapable that it is chiefly desired. Those whose
abilities do not warrant an expectation that they will succeed
in the open professions, where they must encounter the competition of their contemporaries, and those whom indolence of
temperament or physical infirmities unfit for active exertions,
are placed in the Civil Service, where they may obtain an
honourable livelihood with little labour, and with no risk;
where their success depends upon their simply avoiding any
flagrant misconduct, and attending with moderate regularity
to routine duties; and in which they are secured against the
ordinary consequences of old age or failing health by an
arrangement which provides them with the means of supporting themselves after they have become incapacitated. It may
be noticed in particular that the comparative lightness of the
work, and the certainty of provision in case of retirement
owing to bodily incapacity, furnish strong inducements to the
parents and friends of sickly youths to endeavour to obtain for
them employment in the service of the Government; and the
extent to which the public are consequently burdened, first
with the salaries of officers who are obliged to absent themselves from their duties on account of ill health, and afterwards with their pensions when they retire on the same plea,
would hardly be credited by those who have not had opportunities of observing the operation of the system. It is not our
intention to suggest that all public servants entered the
employment of the Government with such views as these; but
we apprehend that as regards a large proportion of them these
motives more or less influenced those who acted for them in
the choice of a profession; while on the other hand there are
probably very few who have chose this line of life with a view
to raising themselves to public eminence. The result naturally

is that the public service suffers both in internal efficiency and in public estimation. The character of the individuals influences the mass, and it is thus that we often hear complaints of official delays, official evasions of difficulty, and official indisposition to improvement.

I think that attention should be called to the then actual state of the Civil Service; because, happily, it is a bygone state of things. . . . The remedy is mentioned at page 343, where we say:—

We accordingly recommend that a central board should be constituted for conducting the examination of all candidates for the public service whom it may be thought right to subject to such a test. Such board should be composed of men holding an independent position and capable of commanding general confidence. It should have at its head an officer of the rank of privy councillor, and should either include or have the means of obtaining the assistance of persons experienced in the education of the youth of the upper and middle classes and persons who are familiar with the conduct of official business. It should be made imperative upon candidates for admission to any appointment (except in certain special cases which will presently be noticed) to pass a proper examination before this board, and obtain from them a certificate of having done so. We are of opinion that this examination should be in all cases a competing literary examination. This ought not to exclude careful previous inquiry into the age, health, and moral fitness of the candidates. Where character and bodily activity are chiefly required more comparatively will depend upon the testimony of those to whom the candidate is well known; but the selection from among the candidates who have satisfied these preliminary inquiries should still be made by a competing examination. This may be so conducted as to test the intelligence as well as the mere attainments of the candidates. We see no other mode by which (in the case of inferior no less than of superior offices) the double object can be attained of selecting the fittest person and of avoiding the evils of patronage. For the superior situations endeavours should be made to secure the services of the most promising young men of the day by a competing examination on a level with the highest description of education in this country . . .

I submit that the remedy proposed by the report has been successful, patronage has for the time become a thing of the past, and we obtain a very superior class of candidates compared with those whom we had before.

1.6   The Poor Law and charity

From Macmillan's Magazine, *Vol. 15, December 1866. The author, the Rev. J. Llewellyn Davies, himself a Poor Law Guardian, is anxious about the demoralising effects of the New Poor Law (1834). This abolished the 'Speenhamland System', which allowed the wages of the agricultural poor to be supplemented by rates from the parish, without ensuring at the same time that a living wage was paid. The workhouse was now often the only alternative to starvation — and the Act also made sure that conditions in the workhouse were harsher than the life of free labour outside.*

Who can help desiring that the respectable poor who have fallen into misfortune should be treated more indulgently, or less sternly, than those who make themselves destitute through idleness and profligacy? . . . The following considerations are reasons . . . why all decent poor people should shrink from the workhouse.

1. Poor-law relief must open its doors to the very dregs of the population. Pauperism is not necessarily a crime; but paupers are sure to consist in no trifling proportion of the worthless and vicious, if not of actual criminals . . .

2. Poor-law relief may be claimed as a matter of right. The poor are perfectly aware of this. . . . They need ask no favour, and show no gratitude; all that they have to do is to force themselves with determination upon the officials and the Board.

3. Relief being thus guaranteed as a matter of right to all who are miserable enough to claim it, a perpetual siege is kept up by those who are not above parading and feigning misery against the resolution and watchfulness of the official relief-givers. . . . One of the notorious difficulties of Poor-law management in London and other large towns is the extremely low and savage kind of life which prevails amongst the Irish immigrants. Many of these poor creatures can exist, and even live with some cheerfulness, in a condition to which it seems impossible to refuse aid. In the great

poor districts of London, Boards of Guardians and their servants are necessarily in a constant attitude of defence against the appeals and the artifices of the uncivilized class. . . .

4. It is impossible to adopt the expedient which all would desire if possible to introduce, of treating applicants according to their character. You cannot safely attempt a moral classification. . . . This is a sad drawback to every department of our workhouse system. . . . The people of the best character are always exposed to the profane and vile language, to the lies, to the quarrelsome and slanderous tendencies of the most degraded. . . .

5. Discipline may no doubt do a great deal to make life endurable in such circumstances. But at what a cost is this done! Those who enter the region of dreary unbending uniformity situated within our workhouse walls may not quite leave all hope behind; but they unquestionably leave all personal freedom at the gate. With the important exception that they may at any time 'take their discharge,' the inmates of our workhouses are slaves, with a slavery only exceeded by that of the prison. Apart from the regulations by which every hour of their life is inexorably governed, think of the single fact that paupers are incapable of owning the very smallest piece of private property. An inmate, when he has passed the door, ceases to own the poor clothes he stands up in. They are taken from him, and he puts on a uniform which is the property of the house. If he is allowed to leave the house for an hour, his pockets are searched when he returns. He must open any letters he receives in the presence of an official, lest he should receive postage-stamps or other gifts in an envelope. In the eye of the law he cannot call even his Bible or his Prayer-book his own . . .

And I never heard of any agitation for the purpose of abolishing this slavery. There used to be protests made, I remember, against the separation of husband and wife, of parents and children. But these protests, so far as I know, have died out; and philanthropists have of late accepted the leading features of workhouse system as inevitable . . .

A large amount of money is now expended by societies and by individuals in relieving distress in the metropolis. . . . Consider what is given away in a poor London locality. There is first the Church relief, dispensed by clergymen and district visitors and lay agents. Then there are the alms which radiate from every dissenting chapel, the alms which follow in the wake of the City Missionary and his meeting, of Mrs. Ranyard's Bible-women and her meeting, the alms given by the Ragged School to the children and their parents. Add what is diffused by the almoners of the Associations for the Relief of Distress. Time would fail me to speak of the Kitchens, and Dinner-tables, and Coal and Bread Associations, and local Samaritan or Philanthropic Societies, and Lying-in Charities, which one after another recur in the memory, all working independently in the same field. . . . Any one who studies closely the history of a parish can see only too plainly the symptoms of the demoralization caused by irregular alms-giving. . . . But cannot our present chaotic alms giving be organized? . . . All distress caused immediately by vice or wilful folly should belong to the province of the law. For a different reason, but under the pressure of a strong necessity, all distress arising from want of employment should be similarly dealt with, — except when the loss of employment has an exceptional origin, as in the case of the cotton famine. These two heads comprise both the largest portion and the obviously impracticable portion, of existing pauperism. Voluntary charity might hope to provide for those who are brought to want by a visitation of illness, and for those who are permanently disabled and without relatives to support them. These would be the two great classes to be saved from the humiliations of the workhouse, and within the latter might be comprised the class of widows who have young children to maintain. . . .

We cannot by these schemes prevent misery, we can only mitigate it; and we may often fail to do even that. When scandals of destitution, such as deaths from starvation,[1] occur, I think it is far more melancholy that our social system should be one that generates such accidents than that our remedial measures should not have been at hand to relieve them . . .

Note

1. *deaths from starvation*: Ruskin made one example famous in *Sesame and Lilies*.

1.7   Mr. Gladstone and our Empire

From The Nineteenth Century, *Vol. 2, September 1877. The author is Edward Dicey (1832–1911), author and journalist, editor of* The Observer.

It does not logically follow that because a politician objects to any further extension of our Empire he should therefore be in favour of its dismemberment. But if once this country comes to the conclusion that we have had enough of empire, and that we should do wisely to reduce our Imperial liabilities as soon as we can do so consistently with the moral obligations we have undertaken, then the days of our rule as a great Power beyond the four seas are clearly numbered. Englishmen who live out their lives in these small islands, who give the best of their labour to the questions, conflicts, issues of our insular existence, are apt to forget what England is in truth. Take up any gazeteer and you will find there what every schoolboy is supposed to know, but what to scores of Englishmen out of every hundred will read like a new discovery, the dimensions of the Empire of Great Britain. The United Kingdom, with an area of 120,000 square miles and a population of thirty-three millions, rules over eight million square miles of the globe's surface and two hundred millions of the world's inhabitants. Open any map, and glance for one moment at the dominions in which the Union Jack is the standard of the ruling race! Canada, stretching from the Atlantic to the Pacific, the peninsula of India, the continent of Australia, the South of Africa, are only the largest blotches so to speak, in a world chart blurred and dotted over with the stamp marks of British rule. Spread-eagle declamation about the Empire over which the sun never sets is not in accordance with the taste of our day, or the tone of thought which prevails amidst our governing classes. Facts and not fancies are the cry of the age. But it is well to remember that, after all, the existence of the British Empire is a fact and not a fancy. . . . Wherever the Union Jack floats, there the English race rules; English laws prevail; English ideas are dominant: English speech holds the upper hand. Our Empire may or may not be a benefit to England or to the countries over which she holds dominion; but its reality is as certain as its magnitude. . . . All I do assert is that England, like Rome, is the corner-stone of an imperial fabric such as it has fallen to the lot of no other country to erect, or to uphold when erected. This being so — and that it is so even the most fanatical of anti-imperialists will admit — the burden of proof surely rests with those who would pull down this Greater Britain, or allow it to fall to pieces, not with those who would consolidate or, if need be, extend the inheritance handed down to us by the labour, self-sacrifice, and courage of bygone generations of Englishmen.

The general issue of Empire or no Empire is not affected by considerations as to individual augmentations or cessions of territory. I may admit, as a matter of argument, that England gained, rather than lost, by the secession of her American colonies; that the cession of the Ionian Islands was a wise measure and the annexation of Fiji an unwise one. I may even acknowledge that the secession of Canada from the mother country is an event to be looked forward to without regret. Personally I should dissent from most of these conclusions; but, even if I accepted them, I should see no cause to alter my view, that the maintenance of the Empire — that is of British authority over a vast outlying territory — ought to be one of the chief, if not the chief, object of British statesmanship. . . . What I want to point out is that our Empire is the result not so much of any military spirit as of a certain instinct of development inherent in our race. We have in us the blood of the Vikings; and the same impulse which sent the Norsemen forth to seek new homes in strange lands has, for century after century, impelled their descendants to wander forth in search of wealth, power, or adventure. 'To be fruitful, and multiply, and replenish the earth', seems to be the mission entrusted to us, as it was to the survivors of the deluge. The Wandering Jew of nations, it is forbidden to us to rest. The history of all our conquests, settlements, annexations, is, with rare exceptions, substantially the same. Attracted by the hope of gain, the love of excitement, or, more still, by the mere migratory instinct, English settlers pitch their tents in some foreign land, and obtain a footing in the country. But, unlike the colonists of other races, they carry England with them; they keep their own tongue, marry amidst their own people, dwell after their own fashion, and, though they may live and die in the land of their adoption, look to the mother country as their home. As their footing becomes established their interests clash with those of the native population. Whether with or without due cause, quarrels ensue; and then, sometimes by their own energy, sometimes by the aid of England, sometimes by both combined, they establish their own supremacy and become the ruling race in the regions which they entered as traders . . . [T]he point I wish to have placed in a clear light is that our Empire is due, not to the ambition of kings, not to the genius of generals, not even to the prevalence of one of those phases of military ardour through which most nations have to pass, but to the silent, constant operation of the instincts, laudable or otherwise, which have filled the world with the sound of the English tongue.

1.8   Two Trips to Gorilla Land

From Two Trips to Gorilla Land *(1876). Sir Richard Burton (1821 – 90), explorer and scholar, expresses scant respect for English colonial policy in Africa.*

After a languid conviction during the last half-century of owning some ground upon the West Coast of Africa,[1] England has been rudely aroused by a little war which will have large consequences. The causes that led to the 'Ashantee Campaign' . . . may be broadly laid down as general incuriousness, local mismanagement, and the operation of unprincipled journalism.

It is not a little amusing to hear the complaints of the public that plain truth about the African has not been told. I could cite more than one name that has done so. But what was the result? We were all soundly abused by the negrophile; the multitude cared little about reading 'unpopular opinions'; and then, when the fullness of time came, it turned upon us, and rent us, and asked why we had not spoken freely concerning Ashanti and Fanti, and all the herd. My '*Wanderings in West Africa*' is a case in point: so little has it been read, that a President of the Royal Geographical Society could state, 'If Fantees are cowardly and lazy, Krumen are brave'; the latter being the most notorious poltroons on the West African seaboard.

The hostilities on the Gold Coast might have been averted with honour to ourselves at any time between 1863 and 1870, by a Colonial Office mission and a couple of thousand pounds. I need hardly say what has been the case now. The first steps were taken with needless disasters, and the effect has been far different from what we intended or what was advisable. For a score of years we [travellers] have been advising the English statesman not to despise the cunning of barbarous tribes, never to attempt finessing with Asiatic or African; to treat these races with perfect sincerity and truthfulness. I have insisted, and it is now seen with what reason, that every attempt at deception, at asserting the 'thing which is not', will presently meet with the reward it deserves. I can only regret that my counsels have not made themselves heard.

Yet this ignoble war between barbarous tribes whom it has long been the fashion to pet, this poor scuffle between the breechloader and the Birmingham trade musket, may yet in one sense do good. It must perforce draw public attention to the West Coast of Africa, and raise the question, 'What shall we do with it?' My humble opinion, expressed early in 1865 to the Right Honourable Mr. Adderley,[2] has ever been this. If we are determined not to follow the example of the French, the Dutch, the Portuguese, and the Spaniard, and not to use the country as a convict station, resolving to consume, as it were, our crime at home, we should also resolve to retain only a few ports and forts, without territory, at points commanding commerce, after the fashion of the Lusitanians in the old heroic days. The export slave-trade is now dead and buried; the want of demand must prevent its revival; and free emigration has yet to be created. As Mr. Bright[3] rightly teaches strong places and garrisons are not necessary to foster trade and to promote the success of missions. The best proof on the West African Coast is to be found in the so-called Oil Rivers, where we have never held a mile of ground, and where our commerce prospers most. The great 'Tribune' will forgive my agreeing in opinion with him when he finds that we differ upon one most important point. It is the merchant, not the garrison, that causes African wars. If the home authorities would avoid a campaign, let them commit their difficulty to a soldier, not to a civilian.

The chronic discontent of the so-called 'civilized' African, the contempt of the rulers if not of the rule, and the bitter hatred between the three races, white, black, and black-white, fomented by many an unprincipled print, which fills its pocket with coin of cant and Christian charity, will end in even greater scandals than the last disreputable war. If the *damnosa licentia* be not suppressed — and where are the strong hands to suppress it? — we may expect to see the scenes of Jamaica[4] revived with improvements at Sierra Leone. However unwilling I am to cut off any part of our great and extended empire, to renew anywhere, even in Africa, the process of dismemberment. . . . it is evident to me that English occupation of the West African Coast has but slightly forwarded the cause of humanity, and that upon the whole it has proved a remarkable failure.

Notes

1. *West Coast of Africa*: awarded to England at the Congress of Vienna, 1815.
2. *Mr. Adderley*: C. M. Adderley, Conservative Member of Parliament for North Staffordshire.
3. *Mr. Bright*: See note under 'Mr. Bright and Democracy'.
4. *Jamaica*: Governor Eyre had put down a black revolt in 1866 with notorious brutality.

2

The Gentleman

One interesting thing to emerge from the middle decades of the century is the parallel between the gradual democratisation of society and the growing tide of debate in every medium about the Gentleman — his definition, his nature, his function — as old aristocratic ideas were challenged and exploded. As the change in every sphere of life gained momentum, old status distinctions were realigned and the traditional hierarchy questioned. While preceding ages seemed to have been shaped largely by individual energy, a lot of the energy of the Victorians went into the development of institutions and corporate organisations, and this restructuring of society created areas of human life unrecognised by earlier tradition. It was a phenomenon discussed by every commentator on society, though most notably, perhaps, by Matthew Arnold.

Concepts and definitions of 'the middle class' and 'the gentleman' — Arnold's Philistines among them — took on fresh layers of meaning, and were endlessly debated. Social mobility made it obsessively interesting to try to establish the criteria for membership of the power élite; while more radical thinkers proposed that all men, regardless of their rank, should be esteemed according to their moral worth. New professions came into existence, and old ones expanded, as these new corporations recruited trained administrators for growth industries like transport or mining, and the Industrial Revolution created a need for technologists and engineers. In addition, the Post Office had been reorganised, the medical professions expanded, teaching recognised as a profession that needed manpower. With the Municipal Reform Act of 1835, local government had been established as a profession, and in 1875 the civil service was thrown open to competitive examination, making it, in principle, accessible to all. These were all new professions — but was the new professional man automatically a gentleman? Moreover, in the army (an old and gentlemanly profession) the purchase of commissions was abolished; and even the church, long the bastion of the old landowning classes, ceased to recruit exclusively from the universities, and took non-graduate ordinands from the new theological colleges. The Empire too provided fresh grounds for the expansion of the middle classes: an undiminishing stream emigrated beyond the seas to supply the needs of this new world.

J. S. Mill was afraid that all this activity would result in complete heterogeneity and the disappearance of the individual in society; but Samuel Smiles might have reassured him. Despite the institutionalising of society, the spirit of self-help and individual initiative produced as many great men as any previous age, and Smiles popularised the principle with his biographies of self-made men like George Stephenson and Josiah Wedgwood, and his enormously popular *Self-Help*. Trenchant evidence for the phenomenon, from several different points of view, is found in the contemporary fiction which made its own contribution to the debate, in Josiah Bounderby in *Hard Times* (1854) and *John Halifax, Gentleman* (1857), or even Jo Gargery and Pip in *Great Expectations* (1860). There was no lack of advice or direction on how to get to the top, in fact.

Undoubtedly the extension of the franchise was the first and most powerful force in the breakdown of familiar class distinctions. The other, which grew from it, was education. Education generally, and for the growing middle class in particular, had become a priority. This period marks the heyday of the public school, which proved a melting-pot for the old gentry and the new. To the ten traditional schools identified by the Royal Commission set up in 1866 to investigate the question were added dozens of new schools, including the Woodard Schools, founded after the Oxford Movement on church principles, specifically for the less affluent middle classes; and schools with a specific bias towards, for example, the army, or the Empire. They all took a common tone from the Rugby of Thomas Arnold, depicted in *Tom Brown's Schooldays* (1857). Squire Brown sent his son to Rugby to become 'a brave, helpful, truth-telling Englishman, and a gentleman'.

The universities, too (in the ideal defined by Newman in 1852), had a similar function, 'the nurturing . . . of gentlemen'; and in these exuberant days of reform their degrees continued to be one hallmark of a gentleman. Now to Oxford and Cambridge were added new Utilitarian universities, founded to educate the new middle classes excluded till now from the old universities. Meanwhile Oxford and Cambridge abolished the religious qualifications, first for undergraduates and then all members of the university; and these traditional fastnesses of the gentleman were finally accessible to all.

2.1   Character — the true Gentleman

From Self-Help, *(1859). The author, Samuel Smiles (1812 – 1904), was a popular writer and moralist who promulgated the contemporary spirit of self-help and personal initiative in his works on political and social reform.* Self-Help *was enormously popular, and was translated into many languages.*

As daylight can be seen through very small holes, so little things will illustrate a person's character. Indeed, character consists in little acts, well and honourably performed; daily life being the quarry from which we build it up, and rough-hew the habits which form it. One of the most marked tests of character, is the manner in which we conduct ourselves towards others. A graceful behaviour towards superiors, inferiors, and equals, is a constant source of pleasure. It pleases others because it indicates respect for their personality; but it gives tenfold more pleasure to ourselves. Every man may, to a large extent, be a self-educator in good behaviour, as in every thing else; he can be civil and kind, if he will, though he have not a penny in his purse. Gentleness in society is like the silent influence of light, which gives colour to all nature; it is far more powerful than loudness or force, and far more fruitful. It pushes its way quietly and persistently, like the tiniest daffodil in spring, which raises the clod and thrusts it aside by the simple persistency of growing. . . .

Morals and manners, which give colour to life, are of much greater importance than laws, which are but their manifestations. The law touches us here and there, but manners are about us everywhere, pervading society like the air we breathe. Good manners, as we call them, are neither more nor less than good behaviour; consisting of courtesy and kindness; benevolence being the preponderating element in all kinds of mutually beneficial and pleasant intercourse amongst human-beings. 'Civility,' said Lady Montague,[1] 'costs nothing and buys everything.' The cheapest of all things is kindness, its exercise requiring the least possible trouble and self-sacrifice. 'Win hearts,' said Burleigh to Queen Elizabeth, 'and you have all men's hearts and purses.' If we would only let nature act kindly, free from affectation and artifice, the results on social good-humour and happiness would be incalculable. Those little courtesies which form the small change of life, may separately appear of little intrinsic value, but they acquire their importance from repetition and accumulation. They are like the spare minutes, or the groat a day, which proverbially produce such momentous results in the course of a twelvemonth, or in a lifetime.

Manners are the ornament of action; and there is a way of speaking a kind word, or of doing a kind thing, which greatly enhances their value. What seems to be done with a grudge, or as an act of condescension, is scarcely accepted as a favour. Yet there are men who pride themselves upon their gruffness; and though they may possess virtue and capacity, their manner is often such as to render them almost insupportable. . . .

The cultivation of manner — though in excess it is foppish and foolish — is highly necessary in a person who has occasion to negotiate with others in matters of business. Affability and good breeding may even be regarded as essential to the success of a man in any eminent station and enlarged sphere of life; for the want of it has not infrequently been found in a great measure to neutralize the results of much industry, integrity, and honesty of character. There are, no doubt, a few strong tolerant minds which can bear with defects and angularities of manner, and look only to the more genuine qualities; but the world at large is not so forbearant, and can not help forming its judgments and likings mainly according to outward conduct.

Another mode of displaying true politeness is consideration for the opinions of others. It has been said of dogmatism, that it is only puppyism come to its full growth; and certainly the worst form this quality can assume, is that of opinionativeness and arrogance. Let men agree to differ, and, when they do differ, bear and forbear. Principles and opinions may be maintained with perfect suavity, without coming to blows or uttering hard words; and there are circumstances in which words are blows, and inflict wounds far less easy to heal. . . .

The inbred politeness which springs from right-heartedness and kindly feelings, is of no exclusive rank or station. The mechanic who works at the bench may possess it, as well as the clergyman or the peer. It is by no means a necessary condition of labour, that it should, in any respect, be either rough or coarse. The politeness and refinement which distinguish all classes of the people in many continental countries amply prove that those qualities might become ours too — as doubtless they will become with increased culture and more general social intercourse — without sacrificing any of our more genuine qualities as men. From the highest to the lowest, the richest to the poorest, to no rank or condition in life has nature denied her highest boon — the great heart. There never yet existed a gentleman but was lord of a great heart. And this may exhibit itself under the hodden grey of the peasant as well as under the laced coat of the noble. Robert Burns was once taken to task by a young Edinburgh blood, with whom he was walking, for recognizing an honest farmer in the open street. 'Why, you fantastic gomeral!' exclaimed Burns, 'it was not the great coat, the scone bonnet, and the saunders-boot hose that I spoke to, but *the man* that was in them; and the man, sir, for true worth, would weigh down you and me, and ten more such, any day.' There may be a homeliness in externals, which may seem vulgar to those who can not discern the heart beneath; but, to the right-minded, character will always have its clear insignia. . . .

The True Gentleman is one whose nature has been fashioned after the highest models. It is a grand old name, that of Gentleman, and has been recognized as a rank and power in all stages of society. 'The Gentleman is always the Gentleman,' said the old French General to his regiment of Scottish gentry at Rousillon, 'and invariably proves himself such in need and in danger.' To possess this character is a dignity of itself, commanding the instinctive homage of every generous mind, and those who will not bow to titular rank will yet do homage to the Gentleman. His qualities depend not upon fashion or manners, but upon moral worth — not on personal possessions, but on personal qualities. The Psalmist briefly describes him as one 'that walketh uprightly, and worketh righteousness, and speaketh the truth in his heart'.

The Gentleman is eminently distinguished for his self-respect. He values his character — not so much of it only as can be seen by others, but as he sees it himself; having regard for the approval of his inward monitor. And, as he respects himself, so by the same law, does he respect others. Humanity is sacred in his eyes; and thence proceed politeness and forbearance, kindness and charity. It is related of Lord Edward Fitzgerald that, while travelling in Canada, in company with the Indians, he was shocked by the sight of a poor squaw trudging along laden with her husband's trappings, while the chief himself walked on unencumbered. Lord Edward at once relieved the squaw of her pack by placing it upon his own shoulders — a beautiful instance of what the French call *politesse de coeur* — the inbred politeness of the true gentleman.

The true gentleman has a keen sense of honour — scrupulously avoiding mean actions. His standard of probity in word and action is high. He does not shuffle, or prevaricate, dodge nor skulk; but is honest, upright, and straightforward. His law is rectitude — action in right lines. When he says *yes*, it is a law: and he dares to say the valiant *no* at the fitting season. The gentleman will not be bribed; only the low-minded and unprincipled will sell themselves to those who are interested in buying them. . . .

Riches and rank have no necessary connexion with genuine gentlemanly qualities. The poor man may be a true gentleman — in spirit and in daily life. He may be honest, truthful, upright, polite, temperate, courageous, self-respecting, and self-helping — that is, be a true gentleman. The poor man with a rich spirit is in all ways superior to the rich man with a poor spirit. To borrow St. Paul's words, the former is as 'having nothing, yet possessing all things', while the other, though possessing all things has nothing. The first hopes every thing, and fears nothing; the last hopes nothing, and fears every thing. Only the poor in spirit are really poor. He who has lost all, but retains his courage, cheerfulness, hope, virtue, and self-respect, is still rich. For such a man, the world is, as it were, held in trust; his spirit dominating over its grosser cares, he can still walk erect, a true gentleman. . . .

Above all, the Gentleman is truthful. He feels that truth is the 'summit of being', and the soul of rectitude in human affairs. Lord Chesterfield, with all his French leanings, when he came to define a gentleman, declared that Truth made his success; and nothing that he ever said commanded the more hearty suffrage of his nation. The Duke of Wellington, who had an inflexible horror of falsehood, writing to Kellermann, when that general was opposed to him in the Peninsula, told him that if there was one thing on which an English officer prided himself more than another, excepting his courage, it was his truthfulness. 'When English officers,' said he, 'have given their parole of honour not to escape, be sure they will not break it. Believe me — trust to their word; the word of an English officer is a surer guarantee than the vigilance of sentinels.'

True courage and gentleness go hand in hand. The brave man is generous and forbearant, never unforgiving and cruel. It was finely said of Sir John Franklin by his friend Parry,[2] that 'he was a man who never turned his back upon a danger, yet of that tenderness that he would not brush away a mosquito.' A fine trait of character — truly gentle, and worthy of the spirit of Bayard — was displayed by a French officer in the cavalry combat of El Bodon in Spain. He had raised his sword to strike Sir Felton Harvey, but perceiving his antagonist had only one arm, he instantly stopped, brought down his sword before Sir Felton in the usual salute, and rode past. . . .

Notwithstanding the wail which we occasionally hear for the chivalry that is gone, our own age has witnessed deeds of bravery and gentleness — of heroic self-denial and manly tenderness — which are unsurpassed in history. The events of the last few years[3] have shown that our countrymen are as yet an undegenerate race. On the bleak plateau of Sebastopol, in the dripping perilous trenches of that twelve-months' leaguer, men of all classes proved themselves worthy of the noble inheritance of character which their forefathers have bequeathed to them. But it was in the hour of the great trial in India[4] that the qualities of our countrymen shone forth the brightest. The march of Neill on Cawnpore, of Havelock on Lucknow — officers and men alike urged on by the hope of rescuing the women and the children — are events which the whole history of chivalry cannot equal. Outram's conduct to Havelock, in resigning to him, though his inferior officer, the honour of leading the attack on Lucknow, was a trait worthy of Sydney, and alone justifies the title which has been awarded to him of, 'the Bayard of India' . . .

There are many tests by which a gentleman may be known; but there is one that never fails — How does he *exercise power* over those subordinate to him? How does he conduct himself towards women and children; How does the officer treat his men, the employer his servants, the master his pupils, and man in every station those who are weaker than himself? The discretion, forbearance, and kindliness with which power in such cases is used, may indeed be regarded as the crucial test of gentlemanly character. He who bullies those who are not in a position to resist may be a snob, but cannot be a gentleman. He who tyrannizes over the weak and helpless, may be a coward, but no true man. The tyrant, it has been said, is but a slave turned inside out. Strength, and the consciousness of strength, in a righthearted man, imparts a nobleness to his character; but he will be most careful how he uses it. . . .

Gentleness is indeed the best test of gentlemanliness. A consideration for the feelings of others, for his inferiors and dependants as well as his equals, and respect for their self-respect, will pervade the true gentleman's whole conduct.

Notes

1. *Lady Montagu*: Lady Mary Wortley Montagu (1689–1762), writer and leader of society.
2. *Sir John Franklin:* [*Sir William*] Parry: Contemporary Arctic explorers.
3. *The events . . . few years*: The Crimean War, fought against Russia, who was attempting to oust Turkey from the Balkans.
4. *great trial in India*: The Indian Mutiny (1857). Cawnpore and Lucknow both fell to the mutineers.

2.2   The grand old name of Gentleman

From The Contemporary Review, *Vol. 11, August 1869. This is a typical item, by J. R. Vernon, from the Victorian quest for the definition of the Gentleman, which they worried at with absorption.*

And thus he bore without abuse
  The grand old name of Gentleman;
  Defamed by every charlatan,
And soiled with all ignoble use.

In Memoriam

Many hues make up light; many ingredients a salad; many qualities the Gentleman. Like both the above, he is no heap of unamalgamated parts, but a perfect whole. And as, again, beautiful sounds amid discords and without connection are not music, so noble traits may be found in a person, and yet, being rare, unsustained, unbalanced, undovetailed into others, will not constitute the Gentleman. Many a one performs at times isolated acts that are gentle and noble. But what we want is the Gentleman; the man always noble — the perfect cube. . . . There is need that it be defined, for the words are true that the name, the grand old name, is nowadays more than ever 'defamed by every charlatan', and 'soiled with all ignoble use'. Not only are mere accidents or accessories regarded as though of the essence, but things which are quite foreign to it, and which sometimes actually encumber and obscure it, are regarded as though constituent parts of it. A large house, a carriage, much ostentation — what have these really to do with the character? Nor will those of the blood be deceived by them. But, with many, do they not pass off paste for jewels by their showy setting? . . .

We must start, then, by disencumbering ourselves of things external merely — rank, wealth, power, show — all the mere setting of the stone. And further, of things also which, though undeniably advantages and adornments, are yet not of the *essence* of this character; are accidental — can be dispensed with — though they adorn where they may be had. High breeding; liberal education; familiarity with the ways of the best society; polished behaviour; easy manners; experience of books, and men, and countries; absence of shyness; an acquaintance with what is not mere littleness in etiquette; — these may be the *cutting* of the jewel. Yet, though many of them will be assumed in this sketch, let it be declared at the outset that the *jewel* can exist without them. . . . The true gentleman is never a suspicious man, never a depreciator. He never gratuitously supposes meanness in another; in the general he is hopeful, and hardly made to distrust. Thus, in a world of extreme littleness and meanness, especially in the imputing of motives and in low suspicions, you are, in the society of the Gentleman, raised into a higher atmosphere; you breathe freer. Without effort, and naturally, he is walking on an eminence above those pettinesses, low considerations, and spites; and even if you stand not on it usually, you are, in your intercourse with him, raised to his level. You left the stinging midges, the foul vapours, below in the valley. Your point for the time is higher, your view less narrow; you stand and look down upon the dull mist that roofs the petty world.

It may be laid down as a first condition that the Gentleman has that just appreciation of self which constitutes self-respect. Now it is difficult to convey a true idea by this word; for some would understand *pride* by it, it being of the flattering names invented to mask the ugliness of the devil's sin. And of all qualities that the

Gentleman must *not* have, perhaps I would point out pride especially. A proud man cannot possibly be a true gentleman. But the Gentleman has a just appreciation of self — he respects himself. Now this *just* appreciation will be the very thing which prevents pride. He will have a mournful humility, possessing an ideal, short of which he finds himself to be ever falling. Still the very possession of this ideal will make him respect himself — will raise him above aught undignified and unworthy by the consciousness of a latent greatness. Of necessity, therefore, and essentially a humble man, he is not in the least cringing or abject. A gentleman is a MAN. And he realizes what is contained in that word, — the high descent, the magnificent destiny. So in the presence of his God and of his fellow-men he is never abject; he is always manly, always keeps self-respect; his humility is never a mean thing, it is a power that raises, not degrades. In him the taking the lower room leads surely to the going up higher, not from intention, but in result.

And this self-respect prevents his being over-sensitive to slight or affront. He is in a measure . . . *self-sufficient*, . . . So that upon occasion he can retire into this castle of his own self-respect, and consciousness of worth though but in embryo, and thus mildness and dignity can in him go hand in hand, commanding probably in the event the respect also of others. Quite feeling that there are in him such inadequacies and defects that it is always excusable and often just that others should think slightly of him, he yet is conscious of at least incipient, struggling worth and nobility that make him, in the Divine and in the larger human view, no object merely of contempt. He is company for himself; he has sympathy with himself; he understands himself, and retires on this inner consciousness when misunderstood by others; he is, in a sense, independent of them. . . .

I think that his manner and bearing towards Superiors are a delicate test. He avoids that tendency to over-deference which is the commoner fault; *also* that slight inclination to an over-independent manner, that standing on their guard to which minds above the more common weakness are apt to swerve. . . . the self-respect which averts the constant fear lest he should be humbled or mortified. The great thing, the result of these principles, is that he is at his ease. Due deference to others is natural to him, so also is the consciousness of what is due to himself. He can quite well do without the notice of those above him in the social scale, but he has stamina and ballast enough to enjoy their society without an ever-present sense of difference whispering him to be on his guard against a slight. And if the superior in position should not be a gentleman, *i.e.*, should obtrude that superiority, why the advantage instantly changes round and is on the side of the Gentleman, and he knows it, though too true to his character to make this knowledge patent. True gentleman meets true gentleman, recognising the brotherhood through the accidental and trivial distinctions of this brief state: they acknowledge these differences, but are not encumbered by them. . . .

I have already touched on the conduct of the Gentleman towards inferiors. Much lies in what I have hinted — namely, that he will be careless to any others rather than to them; he will err rather on the side of punctiliousness than of slovenliness. Of course he is not clumsy enough to make this noticeable, or to obtrude it. He would steer clear of an awkwardness which would make over-ceremony offensive by betraying the motive, and therefore the idea in his mind. Thus also he can afford to dispense, in his intercourse with them, with the very tiniest giving to understand that he is condescending. Indeed, he does not feel himself to be doing so, having a larger view of things than from this world's hillocks, and so he is able to be simple and natural. . . .

And now we come to the gentleman *at home*. This is certainly the crucial test. It is undoubtedly of all others the far most difficult sphere of action. There is the familiarity, the sense of undress, and of there being no need for '*company manners*'. (How this well-used word witnesses for the truth of what I am saying!) Certain positive restraints and obligations no longer hold back or bind a man in his own home. The gentleman has, therefore, to be on his guard, and to keep a vigilant watch against the creeping over his behaviour of the least slovenliness or tarnish.

> 'Love's perfect blossom only blows
>   Where noble manners veil defect:
> Angels may be familiar; those
>   Who err, each other must respect.'

This I take from a very manual upon this branch especially of my subject, full of delicate subleties — Coventry Patmore's *Angel in the House*.

The true gentleman, then, at home does not drop any of those attentions and courtesies to wife, sister, father, mother, which he is in the habit of paying to other ladies and gentlemen when in society. . . .

It seems an absurd truism to say, Let the husband who is ashamed to be attentive to his wife or sister, the son who is ashamed of being deferential to his father, — let these make no pretension to name of Gentleman; neither let him stain it with his touch, who, though he be the most polished gentleman in society, is yet a sloven in his manner at home. . . .

The Gentleman, I say, is always a student, for this character is greatly a matter of learning. . . . A finished artificial gentleman has attained to the art which veils art. A perfect real gentleman has nothing to conceal — he is acting naturally.

2.3   Mill on Liberty

From The National Review, *Vol. 8, April 1859. Review by R. H. Hutton of J. S. Mill's* On Liberty. *J. S. Mill's* On Liberty *(1859) had raised a questioning voice about the effects on society of the growing movement towards democracy. R. H. Hutton, critic, journalist and Unitarian theologian, protests that Mill's fears for individual freedom are overstated.*

We do not for a moment doubt that English 'public opinion' is a much more intelligible and homogeneous thing in our own day than it has ever been at any previous time; that it comprehends much fewer conflicting types of thought, much fewer distinctly divergent social tendencies, much less honest and sturdy controversy between diametrical opposites in intellectual theory. Sectarian lines are fading away, political bonds are sundering, even social attractions and repulsions are less marked than they used to be; and to this extent we willingly concede to Mr. Mill[1] that considerable progress is rapidly making towards that universal assimilation of the social conditions of life which he so much dreads. 'William von Humboldt',[2] says Mr. Mill, 'points out two things as necessary conditions of human development, — freedom, and variety of situations. The second of these two conditions is in this country every day diminishing; the circumstances which surround different classes and individuals, and shape their characters, are daily becoming more assimilated.' No doubt this is true; and it is true also, as Mr. Mill says, that 'the very idea of resisting the will of the public, when it is positively known that they have a will, disappears more and more from the minds of practical politicians'. But to what do these facts point? Mr. Mill believes that they point to an increasing despotism of social and political masses over the moral and intellectual freedom of individuals. To us his conclusion appears singularly hasty, and utterly unsustained by the premises he lays down. . . . [W]e would suggest that any moral monotony which springs exclusively from the assimilation of social conditions is not only inevitable, but a necessary result of social and political *liberty*, instead of a menace to it.

And what *are* the varieties of character which disappear as the process of social assimilation goes on? Surely *not* individual varieties of character, — varieties, that is, proper to the natural development of an individual character; but simply class types, — the varieties due to well-marked sectional groups, — to widely-severed phases of custom, — to the exclusive occupations of separate *castes*, — in short, to some local or social organisation, the sharp boundary of which is gradually becoming softened or altogether dissolved by the blending and fusing influences of civilisation. That this process has been going on very rapidly during the last century, we believe. But so far from holding, with Mr. Mill, that it is a process fatal to the due development of individualities of character, we conceive that it has not contracted, but rather enlarged, the sphere of individual freedom. The country gentleman stands out no longer in that marked contrast to the tradesman or the man of letters which was observable in the days of Sir Robert Walpole;[3] the dissenter is no longer a moral foil to the churchman; and the different shades of English religious opinion can not any more be mapped out as distinctly as the different counties in a map of England. But what individual freedom has any one lost by the fading away of those well-defined local and moral groups? That there has been a loss of social *intensity* of character in consequence, we admit. The exclusive association of people of the same habits of life and thought has no doubt a tendency to intensify the peculiarities thus associated, and to steep the character thoroughly with that one influence, to the exclusion of all others. But this intensification of local, or social, or religious one-sidedness is as far as possible from the development of that individuality of character for which Mr. Mill pleads so eagerly. Rather must the impressed force of such social moulds or stamps have tended to overpower all forms of individual originality which were not consistent with those special moulds or stamps. No doubt if there were any remarkable element of character in the individual which also belongs specially to the group or caste, we might expect that it would be fostered by such association into excessive energy. But any peculiarly individual element of character, on the other hand, would have been in danger of being overwhelmed. And it is therefore mere assumption to say that because there are now fewer striking varieties of type and class than there were in former generations, there is less scope for individual freedom. The very reverse must be the case, unless the assimilated public opinion of a whole nation be supposed to be more minute, more exigeant and irritating in its depotism, than the sectarian opinion of small local bodies or social castes.

[N]otwithstanding his running eulogium, Mr. Mill has missed something of true respect for individual liberty, exactly because he has systematically and profoundly underrated the significance and value of social liberty. In his effort to guard an absolute sphere of liberty for the individual, he would put most unwarrantable constraints on that social freedom which is quite as necessary to all mighty and rapid currents of human faith. Mr. Mill maintains, in fact, that every individual mind should be surrounded with an element that is a perfect non-conductor of social authority; a private sphere, from which social life should be jealously excluded. We maintain that this would be as fatal to the due development of individualities as to the due growth of social and national life. We hold that society has, and ought to have, a common life, which sends its pulses through every individual soul. If St. Paul's teaching, that different men are all '*members*' of one body, appears to represent insufficiently the independence of moral and individual character, yet the opposite conception of society as a mere aggregate of independent units implies a much more delusive and much commoner mistake. There *is* a common life and common conscience in society; and every individuality soon becomes a mere loose atom of eccentricity which does not feel, acknowledge, and show clear indications of its influences. The man who is most willing to open his mind to the stirrings of social faith and social conscience, is the one whose individual thought and powers will react most strongly upon society.

Notes

1. *Mr. Mill*: John Stuart Mill (1806–73), philosopher and representative thinker of the age. *On Liberty* is a monumental treatise on human freedom, which deplored the modern movement towards uniformity, and therefore mediocrity.
2. *William von Humboldt*: Baron von Humboldt (1767–1835) established the University of Berlin, 1809.
3. *Sir Robert Walpole*: Prime Minister 1721–42. The first statesman to hold this title.

2.4 Professions and professional classes

From Henry Byerley Thomson, The Choice of a Profession, *1857. H. B. Thomson (1822–67), a colonial judge, gives advice to parents wishing to establish their sons in one of the older or new professions.*

Everybody will be ready to acknowledge that the first most important step in a man's life is the choice of his future calling. On the circumstance of his having chosen one adequate to his powers, not hostile to his tastes, parallel to his interests, and the pursuit of which is within the range of his capital, not only his chance of failure or success, but, even if successful, much of his happiness depends. There can scarcely be a greater social misfortune than the erroneous choice of a profession. It is an error that is often not discovered until it is too late to change or to retreat. How often is a talented, but mild and retiring man, found getting grey as a brief-less barrister; the rough, though good-natured physician, unable, with all his experience, to gain patients; or the man of energy and worldly wisdom, in the garb of the priest, wasting his irritable powers in parish squabbles. In choosing a business or a trade the same difficulty does not occur; the operations of the mind are much the same, whether a man sells cotton or corn; and therefore a father, in determining whether his son shall be a cotton broker or a corn factor, looks to considerations not immediately dependent on the intellectual capacity of the future business man. Business is nearly the same kind of thing in all its branches; and if a lad is fit for one kind of mercantile operation, he is in general fitted (with the addition of the necessary knowledge and experience) for any

other. It is far different with the choice of an intellectual calling, —
that is, a profession. There is scarcely any resemblance between
any two, and success in any depends in no small degree on natural
fitness, and the grant of a fair opportunity. . . .

In attempting to define a profession, according to the modern
acceptation of the term, it is almost impossible to set out the limits
where a profession merges into a business. At no great length of
time back, the term was limited to the learned professions —
divinity, law, and medicine, and the professions of the army and
navy. Even all these have not at all times held the position and
dignity they now hold as professions. The professors of divinity,
and the law, always have held a superior position in virtue of their
connection with the State; but it was not until after the establishment of the College of Physicians, or, indeed, until the time of
Sydenham, that medicine achieved the position of a profession. It
was even later that the profession of arms, in the person of the
army, began to assume a form; and the separation of the king's
naval officer from an equality of position with the privateer
captain, and merchant skipper, was of date yet later.

The advance of education, and the liberality of an improved
social condition, have extended the honourable term to other
callings not originally included in it. The first admitted were the
artists, sculptors, and architects: then the civil engineers. Still
more lately have actuaries, and other scientific men claimed, and
been readily accorded, the denomination of professional men, and
endeavoured, with more or less success, to unite themselves into a
professional body. Quite recently have a most important body,
long looked down upon, but now of necessity pushing their way,
endeavoured to mould themselves into a professional class —
namely, the professors of education. It is to be hoped that the
gradual obliteration of ancient prejudice, and narrow views, will at
no distant period enable these useful members of the commonwealth to assume their right position. By the followers of music,
and the stage, the term has always been claimed, and has been by
society accorded with a degree of reluctance, if not at first even
with ridicule.

With so many examples it might be supposed to be easy to
define the term 'profession', yet almost any general definition
presents many exceptions, and difficulties. It is far easier to
enumerate than to define. With much doubt it is suggested that
that calling is a profession, according to the present meaning of the
word, in which 'a man for a reward places at the public service his

intellectual labour, and the fruits of intellectual knowledge, and experience'. . . . It is more than probable that on a close examination of the definition, many persons may be included that are not generally included in professions, or at least in the higher professions. It is the latter order, that it is the intention of this work to touch upon, and they may be enumerated as follows:—

Divines, lawyers, medical men, officers in the army, officers in the navy, persons in the higher branches of the civil service of the crown, painters, and sculptors, architects, engineers, actuaries, &c., musicians, and actors, educators, and men of letters. There are many callings, professional in character, but too confined in their operations to be noticed here — such as linguistics, average calculators, agricultural chemists, &c.

The professions naturally divide themselves into two principal classes — the *privileged* and the *unprivileged* professions. Amongst the privileged professions are reckoned: 1. the church; 2. the law; 3. the medical profession; 4. the army; 5. the navy; 6. the mercantile marine; 7. the public service. The entrances to these professions are regulated by law, and are closed (except partially in the case of the medical profession) to free competition from without.

The unprivileged professions are those of the painter, architect, sculptor, civil engineer, educator, parliamentary agent, actuary, average calculator, &c. To these professions there is no legal restriction of entrance.

The privileges granted to the first are less in the light of benefits to themselves than as a protection to the public. Some public evidence of competency being required before permission to practice is granted, all are excluded who have not passed through the regulated curriculum. The privileged professions (except the mercantile marine) take a higher position than the others. They are more, or less connected with the State; their importance is recognised by the law; they excel the others in numbers and wealth, receive a superior education, and are generally drawn from a superior class. Yet the unprivileged professions are not the less difficult to enter, the less arduous to succeed in. In the privileged professions, the candidate has but to enter his name at the proper institution, to pay his fees, and, in due course of time, by no very extraordinary exertions, to obtain his diploma. This diploma, in some cases, gives him almost an absolute right to employment, and in all is an authorised warrant to the public of fitness. Except as to the place of education, little minute inquiry is made with regard to a person so coming before the public; — he is so far supposed to be competent, and he has only his character for experience, and intelligence to make. In the unprivileged professions it is generally different. The neophyte here comes before the public with no guarantee of competence, or even of a regular education. Whatever name he assumes, he has dubbed himself by that title, whether worthy, or not to assume it. Those, then, who are the client, or employers of his particular calling, having no institutional education, public examination, or diploma, to look to as a declaration of fitness, are more particular in their inquiries, and require a more personal knowledge of the individual than in the privileged professions. The character, and reputation of the teacher takes the place of the fame of the institution in the other case; it is not enough to have even a good teacher, but that teacher must himself be a man of reputation, in order that his certificate may carry any weight with it. So that it happens, that the student of the unprivileged profession seeks for his instructors men of acknowledged ability, and established reputation alone. The number of masters are therefore of necessity small, the number of students they can take few; consequently, the premium is high, and the expense of professional education, of a good order, not much less than that required in the privileged professions. Much of this is modified in those professions in which public exhibition admits of free competition; but, nevertheless, the natural anxiety to attend the schools, or classes of only the first-rate, confines the means of education, and imposes difficulties in the progress of their undertaking.

The importance of the professions, and the professional classes can scarcely be over-rated, they form the head of the great English middle class, maintain its tone of independence, keep up to the mark its standard of morality, and direct its intelligence. The best estimate of them is obtained by their numbers.

In referring them to the numbers of the professional classes, taking the learned professions first, it is found that the clergymen of Great Britain of the established churches amount to 18,587; that is, 17,320 in England and Wales, 143 in the isles of the British Seas, and 1124 in Scotland; the other Protestant ministers to 8251; the Roman Catholic priests to 1093; theological students, and various real or pretended religious teachers to 1477. The total number is 30,407.

The lawyers comprise 18,422 persons, or, exclusive of law-students, 16,763; namely, 85 superior or local judges, of whom, generally, 60 are fifty years of age, and upwards; 3111 are barristers or advocates, practising, and not practising inclusive; 13,256 are solicitors, attorneys, or writers to the signet. These are assisted by 19,159 persons; *i.e.* 1436 officers of courts of justice; 16,626 law-clerks, of whom 9270 are under twenty-five years of age; and 1087 law-stationers.

The medical profession has not, like the professions of divinity, and law, any direct connection with the state; its numbers are 22,383, or, exclusive of students and assistants, 18,728: of whom 2238 are returned as physicians, 15,163 as surgeons or apothecaries. The best oculists, aurists, and dentists have the licenses of surgeons, and are so returned. But many of the 1167 dentists are mechanists. Those who supply the drugs, and instruments which the medical profession use are 16,460, of whom 15,333 are druggists, and 430 are surgical instrument makers. A large number of empirics of various kinds, — worm doctors, homoeopathic professors, herb doctors, and hydropathic practitioners, add a doubtful aid to the profession.

The members of the profession of the law are the least numerous body, and sustain no competition from without, such as that to which the clergy, and medical men are exposed — a competition which, however, chiefly affects the income of the latter class only, as the incomes of the clergy are generally secured. The clergy of the Established Church (18,587), the lawyers (16,763), and the medical men (18,728), differ little from each other in numbers, and in the aggregate amount to 54,078. The three professions, with their allied and subordinate members, not differing greatly from the average of 37,000 to each, amount to 110,730, and their importance cannot be over-rated; yet, in point of numbers, they could be out-voted by the tailors of the kingdom.

The poet, the historian, the painter, the sculptor, the musician, the architect, and the natural philosopher, as well as the professors and teachers of literature and science, may next draw our attention. To these belong the Shakespeares, Humes, Handels, Raphaels, Michael Angelos, Wrens, and Newtons, of the present day, and the humblest as well as the highest teachers of mankind. In the middle ages they formed a part of the clergy, and enjoyed endowments; but, except fellows of colleges, the members have latterly had, as an order, no rents or settled incomes from such sources. They, therefore, often derive their income from other sources than their profession, and their numbers are, therefore, difficult to estimate.

The authors, writers, and literary men, number 2866, of whom 436 are authors, 1302, or writers.

The artists, in the wide sense of all who devote themselves to the fine arts, are returned at 8600: including, however, 4915 painters, some of whom generally call themselves artists, but are often called by others, drawing-masters. Many of the 2971 architects are, undoubtedly, builders.

The professors of science are singularly few, according to the last census the number is 466, but many of them are returned among the learned professions. The actuaries number only 45. The civil engineers, 3009.

Turning to the profession of education, we find the fair sex appearing as an important element, inconsiderable in number in other professions. This calling includes 34,378 men; namely, 23,488 schoolmasters, 4371 general teachers, 3149 music-masters, 1530 professors of languages, 554 professors of mathematics, and a few more. The ladies number 71,966: including 41,888 school-mistresses of all ages, 5259 general teachers, and 2606 music-mistresses.

In the histrionic profession, also, the ladies assert a position. There are in all 2041 actors and actresses — 1398 of the former, and 643 of the latter.

The profession of music (not including teachers) musters 11 music-composers, *i.e.* persons living by that art only; 4200 musicians, of whom 3688 are men, and 432 women; as well as 370 vocalists, 114 being men, and 256 women, which speaks in favour of the popularity of the female voice.

The Civil Service of the country assists in its government, and consequently even in number occupies a prominent position. 71,191 men of the age of twenty and upwards are employed in this important function, or one per cent of the men of the country; 37,698 are in the civil service of the nation; 29,785 are in offices of local government; while 3,708 are officers in the East India Government residing in Great Britain. The civil offices have 105 heads of departments, comprising commissioners; 109 secretaries and chief clerks; 378 special professional and other officers; 1893 heads of particular branches; and 3982 clerks, of whom 506 are temporary or extra clerks.

The army and navy, of course, vary much; but in 1852, pre-vious to the last war, their numbers stood as follows:— Officers in the army, 806 cavalry; 5066 infantry; in all, 5872 officers; 943 artillery and engineer officers. In the navy the numbers were —

198 admirals, &c., and their staffs. 31 dock-yard officers, and 3746 ship-officers. 260 marine officers, 37 marine artillery officers.

These numbers represent the professional classes *in* England, but not professional classes *of* England, born in this country, and established on an English professional education. We have no means even approximate of estimating the numbers (especially of divines, lawyers, doctors, and engineers) that annually leave the country in search of wider fields of enterprise; yet they are not to be left out of consideration in estimating the amount of opportunity presented by a professional career. With the extension of the empire has extended the colonial church, and with it there is a constantly increasing call for English divines. English physicians find no want of opportunity in the colonies, and even on the continent of Europe. The rapid extension of the colony of Australia has lately called away many a hopeless and briefless barrister to employment and prosperity in Melbourne and its vicinity; and the necessity of reforming the Suddar courts and local jurisdictions of the Presidencies seems to be opening a new field for this class in India. The continent of Europe attests to the foreign employment of the civil engineers, in numerous railroads and public works, wrought by English genius. Even the small and select profession of the actuaries are beginning to find profitable arenas for assurance in countries beyond the four seas.

When, in addition to these numbers, it is remembered that the majority of those contained in them are heads of families, the importance of the professional classes, even in point of number, is not inconsiderable. . . .

In point of social position the professions have vastly, the superiority over the business world. The man of business has, as a rule, no position in respect of his occupation. If *in society*, his position is the result of his wealth, his education or the accident of his birth, and breeding. He has not gained it by his mercantile pursuits, and he will not lose it should he abandon them. The member of the higher professions on the other hand, at once takes a place in society by virtue of his calling; the poor man of business is nowhere in social position, yet the poor curate is admitted readily to that coveted country society that the millionaire has even to manoeuvre for. It is true that some merchants and manufacturers have been raised to the peerage, and that some professional men are not even gentlemen, but the former circumstance is as incapable of raising the general mercantile body in social position, as that the latter is able to bring any general degradation upon the professional body. I refer always to the plateau, and not to the lofty mountains, or deepest valleys, in estimating the general level. No doubt the mercantile classes have much advanced of late years, and the distance between the trading, and professional communities has been very much lessened, and numerous points of contact established; nevertheless the professions still maintain that superiority which their nature must ever give them.

On the whole it will be perceived that the entrance to a business is not so expensive as to a profession, that it gives an earlier return, but that only in the form of a small independence. Unless a man is possessed of capital, or is early adopted into an established connection, from motives of relationship, or otherwise, the man of business will be longer rising to a position to command a good income, or acquire a fortune than in a profession; that the man of business will be obliged to commence life with a defective education, and to assert a position in society, by means of his own force only.

The entrance to a profession is no longer delayed, but the education is completed, and a social position at once acquired. Success is independent of any capital beyond the necessary support until success arrives, and depends more on the man himself, and less on surrounding accidents, than in a business. That of a position attained in a profession is easily maintained, and is independent generally of the defalcations of others. The objects of a profession are nobler, more intellectual, of wider range, and confer more happiness than those of a business.

2.5   The Gentleman's House

From Robert Kerr, The Gentleman's House; or, How to Plan English Residences, from the Parsonage to the Palace *(1864). The newly enfranchised middle class began, in imitation of the established gentry, to build themselves houses and villas, ranging, in style and expense, from the kind described here, to that owned by Mr. Pooter in* The Diary of a Nobody, *by George and Weedon Grossmith! The author, Robert Kerr (1823–1904), was the first president of the Architectural Association, 1847–48.*

Primarily the House of an English gentleman is divisible into two

departments, namely, that of THE FAMILY, and that of the THE
SERVANTS. In dwellings of inferior class, such as Farmhouses and
the Houses of tradesmen, this separation is not so distinct; but in
the smallest establishment of the kind with which we have here to
deal this element of character must be considered essential; and as
the importance of the family increases the distinction is widened,
— each department becoming more and more amplified and
elaborated in a direction contrary to that of the other.

In a few Mansions of very superior class another special department is constituted by the STATE-ROOMS.

As outdoor departments or appendages, if any, there are the
STABLES and the FARM OFFICES. . . .

Let it be again remarked that the character of a gentleman-like
Residence is not a matter of magnitude or of costliness, but of
design, — and chiefly of plan; and that, as a very modest establishment may possess this character without a fault, all unadorned; so
also the stately Seat of a millionaire may perchance have so little of
it that the most lavish expenditure shall but magnify its defects.

The points which an English gentleman of the present-day
values in his house are comprehensively these:

Quiet comfort for his family and guests,—
Thorough convenience for his domestics,—
Elegance and importance without ostentation. . . .

It is a first principle with the better classes of English people that
the Family Rooms shall be essentially private, and as much as
possible the Family Thoroughfares. It becomes the foremost of all
maxims, therefore however small the establishment, that the
Servants' Department shall be separated from the Main House, so
that what passes on either side of the boundary shall be both
invisible and inaudible on the other. The best illustrations of the
want of proper attention to this rule must necessarily be obtained
from houses of the smaller sort; and here cases more or less striking
are unfortunately by no means rare. Not to mention that most
unrefined arrangement whereby at one sole entrance door the
visitors rub shoulders with the tradespeople, how objectionable it is
we need scarcely say when a thin partition transmits the sounds of
the Scullery or Coal-cellar to the Dining-room or Study; or when a
Kitchen window in summer weather forms a trap to catch the con-
versation at the casement of the Drawing-room; or when a Kitchen
doorway in the Vestibule or Staircase exposes to the view of every
one the dresser or the cooking range, or fills the house with

unwelcome odours. Those who are acquainted with the ordinary class of suburban speculation Villas, which, by the standard of rent, ought to be good houses, but are not, will at once recognise the unexaggerated truth of these illustrations; whilst, on the other hand, the facility with which houses of the same size and value are arranged by better hands for the express avoidance of all these evils is equally well known.

On the same principle of privacy, in a somewhat larger house, a separate Staircase becomes necessary, for the servants' use. Advancing further in respect of the style of the establishment, the privacy of Corridors and Passages becomes a problem; and the lines of traffic of the servants and family respectively have to be kept clear of each other at certain recognised points. Again, in the Mansions of the nobility and wealthy gentry, where personal attendants must be continually passing to and fro in all parts, it becomes once more necessary to dispose the routes of traffic so that privacy may be maintained under difficulties. In short, whether in a small house or a large one, let the family have free passage without encountering the servants unexpectedly, and let the servants have access to all their duties without coming unexpectedly upon the family or visitors. On both sides this privacy is highly valued.

It is a matter also for the architect's care that the outdoor work of the domestics shall not be visible from the house or grounds, or the windows of their Offices overlooked. At the same time it is important that the walks of the family shall not be open to view from the Servants' Departments. The Sleeping-rooms of the domestics ought also to be separated both internally and externally from those of the family, and as far as possible separately approached.

The idea which underlies all is simply this. The family constitute one community; the servants another. Whatever may be their mutual regard and confidence as dwellers under the same roof, each class is entitled to shut its door upon the other, and be alone. . . .

What we call in England a comfortable house is a thing so intimately identified with English customs as to make us apt to say that in no other country but our own is this element of comfort fully understood; or at all events that the comfort of any other nation is not the comfort of this. The peculiarities of our climate, the domesticated habits of almost all classes, our family reserve, and our large share of the means and appliances of easy living, all combine to make what is called a comfortable home perhaps the most cherished possession of an Englishman. To dwell a moment longer on this always popular theme, it is worth suggesting that *indoor comfort* is essentially a Northern idea, as contrasted with a sort of outdoor enjoyment which is equally a Southern idea, and Oriental. . . .

In its more ordinary sense the comfortableness of a house indicates exemption from all such evils as draughts, smoky chimneys, kitchen smells, damp, vermin, noise, and dust; summer sultriness and winter cold; dark corners, blind passages, and musty rooms. But it has also to be said that in its larger sense comfort includes the idea that every room in the house, according to its purpose, shall be for that purpose so contrived as to be free from awkwardness, inconvenience, and inappropriateness, — so planned, in short, considered by itself, as to be in every respect a comfortable room of its kind. . . .

The very qualities which constitute the characteristics of the better classes of this or any other community must, of course, turn necessarily upon the possession of a taste for beauty of every kind; and the advancement of society is in a great measure the improvement of this description of judgement. But the more advanced this taste becomes, the more fastidious is it found to be; and this, not altogether in demanding graces that shall excel, but much more in rejecting those that are too ambitious. Subdued power becomes the perfection of design; and to such an extent may this feeling go, that repugnance to the meretricious or obtrusive has sometimes even led to a sort of repudiation of the element of elegance itself, and the preference of what used to be called archaic simplicity, the crudeness of unrefined thought, the barrenness of an imagination devoid of resources.

Again, it is easy to understand that the state and luxury which surround opulence and rank must sooner or later pall upon the sense and become irksome; so that persons even the most exalted in station and dignified in demeanour shall seek relief in their private retreats by the adoption of simplicity and the abandonment of ceremonial. And the higher the standard of intellectual eminence, and the more overflowing the supplies of material wealth, the more decided will be the development of this reactionary principle.

There is, however, a medium here; the luxury of grandeur may be reduced to a limit without involving the rejection of grace. This limit is indicated — colloquially, at least — by the term Elegance. It displays finish, precision, quiet beauty, without ostentation of any kind; it is not rich, or elaborate, or sumptuous, or gay; it is the subdued power which corresponds to cultivated, perhaps satiated, taste.

It is beyond a doubt, as we have already stated, that the better classes of this country are almost universally disposed to make it a condition in respect of their houses that decoration and display shall be kept within moderate limits. Not that these are the limits of severe simplicity (indeed, they vary considerably in various circles of society, and fashion rules not only their style but their extent), but at the present time the general sentiment is such that in most instances the architect has to restrain his natural inclination towards adornment within a line which, to an imaginative man, is not always easily kept. And as architects are proverbially difficult of restraint here; as they persist in introducing an ornate character, even when it is precisely what their clients desire to exclude; and as it is natural that this should be so — natural in the extreme that a professor of embellishment should forget that embellishment may be a bore; — it therefore becomes necessary to point out that he who would be a successful designer of a Gentleman's House must keep this principle of self-denial in view as one of the most essential of all. Grandeur and artistic ambition must be spared even in places of state: mere richness will often be pronounced vulgar; simple grace, and elegance, and perfect finish are generally enough; their absence, it is true, will at once be detected, but any endeavour to reach beyond them will be labour in vain. . . .

It must strike any one who compares the practice of the English in respect of decorative art with that of the French, that one of the most important distinctions lies here; on one side of the Channel the work is not done so substantially perhaps as might be, but is carefully kept in order; while on the other, the work, if done more solidly, is somehow left to keep itself in order. Observe the periodical cleaning of the public buildings in Paris; and imagine the reception which would meet a proposal that the Gresham Committee should now and then brush down the walls of the London Exchange! Now there is here indicated another principle upon which English self-denial in respect of embellishment may be said to rest. The greater the amount of enrichment, the worse the result of its being left to its own resources for repair; the more the simplicity the more likelihood of its preserving a presentable condition.

A last word on this important point:— elegance unassuming and unelaborated, touching in no way the essentials of home

75

comfort, never suggesting affectation and pride, moderated by unimpassioned refinement, and subdued even to modesty, will be almost invariably accepted. Even where extreme wealth and exalted rank render it incumbent upon a family to surround itself with the most cherished products of industry and genius, it will be rarity and cost, perfection of workmanship and pure or piquant excellence of design, rather than splendour or luxurious richness or imposing grandeur, which will be esteemed; simplicity still, and subdued power — the greater the power the stronger the subduing hand — will be cherished even in magnificence, and the glare of pomp despised.

3

The Religious Debate

Religion has probably never seemed so important, to so many people, as in Victorian England. It was part of every area of life, subsuming the political, educational, professional, social, familial. What you believed, what you didn't believe, was of the greatest account in and to society, and every aspect of Victorian life had its religious dimension. On the visible level, organised religion was most obvious in the steady pace of church building throughout the period (a half of all parish churches now existing were built at this time, and considerably more than that of Nonconformist chapels), as the government sought to accommodate the frightening rise in population in the cities with grants for cheap churches.

The period had opened in the wake of two major religious movements, the Evangelical revival at the turn of the century, and, just before that, the wildfire spread of Methodism. The Test and Corporation Act of 1698, which prevented Nonconformists from holding state or municipal office, was repealed in 1828 and both parties flourished throughout the century. Then, from 1833, the spirit of revival spread to the Anglican Church, with the inception of *Tracts for the Times* and the Oxford Movement, which were designed to remind the National Church of its Catholic foundation, and led to agitation in the church that rippled through society for the rest of the period, and longer. The Roman Catholic Church, the traditional enemy, also flourished as never before in the United Kingdom. The increasing population was swelled by waves of immigration from, for example, Ireland, which Wellington and Peel had reluctantly recognised with the Act of Catholic Emancipation in 1829, which established the right of Roman Catholics to sit in Parliament. (They had been free to practise their faith since 1791.) Then, after the Oxford Movement, a steady stream of notable converts entered the Church, beginning with Newman in 1845, and by 1850 the Vatican was confident enough to restore the Roman Hierarchy, unthought of in Britain for 300 years. As the century progressed, more and more converts were turning hopefully to the Roman Church as old certainties crumbled, and in face of the divisions and controversies in the churches, particularly in the Church of England. Meanwhile the Nonconformists, who represented at least half of the population, and a significant part of the middle class, felt themselves to be second-class citizens. Though their remaining legal handicaps were disappearing, they were still largely (till 1867) disenfranchised; till 1871 all positions at Oxford and Cambridge were closed to them; and even compulsory church rates were not abolished until 1868.

The growth of atheism, or, even more, agnosticism (a word coined during this period) was another element of the Victorian debate. Though 'infidelity' was no new thing, its growth and spread were a spectre which haunted the Victorians, who associated it with the political lawlessness of France and the *sansculottes*, and were the more frightened to detect signs of it among their own middle class, and even, it seemed, in the church itself. Victorian doubt sprang from several sources: the Romanising tendency of the Church was one factor, but more significant was the 'Higher Criticism' of the Bible, which called in doubt, in the light of new information, the literal truth of the Bible. Also, from early on in the period, the foundations of faith were being chiselled away by the scientists, first the geologists (men like Lyell and Chambers), whose conclusions disproved the literal accuracy of the Bible. Darwin has become simply the most notorious of such scientists, and his *Origin of Species* a symbol of what science was doing to the faith of the Victorians. A new level of panic was reached in society when even the church itself seemed to share these doubts, and Bishop Colenso and a clerical contributor to *Essays and Reviews* were victimised for publishing their alarming views. Yet by the end of the period, no area of public life was closed even to the atheist, as first the universities and then Westminster came to admit them to full membership.

3.1   The causes of unbelief

From C. J. Ellicott, Modern Unbelief: Its Principles and Characteristics, *1877. The Bishop of Gloucester and Bristol is expressing in a
lecture of 1877 the dismay of churchmen at the tide of unbelief which threatens
the faithful.*

. . . [Y]esterday I stated generally the subject on which I felt it my
especial duty to speak at the present time, — existing unbelief, its
nature and prevalence, and the best means of counteracting it.

If I may now assume that the subject does demand our attention, and that even the most hopeful can hardly deny that an
unbelief of the most grave and menacing character is now stealing
into the hearts of the young and speculative, if this be so, why is it
so?

Of the many causes which may be assigned, there are three
which seem to claim our more especial consideration, — the tone
and direction of recent historical criticism, the deductions that
have been drawn from the real or alleged discoveries of modern
science, and the moral and metaphysical difficulties which have
been supposed to be involved in or connected with the fundamental doctrines of Christianity.

Let us speak first of recent historical criticism,[1] and the injurious
influence it has certainly exercised in reference to Revealed
Religion. Its leading position has always been the same — that any
narration of facts which involves the miraculous element in it
must, for this very reason, be regarded with the gravest suspicion.
. . . Why . . . is the . . . miraculous element in the history of the
New Testament to be regarded otherwise than as involving a *prima
facie* reason why the narrative should not be accepted as historically
credible? . . .

The answer to these objections is, happily, fair and reasonable.
. . . The narrative of the Old Testament, and still more so that of
the New Testament, is so essentially different in nature and
character from that of the early and legendary narratives with
which they have been compared, that the presence of the miraculous element in the one suggests no just ground for concluding,
merely because that element is present in the other, that the
associated narrative is consequently mythical and untrust-
worthy. . . .

The narrative of the New Testament does not refer to, or include a remote past, but relates events which, it is alleged, took place at a definite time in the world's history, when the principles of history were generally known and recognized. Unless, therefore, it can be shown that the narrative was composed so long after the events that mythical additions would have had time to grow up around them, no just argument, on historical considerations . . . can be used against the credibility of the narrative on the ground of the presence of the miraculous . . .

I do not wish in any way to represent the case worse than it is, — but I certainly fear that even among sober and religious persons the number of those who feel real difficulties in reference to many things in the Old Testament is distinctly increasing. And this increase is in a great measure due to the evil effects produced by the historical criticism to which I am now alluding, left unchallenged and unexamined as that criticism too often is by the otiose if not receptive reader . . .

And if this, only too often, be the effect of current historical criticism, when applied to the Holy Scriptures, still more serious is the effect produced by the speculative deductions that have been made from the real or alleged discoveries of modern science. I advisedly say real or alleged, — for I am persuaded that many scientific theories of the present day which are now current and popular, will in the sequel have to be seriously reconsidered and modified. Or . . . in reference to the most popular subject of all, evolution, — how is it able to account for that similarity of the ultimate particles of matter which may now be said to have been almost demonstrated? If the molecule is 'incapable of growth or decay, of generation or destruction', how can we reconcile such characteristics with the operation of those purely natural causes which are now so persistently claimed to be the constructive principles of the universe? Such questions . . . could be multiplied almost indefinitely, in reference to several alleged discoveries which are causing considerable anxiety to many religious minds at the present time. The questions, however, are overlooked. . . . The uncertainties of modern physical science are by no means to be regarded as existing only in the minds of prejudiced theologians.

It may be admitted, however, that though most of the more startlingly popular theories are either still utterly uncertain, or, like the principle of Natural Selection, are found to require very serious rehabilitation, there remain some at least that *seem* to militate with received opinions, and are consequently causing to many minds very great disquietude. It may be admitted, for example, that, in a certain sense, the principle of evolution is apparently supported by trustworthy evidence. It seems also probable that the existence of man upon the earth is to be referred to a period slightly more distant than that which has commonly been assigned — and it perhaps may be conceded that, in the origination of species, laws hitherto not recognized may be considered now to rest on sufficient induction.

What, however, does it amount to beyond this — that our adorable Creator has permitted the creatures of His hand to catch clearer glimpses, as the ages roll onward, of the blessed mysteries of His providential wisdom and power. And this which ought really to dispose our hearts to deeper reverence and more adoring love, has been made to become to us a source of hindrances and temptations. These silently disclosed mysteries which ought to awaken in each true and loving soul a more lively apprehension of the mercy and majesty of the Creator, have been perverted by the cold heart of unbelief or the vanity of a spurious science into arguments against the truth of revealed religion, and have been made to minister to distrust in the holy reality of the fatherhood of God.

During the past hundred years, and especially during the last portion of that time, the All-Good, the All-wise, and the All-Merciful has permitted the creatures of His hand to see far, far, more clearly than in any centuries of the past, the glory and the majesty of His works.

I feel, therefore, that it may be truly said, that though it does seem certain that the alleged discoveries of recent science, and, still more, the rash and unlicensed deductions that have been made from them, have caused the greatest possible amount of doubt and disquietude in thousands of hearts, — yet that these two things also are certain. First, that of these alleged discoveries some are, in a very high degree, scientifically doubtful. Secondly, that of these same discoveries, those which apparently seem to be trustworthy are distinctly evidences, not, as it is alleged, against, but *for* the blessed truth of the existence and personality of God, and that, too, in a very marked and even providential manner.

But, in the third place, if much of the unbelief of our own times is to be referred to this misuse of the blessings of which true science is designed to be the minister, still more distinctly may we trace the prevalence of unbelief to the moral and metaphysical difficulties which have been supposed to be involved in the fundamental truths of the Christian dispensation.

The problem of the existence of evil, especially the traces of the misery and suffering of living creatures, ages before man's sin cast its shadow on the creation around, — the still deeper problems connected with the holy mystery of sin's atonement, and the dark and terrible questions that are connected with the doom of the impenitent — these three aspects of physical and moral evil do, beyond all doubt, fearfully try the faith of thousands at the present time. They subtly appeal to the poor doubting heart, and at once ally themselves with the difficulties which may have already been suggested by historical criticism, or scientific speculation. Our very increased knowledge becomes a snare to us. The more science displays to us the wonders of the realms of nature around us, the further we see into the beauty and the glory of the marvellous works of God, — the more terrible seems the difficulty connected with the power and presence of evil. . . . They readily combine . . . with the difficulties arising from other considerations. Each class of difficulties helps to augment the force of the others, — and the result is that tendency to doubt everything, and to consider everything opinionable which I cannot but regard as the very worst and most menacing sign of our times.

Note

1. *Historical Criticism*: Or 'Higher Criticism', is the criticism of the Bible based on contemporary research, which demonstrates that certain 'facts' of authorship, chronology, the miraculous, etc. are scientifically inaccurate, or otherwise unsound.

3.2   Atheism

From The National Review, *Vol. 2, 1856. An article written by R. H. Hutton, the editor.*

If ever the dark shadow of Atheism were suddenly to envelop the earth, would the crash of falling churches, the disbanding of ecclesiastical classes, and the vanishing of all conscious individual intercourse with God, be necessarily accompanied by the yielding of all moral ties and the dissolution of every sacred social organisation? Before we can attempt to answer such a question, we must call to mind a very obvious but a strangely-forgotten truth, that human trust does not create God, and that human distrust would not annihilate Him. There is a thoroughly atheistic way of shuddering over Atheism, which is apt to express itself as if the spread of human disbelief would not only overcloud but *empty* Heaven. . . .

In showing . . . that Atheism is false to human nature, that trust in God is the natural atmosphere of our moral life, we must not take for granted, as is so often done, that belief in God as God, and belief in goodness, are one and the same thing. We must grant the atheist his unexplained impulses to good, the *implicit* God of his conscience, and show how he mutilates and dwarfs human nature by denying it all explained impulses to good, the explicit God of faith. . . . As our ancestors, who did not know that air had weight, reaped unconsciously *most* of the benefits of the all-permeating atmosphere pressure, but of course lost that which depended on the actual recognition and conscious use of its weight, so those who do not know that God is, while they experience, as much as any, most of the blessing which arises only from a knowledge and conscious account of the fact of that existence and character; and therefore . . . the moral loss [is] serious and arises from this mental blindness. . . .

What, then, *is* the atheistic type of character? Vividly to see the import of Atheism to human character, is the first step towards its disproof.

It is clear that Atheism necessarily tends relatively to reduce the influence and independence of the higher intellectual and moral faculties (even where the real existence of these is not disputed), as compared with that of the senses, social impulses, and those energies which tell upon the world. . . . To him [the Atheist] the highest point of *human* culture is the absolutely highest point in the mental universe; mere non-existence roofs us in beyond; and of course, therefore, the highest faculties we possess must derive their sole validity and their sole meaning from the lower nature to which they add the finishing touch. . . .

The atheist says, 'Even you admit that God only helps those who help themselves. Well, we help ourselves, and therefore God, if He exists, helps us; if He does not, we have all the help we can. *Science* is the true providence of man. We lay no faith on "personal god"; we use our own faculties'. Very well; but let men only realise your negative creed, and you will find they have not the heart, or perhaps the temerity, on great occasions, to help themselves any longer. *Trust* is the postulate of the capacity to help ourselves in any great or noble work. It becomes *impossible* to do our part bravely without this perfect reliance in the co-operation of God. . . .

Again, a fully realised Atheism will undermine the worth of personal human affections; not merely indirectly, by losing sight of immortality, but still more directly by cutting off the chief spring of their spiritual life. . . . The atheistic theory thus tends to reduce the life of human affection to a close dependence on the *visible* moral relations between man and man. It leaves some sense of responsibility towards the living and present object of affection, but it cancels all idea of moral responsibility to the Inspirer of affection. It would tend to make us measure the self-sacrifice *deserved* by others, instead of measuring it by the eternal purposes and the immeasurable love of God. . . .

We have thus sketched the main features of the character which Atheism, fully realised, would tend to generate in an *awakened* moral nature. We have attempted to show that it would tend to weaken and even shatter the authority of conscience, to show despondency in the heart both as to personal and human progress, to reduce personal affection to a narrow and selfish type, and to exorcise all the fascination and grandeur in the conception of truth. Still, the atheist may reply that even if he admit all this, it only goes to prove that the existence of God is *desirable* — not that it is real . . .

We are not attempting to *prove* the existence of God. We firmly believe that God alone can finally convince any man of His own existence. But it is possible to point out the lines of ascertained fact which converge on this truth. It is possible to *prepare* men's minds for the discernment of truth, — to point out the directions in which it may be most clearly seen. . . . There is . . . a vague, general dread that Science if fairly faced, is atheistic in its tendency. Men are haunted with a phantom of a power that they dare not challenge, which is rumoured to have superseded and exposed natural theology, and to be gradually withdrawing, with inexorable hand, every fold of mystery from the universe, without disclosing any trace of the everlasting God. So far are we from believing this to be true, that we are satisfied there is striking indication of the fundamental necessity of Theism in the incredible incoherence of texture which Science, as a whole, presents to the thought without the theistic nexus. . . .

We have barely touched on some of the most remarkable indications that man's nature is every way dwarfed by Atheism, and that Science, so far as it gives evidence at all, gives strong evidence of the same kind. Instead of being a source of uneasy fear and suspicion, we have tried to show that, fairly faced, Science adds all its strength to the side of trust. . . . No one can actually *manifest* God to another. But there are few, we believe, of those who anxiously seek, who do not ultimately attain a clear vision of the truth that '*no* man hath quickened his own soul', and that in this truth is involved not the despair, but the deepest peace of man.

3.3   The tendencies of science

From The Theological Review, *Vol. 2, 1865. The writer acknowledges that received opinion on the Creation has been challenged by science, but argues that no current theory has disturbed the First Cause.*

When the geologist examines a bed of ancient drift, he observes that the pebbles have their longer diameters all in one direction. They tell him almost as clearly as if they could speak, that a great current of water has anciently passed over them; they indicate the line in which that current must have swept. In like manner the future historian of civilization, when looking back on these present times, will observe the tendencies of thought of all the most eminent thinkers in every department of human knowledge turned in the same direction. He, too, will read here the fact, that some great current of influence — some one powerful law of thought — has been sweeping over the educated mind, bearing all intellectual development on in the line of its own great stream. He will notice that the thinkers are tending everywhere towards the utmost possible unity in their explanation of the universe. They seek to make one law explain as many phenomena as possible, and one more comprehensive law explain as many lesser laws as possible. In like manner they seek to make the laws acting at present in the sphere of our own observation explain whatever they can possibly explain in the past time and in the distant space.

What is this gulf-stream flowing over the modern mind? It is what Newton calls the Law of Philosophizing, which has been followed more or less consciously or instinctively in building up the whole structure of our modern science. Sir William Hamilton[1] calls it the Law of Parsimony. It is a law or habit of thought which determines the mind to be as parsimonious as possible in the use of laws and causes. It assumes that the Divine Mind does nothing needlessly; that God never employs more methods or agencies to effect His purposes than are absolutely necessary; and that He never changes His agencies or methods as long as they are sufficient to effect His purposes . . .

But we turn now to notice the effect of this great tendency of modern thought in the world of theology. Here, it must be confessed, it has shown itself less than in other departments of knowledge. The truth is, that until lately it has scarcely dared to enter here. Science has almost from the first been separated from theology . . .

Let the reader, then, take this ultimate oracle which science is compelled to utter, and he need not fear that in any of her discoveries, now or hereafter, she can tell·us there is no God. The theories of Darwin and Huxley, even if they are true, are only discoveries as to the modes of God's operations; they are only discoveries that He acts by development, instead of by creation according to the old conception. The Great Cause Himself they do not touch; they neither truly put Him farther from nor bring Him nearer to us, for science beforehand shews us that He is the beginning and the end. He is the Infinite Being from whose living will issued the primal forces that clothed themselves with the first forms in the vast scale of development. . . .

Darwin and Huxley are dissatisfied with the old theories of creation, in which causes or laws were imagined that are not seen in action now. The old doctrine supposed miraculous interventions in the regular course of nature. It assumed that there were, at epoch after epoch, fresh acts of creative energy by which new species were introduced upon the earth. But Darwin attempts to explain the variety of species, both of plants and of animals, and the introduction of all new species in the past, by the operation of laws of variation and selection which are observed in the present. The grazier and the gardener find constant but small variations in the individuals composing their stock. They select for breeding the animals or plants possessing any variation which makes them more valuable than the rest, and then from their offspring select again the individuals possessing the variation in greatest perfection, and thus by this accumulative selection in the course of a few generations a new variety — cattle with shorter horns, sheep with finer wool, race-horses with more and more resemblance to the greyhound, fruit trees with richer and larger fruit — is produced. There has been similar variation, says Darwin, through all the past; and nature, by the constant struggle for existence of every creature, makes selection of the individuals possessing any variation that would give them the slightest advantage above their competitors in the race for life. It selects from the offspring of the favoured creatures those which have the useful variation in greatest perfection, and thus are produced new varieties which gradually develop into species.

Darwin is inclined to push his theory so far as to account for the origin of all organized beings. He says:

> Therefore I should infer from analogy that probably all the organic beings which have ever lived on this earth have descended from some one primordial form, into which life was first breathed by the Creator. . . .

We do not pretend to endorse or reject these theories of development. We wait for further light. Many of the most eminent men of science have, it is true, embraced the theory of transmutation; but we frankly confess that our knowledge of all the laws and conditions of variation at present, and of the records of the past entombed in the rocks, is far too restricted to enable us to form satisfactory conclusions on so vast and mysterious a subject. For ourselves, we are prepared to accept whatever explanation of God's method in creation science can verify, knowing that it is only His method with which she is here concerned; and that, whatever may be the method used, He is equally present. And if we should at least be brought to acknowledge that a lower animal form has been gradually developed to humanity — that a reptilian form has been developed into the bird, the fish into the reptile, the medusa into the echinoderm, and the inorganic atoms themselves into the infusoria or sponge — this will not in the slightest degree disturb our religious faith. We shall only say,

> God has chosen to adopt this method of creation, instead of the method which we once believed; but He has been present at every step. It is His outflowing, all-pervading Life that has quickened the lower forms and developed them into higher.

We shall think of Him as quickening into higher organisation the embryo of some anthropoid animal, and breathing into it the breath of human life, just as we used to believe He quickened into such an organisation the dust of the inorganic earth. And we shall feel it no more degrading to have created from material already vitalized in an animal form, than to have been created from dead inorganic matter, the very 'dust of the earth'.

Note

1. *Sir William Hamilton*: (1805–65), mathematician and scientist. (See also 'Universities of England — Oxford' in Education.)

3.4   The attitude of the clergy towards science

From The Contemporary Review, *Vol. 6, September 1867. The writer (probably John Hannah (1818–88), Archdeacon of Lewes) argues that the popular reputation of the clergy for prejudice and hostility towards scientific thought is unjustified: science has traditionally been the Church's territory.*

It cannot be denied that, with many individual exceptions, a good deal of mutual suspicion exists at present between clergymen and men of science. While Science is threatening to warn the clergy off its premises altogether, with a vigorous denunciation of theological prepossessions, the clergy are too often disposed to look with both fear and anger on the position assumed by their scientific assailants . . .

It may be worth while to examine what justice there is in the accusations which are currently brought against the clergy on the part of science. Is it true that, as a body, they are narrow-minded and obstructive beyond the average of educated men? Have they always led the chorus of unreasoning remonstrance against every fresh influx of scientific light? Are they incapable, even at their best of defining their position with anything like the same precision with which men of science can define their own? Have they reached their highest tide-mark of charity and intelligence, as soon as they have repudiated the earlier spirit of persecution, and assented to a few obvious propositions on the truth of science as the Gift of God, and the certainty that no real contradiction can be established between the revelations of His Word and the discoveries of His Works?

As there is nothing like a candid friend for telling you the worst of yourself, I will call in a clergyman[1] to furnish the indictment against the clergy:—

It is worth while to take the single instance of the use of science to our clergy. Seeing that the Bible, in page after page (to say nothing of whole books of it), is constantly occupied in directing profound attention to the power of God as proved by the magnificence of His creation, — seeing that the Saviour of the world points, as the special proofs of God's love, to His care for the mountain lily, and the falling sparrow, and the raven's callow brood, — is not our education, and especially that of our clergy, distinctly *irreligious* in neglecting these things, and in elevating the poor words of man, as an instrument of training, unmeasurably above the mighty works of God? And with what results? It would be hardly possible to exaggerate their disastrous importance. Not only do the clergy, who should be the leaders of thought, lose the advantage of assisting in a thousand ways their poorer parishioners but they find themselves actually inferior in these great fields of knowledge to many clerks and artisans in their own congregations, before whom they cannot venture to speak of them without the danger of raising a contemptuous smile.

Let me pause to observe that I quote the above sentences only as an introduction to what follows. No one can dispute the great advantage of every kind of useful knowledge to the clergy; nor need we discuss the transparent fallacy of depreciating the words of man in contrast with the works of God; as though the excellence of the creature were not the glory of the Creator, to whose gift alone man owes the faculty of expressing noble thoughts in graceful language. 'This, however,' he proceeds,

is the least part of the evil. Science has interpenetrated to a wonderful degree the thoughts, the speculations, nay, even the common literature of the age, and yet the clergy are wholly out of sympathy with it; in many instances are suspicious of it; in many more are its bitter and ignorant opponents. Scarcely has there been an eminent philosopher,

from Roger Bacon down to Comte, — scarcely an eminent
discoverer, from Galileo down to Darwin, — who has not
counted the clergy among his most ruthless opponents. . . .
Just as of old 'fops refuted Berkeley with a sneer,' so now
some young ordained B.A. finds it easy to crush Darwin with
a text. Is it, I ask, uncommon to hear some ignorant clergyman, who has laboriously scraped into a poll degree, lay down
the law as though he held the keys of all knowledge in his
hand, and could afford to pity and look down upon those
splendid students whose lives have been one long-continued
heroism of candour and research? . . . Men of science, confounding religion with the anachronisms of its most feeble and
most violent expounders, too often hold aloof from a Church
whose inmost heart is intensely truthful, — a Church which
well knows the delight that deeply religious minds have ever
felt in reverent inquiry into the laws of God, and which sees
more of her own real spirit in the patient labours of science
than in unprogressive idleness and theological hate. (Rev.
F. W. Farrar, *On Some Defects in Public School Education*, pp.
46–8).

The invective exaggerates its small basis of acknowledged fact to
a degree which is as unfair to men of science as to the clergy. The
higher praise which can be given to any kind of education is, that it
makes the judgment just, by training it to form a correct estimate
of things which pass before us. So then Mr. Farrar pays a poor
compliment to scientific education, when he says that those who
have enjoyed its full advantages are in the habit of passing a false
judgment on the most solemn of all subjects, by 'confounding
religion with the anachronisms of its most feeble and most violent
expounders.' There can scarcely be a scientific society in England
which has not numbered clergymen among its leading members.
What excuse can be urged for their scientific companions, if they
turn from the recent memory or the living presence of such men as
Sedgwick and Pritchard and Harcourt,[2] to condemn the clergy in a
mass, and religion along with them, because of the crude lucubra-
tions of 'some ignorant clergyman who has laboriously scraped
into a poll degree'? . . .

It is against human nature to expect that changes can be brought
about in old opinions without resistance from the body which
believes. . . . Scientific men must also lay their account with pro-
voking additional suspicion if they travel out of their province to

assail the religious convictions of their neighbours on alleged scientific grounds. Revealed religion rests entirely on the basis of the supernatural. How then can the teachers of that religion be expected to acquiesce in the assertion that science has proved the supernatural to be a nightmare monster, lingering on from darker ages into days of light? The whole machinery of that religion rests on our faith in the efficacy of prayer. How then can the clergy refrain from remonstrance if the weakness of supposing that prayer can influence the acts of God is made a favourite commonplace with men of science? Let us try if we cannot consider the subject without disturbance from the unjust judgments of either side. The real questions at issue may be stated in this form — Have the clergy contributed the full share of assistance towards the advancement of science which might be expected from a corporation of educated and influential men? . . .

I have no doubt that Mr. Farrar is happy in possessing a far wider acquaintance with the history of science than I can boast of. But his 'challenge' must sound harsh in the ears of a generation which remembers Buckland and Chalmers,[3] and owes so much to Sedgwick and Whewell. . . .[4] The British Association was mainly originated by a clergyman, the Rev. W. Vernon Harcourt, who planned its 'aims and working details,' says Principal Forbes,[5] 'with a completeness which took his hearers somewhat by surprise, but in which they found little to alter or amend; and the constitution proposed by Mr. Harcourt remains in all its important details the working code of the Association to this day.' . . . Mr. Farrar will render no service to the Association if he helps to propagate the idea that this fair alliance has been broken, and that there is now a confessed antagonism between the clergy and that scientific body.

Notes

1. *a clergyman*: F. W. Farrar (1831–1903), schoolmaster and Dean of Canterbury. Author of *Eric, or Little by Little*.

2. *Sedgwick and Pritchard and Harcourt*: All distinguished Victorian scientists. Adam Sedgwick (1785–1873), geologist, was a prebendary of Norwich; Charles Pritchard (1808–93), astronomer and schoolmaster, was an educational reformer; William Vernon Harcourt (1789–1871), President of the British Association, was a canon in York.

3. *Buckland and Chalmers*: William Buckland (1784–1856), geologist, was a canon of Christ Church and Dean of Westminster; Thomas

Chalmers (1760–1847), chemist became Professor of Divinity, Edinburgh. (See also note under 'Conformity Sin, Because Unjust to Nonconformists'.)

4. *Whewell*: William Whewell (1794–1866), mineralogist, mathematician, etc., was Master of Trinity College, Cambridge.

5. *Principal Forbes*: J. D. Forbes (1809–68), physicist, was Principal of St Andrews.

3.5 The clergyman who subscribes for Colenso

From Anthony Trollope, Clergymen of the Church of England, *1866. It was first published anonymously in* The Pall Mall Gazette, *Vols. 2–3, 1865, 1866. Trollope gives an ironic view of one of the crises which threatened to split the Church of England. John Colenso was first Bishop of Natal, 1853. Trained as a mathematician, he found problems in explaining the arithmetic of the Creation, the Flood, etc., to his Zulu converts, concluded that the books were post-exile forgeries, and published his difficulties in* The Pentateuch and Book of Joshua Critically Examined *(1862–79) for which he was dismissed from his see by the Metropolitan of Capetown, Bishop Gray. The Church of England was deeply divided in its reaction to the scandal, as Trollope demonstrates.*

We have heard much of the Broad Church[1] for many years, till the designation is almost as familiar to our ears as that of the High Church or of the Low Church. . . . The liberal clergyman of the Church of England has long given up Bible chronology, has given up many of the miracles, and is venturing into questions the very asking of which would have made the hairs to stand on end on the head of the broadest of the broad in the old days, twenty years since. . . .

But it is when such a one finds himself placed as a parson in a country parish . . . that he calls upon himself the greatest attention. . . . What if the new teaching should be true? So the men begin to speculate and the women quake, and the neighbouring parsons are full of wrath, and the bishop's table groans with letters which he knows not how to answer, or how to leave unanswered. The free-thinking clergyman of whom we are speaking still creates much of this excitement in the country. . . .

Most men who call themselves Christian would say that they believed the Bible, not knowing what they meant, never having attempted, — and very wisely having refrained from attempting amidst the multiplicity of their wordly concerns, — to separate historical record from inspired teaching. But when a liberal-minded clergyman does come among us, — come among us, that is, as our pastor, — we feel not unnaturally a desire to know what it is, at any rate, that he disbelieves. . . . We know that there are some things which we do not like in the teaching to which we have been hitherto subjected; — that fulminating clause, for instance, which tells us that nobody can be saved unless he believes a great deal which we find it impossible to understand; the ceremonial Sabbath which we know that we do not observe, though we go on professing that its observance is a thing necessary for us; — the incompatibility of the teaching of Old Testament records with the new teachings of the rocks and stones. Is it within our power to get over our difficulties by squaring our belief with that of this new parson whom we acknowledge at any rate to be a clever fellow? Before we can do so we must at any rate know what is the belief, — or the unbelief, — that he has in him.

But this is exactly what we never can do. The old rector was ready enough with his belief. There were the three creeds, and the thirty-nine articles; and, above all, there was the Bible, — to be taken entire, unmutilated, and unquestioned. . . . But the new parson has by no means so glib an answer ready to such a question. He is not ready with his answer because he is ever thinking of it. The other man was ready because he did not think. Our new friend, however, is debonair and pleasant to us, with something of a subrisive smile in which we rather feel than know that there is a touch of irony latent. The question asked troubles him inwardly, but he is well aware that he should show no outward trouble. So he is debonair and kind, — still with that subrisive smile, — and bids us say our prayers, and love our God, and trust our Saviour. . . . We can only observe our new rector, and find out from his words and his acts how his own mind works on these subjects.

It is soon manifest to us that he has accepted the teaching of the rocks and stones, and that we may give up the actual six days, and give up also the deluge as a drowning of all the world. . . . Then he has read the *Essays and Reviews*,[2] and will not declare his opinion that the writers of them should be unfrocked and sent away into chaos; — nay, we find that he is on terms of personal intimacy with one at least among the number of those writers. And, lastly, there comes out a subscription list for Bishop Colenso, and we find our new rector's name down for a five-pound note! That we regard as the sign, to be recognized by us as the most certain of all signs, that he has cut the rope which bound his barque to the old shore, and that he is going out to sea in quest of a better land. Shall we go with him, or shall we stay where we are? . . . [W]e may declare that he is, almost always, a true man, — true in spite of that subrisive smile and ill-defined doctrine. He is one who, without believing, cannot bring himself to think that he believes, or to say that he believes that which he disbelieves without grievous suffering to himself. He has to say it, and does suffer. There are the formulas which must be repeated, or he must abandon his ministry altogether, — his ministry, and his adopted work, and the public utility which it is his ambition to achieve. Debonair though he be, and smile though he may, he has through it all some terrible heart-struggles, in which he is often tempted to give way and to acknowledge that he is too weak for the work he has taken in hand. When he resolved that he must give that five pounds to the Colenso fund, — or rather when he resolved that he must have his name printed in the public list, for an anonymous giving of his money would have been nothing, — he knew that his rope was indeed cut, and that his boat was in truth upon the wide waters. . . . He had, by the subscription, attached himself to the Broad Church with the newest broad principles, and must expect henceforth to be regarded as little better than an infidel, — certainly as an enemy in the camp, — by the majority of his brethren of the day . . . It is an accusation hard to be borne; but it has to be borne, — among other things, — by the clergyman who subscribes for Colenso.

Notes

1. *The Broad Church*: The name given to the liberal wing in the Church of England, who were sympathetic to current reforms of most kinds, and to contemporary Biblical research in particular.

The High Church: By the time Trollope was writing this had come to refer to the party most associated with the Oxford Movement, and to describe outward behaviour rather than doctrine.

The Low Church or *Evangelical Church*: This had come to designate the party which preached salvation by conduct as much as by belief. It was the church of many of the famous Victorian reformers and philanthropists. Trollope uses all the terms ironically, of course.

2. *Essays and Reviews*: A book of seven articles of Higher Criticism, six by clergymen, published 1860. One of the clerical contributors, Rowland

Williams, Vice-Principal of St David's College, Lampeter, was prosecuted for his article on Bunsen's Biblical research.

3.6   The aims of the Cambridge Camden Society

From A. J. Beresford Hope, An Essay on the Present State of Ecclesiological Science in England, *1846. Alexander Beresford Hope (1820–87) was the founder and president of the Cambridge Camden Society, also called the Ecclesiological Society, established in 1837 for the study and preservation of Gothic architecture in churches, but also frequently seen as the Cambridge version of the Oxford Movement. The Ecclesiologists saw in ecclesiastical architecture an expression of faith and they were vehement about the godless architecture which succeeded England's secession from the Roman Church at the Reformation. Hence the 'Middle-Pointed' or Decorated style was the last worth considering. Victorian churches are enormously influenced by the Society, in both restorations and new churches.*

We are all more or less familiar with the remarkable events which have characterized the religious history of the last fourteen years. . . .[1] The Church of England as a branch of the Catholic Church, never lost the Catholic faith. The stream of sound doctrine, though shrunk to a narrow thread, had still flowed on continuously through different channels in the darkest and coldest days of the last century. With church-arrangement, however, the case was quite different. . . . Before the existence of such a science as Ecclesiology[2] was contemplated, the natural instinct of newly awakened Catholicism led men to feel that our existing churches were far from being what they should be, that the honour due to the LORD required that His houses should be otherwise dressed than the parsimony of the generation lately passed away had considered needful. . . .

Just at this period however two Societies[3] were established in our two universities. . . . To the establishment of these Societies, . . . was in the main due the preservation of our national architecture. Their founders, as if led by a sort of instinct, seem from the first to have comprehended the truth that the future style of religious architecture to be national must be founded upon that of earlier times.

This study then of our ancient parish churches, viewed with architectural eyes, established one principal point, that they were the true and legitimate models for future religious constructions, and as such deserved the primary attention of architects. This being established, we become possessed of a great half-truth. All that we realized was that the same shell which contained the apparatus of mediaeval worship was, speaking generally, suited to contain that of modern worship . . .

The wide field of Catholic ritualism now opened to us. At this point we may say that ecclesiology, as a separate science, assumed a tangible existence, though as yet its students had not grasped much more than the idea of an English parish church . . .

Henceforward, . . . the researches of the Cambridge Camden Society assumed a thoroughly original form, and one by no means palatable to many who had hitherto been its supporters. Although, as I trust I have shewn, religion and not architecture was the parent and the first nurse of the ecclesiological spirit; although architecture was, we may say, rather forced upon the early church-arrangers, yet the public, naturally enough, did not perceive this. . . . And the result was obvious, our merely architectural friends abandoned us, as absurd unpractical visionaries . . .

When, however, the old English parish church was clearly established as the proper object of imitation, the knot was by no means entirely untied. An old English parish church was a very diverse building; it was, according to its age, an extremely different structure. It might resemble Kilpeck, or Skelton, or Heckington, or Fairford.[4] Were or were not the styles of these respective buildings equally eligible? While this question was being developed, the attention of some leading ecclesiologists was being directed to Durandus,[5] and the other ritualists of the middle ages. This study, as its primary result, established the fact of symbolism, and, as a secondary one, gave shape, reason, and consistency to the adoption of the now-called Middle-Pointed,[6] as the most perfect style hitherto existing, and the one therefore which must be adopted as the basis of future religious structures.

This achievement was one of extreme importance. It conferred unity, form, and method upon hitherto disjointed works. Every stone, every window, was found to tell its own appropriate tale, to bear its own peculiar meaning. The realization of this great fact, and the very general recognition of the superiority of Middle-Pointed, consummated what I shall call the first age of ecclesiological science, . . . Henceforth a bright ideal vision rose before the eyes of enthusiastic ecclesiologists, the type to which they strove to make their restorations, and each new church conform. They saw from far the slender spire broken with row upon row of spire-lights, o'ertopping the churchyard trees. They approach the sacred pile, and enter it by southern porch of stone or rich carved oak. Within the edifice, and at their left hand upon its platform, stands the octagonal font with its lofty tapering canopy, crocket upon crocket, pinnacle upon pinnacle, and bright with gules, azure, and or. The nave is lofty, and crowned with open-timbered or cradle-roof, dark-blue powdered with golden stars; an arcade high and well proportioned, with its clustered pillars and foliage capitals, enriched by the limner's art, separates it from the narrow aisles, while every window is alive with British Saints, venerable figures in glorious vestments, standing awful beneath grotesque and glowing canopies, and all the walls are various with many a symbolic painting. The floor is tesselated with encaustic tiles, and massy broad oak benches receive the worshippers, the rich and poor together. At the north-east angle of the nave the graceful pulpit stands, and near it the eagle with its outspread wings. We admire them, but not for over long, for our eyes are arrested by the glories of the roodscreen, lofty and multiform, enriched with many a fantastic and many a beautiful shape, and beaming all with colour. The holy doors are open, and within them stands the sacred chancel, a more surprising sight, where the painting is richer, the glass more glowing, the tiles more varied, whose western portion is lined with cunningly carved stalls of heart of oak, the venerable seats of clerks; while further on, on triple steps, the sacrarium rises, and in the centre of all, the great and crowning glory of the pile, the holy Altar, costly with the highest gifts of Christian art, and round are duly ranged its sacred accessories, the pelican, the credence-table, the meet piscina, 'vivoque sedilia saxo'.[7]

Notes

1. *the last fourteen years*: He is writing in 1846, some fourteen years after the beginning of the Oxford Movement.

2. *Ecclesiology*: A word coined by Beresford Hope to denote the study of ecclesiastical Gothic.

3. *two Societies*: In Cambridge, the Cambridge Camden Society, founded in 1837; in Oxford, the Oxford Society for Promoting the Study of Gothic Architecture, founded 1840.

4. *Kilpeck, or Skelton, or Heckington, or Fairford*: Famous parish churches, all dating from the tenth to the fifteenth centuries.

5. *Durandus*: William Durandus (*c.*1230–96), Bishop of Mende. His *Rationale divinorum officiorum* is an encyclopedia of mystical interpretations of the liturgy.

6. *Middle-Pointed*: The Ecclesiological Society term for what is usually known as Decorated.

7. *'vivoque sedilia saxo'*: 'and seats of natural rock'. (Page). *Aeneid*, I, 167. The sedilia in an ancient parish church, of course, are the stone seats on the south side of the choir, for the use of the clergy.

3.7   The mode of dealing with popish tendencies

From The Christian Observer, *No. 148, April 1850. An attack on the traditional enemy, the Church of Rome, by the organ of the Evangelical party.*

It is admitted on all hands, that the present are times of remarkable anxiety to the church of God . . . I would venture to regard an old adversary, the Church of Rome, as still retaining the foremost rank amongst the many antagonists of the Gospel. . . . If Popery be thus formidable, — in what a variety of forms is it now assailing us. In the garb of modern liberalism,[1] it is not ashamed to ally itself with infidelity, in order to throw down the religious bulwarks of our constitution. Under the guise of Anglo-Catholicity,[2] it is striving to unprotestantize the Church of England. And, in its own proper garb, and without disguise, it is labouring to extend its English mission through all the important parishes of the land.[3] Books without end are issuing from the press in its defence; and many of them written with much power. And multitudes of artful advocates, both in and out of the pulpit — some showing their colours and some not — are striving to complete what literature has begun.

To the Evangelical clergy, as a body, we must, as I believe, mainly look for successful resistance against this combined and formidable assault; and as Popery has never yet been able to hold its ground against the faithful proclamation of the Gospel, we may confidently believe that, although the struggle may be sharp, in the end the Captain of our salvation will tread this, with all other 'enemies, under His feet'.

Under our present circumstances, however, is it not of the

utmost importance that we should consider carefully the best practical means of prosecuting this holy warfare?

One of the most obvious of these means appears to be the *circulation of substantial and well-authenticated information* upon the subject. The mind of the public is, on the whole, exceedingly ill-informed respecting the real character or history of the church of Rome. Many zealous Protestants are such from mere prejudice; and, if required give a reason for the faith that is in them, have little to say which a subtle antagonist would not tear to pieces in a moment. In like manner those who are in the greater danger of perversion to Popery, are, generally speaking, equally ignorant of its real character. All its more startling features are naturally thrown into the background by the apostles of error. I have known intimately several cases of perversion, but have never known one in which the unhappy victim was well acquainted with the decrees of the Council of Trent, or the creed of Pius the Fourth, and, therefore, with Popery as it really is. It is then in the highest degree necessary that we should fortify the mind of those around us by solid information on the subject . . .

Is it not then to this end important that the ministry should in the first place be *instructive*? Awakened minds are generally anxious on the subject of truth; are prompt to ask with Pilate, 'What is truth?'. In such a state of mind Rome presents herself, and says, 'Be not perplexed, for it is not your business to decide the question; you are not competent for the inquiry and it is alike your privilege and duty to throw yourself upon the teaching of the Church.' Thus all responsibility is taken off the conscience; the sloth of human nature is satisfied; investigation is represented as sin; and blind reliance is honoured by the hallowed name of faith. Hence, then, the importance of a state of mind well furnished with the great truths of Scripture. . . . There are many ways in which this instruction may be conveyed, for example, by Bible Classes, Young Men's Societies, and other parochial means usually devoted to instruction, and which often prove, under the power of God, effective instruments in resisting the aggressions of Popery. But I am inclined to believe that much would be gained by infusing the element of *instruction* more largely into *sermons* . . .

Again, it is surely of the utmost importance, under our present circumstances, that the Gospel should be presented to our people in *its encouraging aspect*. It has already been remarked that those most exposed to Romish influence, are awakened minds struggling after peace. To them Rome offers immediate peace in the confessional. . . . It is of the first importance therefore to present the Saviour to the inquirer with all the encouragement with which he is presented in the Scriptures. . . . But it is one thing to preach no justification by word and another to present a free salvation through grace; one thing to clear away a false foundation, and another to fill the heart with hope. It is one thing to remove a false security, and another to heal a broken heart.

Is it not also a question whether the *present happiness* derived from a sense of our acceptance with God, is a sufficiently prominent object in the Evangelical ministry of the day? . . . If we desire to see our hearers rejoicing in Christ, and rejecting what is false, because they know the joy of what is true, we must not be afraid of addressing them as St. Paul did the Corinthians . . .

Romanism has been described as Christianity without the Holy Ghost. And if this be a somewhat exaggerated statement, it is certain that Romanism often assigns to the Church, or to the Virgin Mary, all the blessed offices of the Spirit. It is the Priest's office to apply the atoning blood of Christ to the conscience; and the office of the Virgin to bring the sinner to the Saviour's throne. — Now what is thus assigned by Popery to a human agent, we must ascribe to the Divine; and teach the troubled conscience where to seek the appropriating witness, and the intercessory voice within us — in the power and presence of the Holy Spirit.

Notes

1. *Liberalism*: See note 1, article 3.5 above, under 'Broad Church'.
2. *Anglo-Catholicity*: The name often used for the High Church party.
3. The Roman Catholic hierarchy had been restored in Great Britain in 1850.

3.8 Auricular confession in the Church of England

From Frances Power Cobbe, Darwinism in Morals, *1877. Frances Cobbe (see* The 'Woman Question'*), well-known contemporary sceptic, is giving voice to popular dismay at the growing influence of the High Church party.*

Certain well-known coarse attempts to 'unmask' the Confessional seem to have effected a purpose very remote from that which their originators designed. By fixing the public mind on gross abuses, which no one seriously apprehends to see revived in the hands of English clergymen, attention has been diverted from the real point at issue, namely, the moral or immoral, spiritual or unspiritual, tendency of the practice of Auricular Confession under ordinary and favourable circumstances. . . . I shall attempt to study as candidly as possible the *inherent* moral character of such an act as regular confession to a priest, and draw such conclusions as may seem warranted regarding the attitude to be observed towards the present revival of the practice. That the inquiry is not untimely may be judged by any one who will take the trouble to inform himself of what the whole High-Church party are now doing in this matter, and to what extent all over the country they are raising a claim to receive the confessions of their flocks as a regular portion of their office.

In a world in which Sin occupies the place it holds to-day on our planet, it would seem almost superfluous to protest against the use of any method which aims at its repression. The evils within and around us may well be thought great enough to occupy all our energies, without turning our hand against those who are honestly contending against them also, even if they employ tactics which we deem ill-advised and indiscreet. 'Let us leave these High-Churchmen', we are inclined to say, 'to make what efforts they please to stem the flood of vice in our great cities. If we do not augur much success for their attempt, at least we honour their zeal, and are fully persuaded that to do anything is better than to do nothing'. Such first impressions are even in a certain way deepened if we chance to read the manuals of penitence prepared by our English Father-Confessors.

But whatever be the good intentions, the honesty and the zeal, of the modern revivers of the confessional in our churches, the question is not altered: Is the practice of Auricular Confession to a priest spiritually or morally expedient? Are its natural results strengthening or weakening to the mind? Must it make a man feel more deeply the burden of his sins, or teach him to cast them off on the shoulders of another? Will it (for this is the crucial question of all) — will it bring the sinful soul nearer, in the deep solitudes of the spiritual world, to the One only Source of purity and restoration, and help it to look straight up into the face of God; or will it, on the contrary, thrust a priest always between man and his Maker to intercept even the embrace of the returning Prodigal in his Father's arms? . . . Our object in the present paper being a practical one, we shall limit our scope to the class and nation which the revival of Auricular Confession in England alone concerns, and ask: How is it likely to affect English men and women from the age of confirmation to the end of life, and from the highest social and intellectual rank down to that level of poverty and stupidity against which the waves of clerical zeal break for ever in vain? We must assume average intelligence, average religious feeling, and, especially, average moral condition. The old Church of England principle, that men burdened with any 'grievous crime' should seek relief from confession to 'any discreet and learned minister of God's work', is one whose wisdom we are not at all inclined to dispute; and it is only with the extension of this reasonable rule from the exceptional to the general and universal, that we are now concerned.

Putting aside . . . cases of offenders who have committed heinous offences, we shall suppose the instance of a person of ordinary character and circumstances in the condition of mind desired by the preachers of Confession. He is sensible of his sinfulness, and (a point to which we shall hereafter refer) very much terrified by fear of hell-fire. His pastors instruct him that his private penitence, whatever may be its intensity, affords no sort of security that the benefits of the 'precious Blood' shall be applied to his particular soul, and that to obtain such security he must confess to a priest who has received at his ordination the commission 'Whose sins thou dost forgive, they are forgiven; and whose sins thou dost retain, they are retained'. . . . Finally, he makes up his mind to come to confession and (as he is assured) become 'clean and safe'. What are the moral and spiritual results likely to follow such an act?

In the first place, the long and close self-examination which is ordered as a preliminary, may, when first practised by a hitherto thoughtless person, very probably open quite a new view to a man of his own character. In some special cases it may perhaps even do the invaluable service of teaching a self-satisfied Pharisee that he ought to put himself in the place of the Publican. Some festering secrets of souls may be healed simply by being brought to light, and spectres dissolved into air by being fairly faced. Long-cherished hatred may be tracked to its root, and a selfish life looked at for once as a whole in its proper colours. All these good results, I freely admit, may follow from the self-examination which is required before Confession, and which (it may be added) has formed a recognized portion of all *metanoia*, from the days of

Pythagoras and David to our own. But how of the Confession itself? What good or harm is to be done to such a mind as we have supposed, by the process of kneeling down in a vestry before a clergyman, making the sign of the cross, and then for about a quarter of an hour (or, in some cases, for five or six hours) going over the events of life *seriatim*: 'I accuse myself of' this falsehood, that unkindness, and so on? If the individual be so ignorant of morals as not to know what is sinful and what is innocent, it must be a great benefit to him to receive instruction from his Confessor, provided always that he is — what priests unfortunately, by some twist of mental confrontation, seem very rarely to be — a sound and healthy moralist. In such a case, the Confessional may obviously be a useful school of ethics. But it is surely no small disgrace to our spiritual guides if it should be needed as such, and if their flocks have been so little instructed in the principles of uprightness and charity, as not to know beforehand what is right and what is wrong, and to require to wait till they have sinned, to know what is sinful.

That the fear of having hereafter to confess a sin may sometimes possibly keep a man from committing it, is another argument for the usefulness of the Confessional as a moral agent, on which I need not enlarge. Such a motive would, of course, have no ethical value, and as to its deterrent force, may plausibly be balanced against the encouragement (found undoubtedly by Romish criminals, bandits, etc., and possibly, therefore, also by Anglicans) in the assurance of pardon, obtainable at any moment, by priestly absolution. When we have descended to so low a level of motive in the one case, we are called on to do the like in the other.

Lastly, there is a very great and important result of the practice of Confession, which to some of its upholders doubtless appears among its chief advantages, but which I must be excused for classing altogether in another category, namely, the enormous influence given thereby to the priesthood over the minds of their flocks. That the influence of the clergy of the Church of England would ever be as evil as that of their brethren of the Church of Rome, I am far from believing; but with the warning of all history before our eyes, I think that he must be a bold man, indeed, who should desire to place in the hands of any priesthood on earth a power whose most partial misuse means ecclesiastical despotism, and the mental and moral slavery of all the weaker minds of the community.

3.9 Conformity sin, because unjust to Nonconformists

From William Robinson, The Sin of Conformity, *1860. The writer voices the resentment felt by many Nonconformists at the disabilities they suffered, though they made up a significant part of the population.*

The Lord Bishop of London, clad in lawn, taunts Dissenters with their supposed difficulty in finding a grievance. Dissenters beg to tell him that to every enlightened freeman, and yet more to every enlightened Christian, his Lordship is a great grievance. For Dr. Tait,[1] as a man, a Christian, and a Christian minister, I have high respect. There are not many of the people of Great Britain who have observed his thorough evangelicism; his admirable decision in proclaiming the great worth of human souls, and the trivial importance of steeples and chancels; and his excellent example in going into the high-ways to seek the lost, with more loving appreciation than the author of these pages. But for his official *status*, I cannot affect to have any other feeling than sorrow and pity . . . Can it be that Dr. Tait's conscience fails to accuse him of bearing a title, and holding an office, thoroughly anti-Christian: an office and title, quite as foreign to both the genius and precepts of the New Covenant, as the title and office of Cardinal or Pope? If Dr. Wiseman[2] choose to protrude himself on the public with 'great swelling words of vanity', assuming the empty title of Lord Archbishop of Westminster, I am grieved by so obvious a violation of the dictates of good sense, and of the Bible: but I suffer no civil wrong. But when Lord Palmerston gives to Dr. Tait a title offensive to more than half the people of the realm, and lavishes on him ten thousand a year of public property, and he uses the influence thus greated in magnifying 'our ecclesiastical establishment,' and repressing and taunting Dissenters, I have, in addition, civil grievances to endure; and, as a citizen, I have the right to demand that such partiality should be brought to an utter end. If the bishop be disposed to make a catalogue of Dissenters' grievances, he may find a tolerably strong example to begin with, in the palace at Fulham.

If Nonconformists complain of church-rates, it is stoutly denied that they have any good ground of complaint. A member of the government to whom I applied on the subject, defended the impost as follows. I give his words as embodying with brevity and force, the argument which seems to have the greatest weight with the supporters of the tax.

> The church rate like all other local taxes is a charge upon the landlord, not upon the occupier; neither having just cause of complaint: the former having either inherited or purchased his property subject to this charge; the latter having in his calculations when hiring the land or tenement, deducted the same from the rent which he has agreed to pay to his landlord.

A house is to be let, the net rating of which is £63. A church rate of 3d. is levied annually. An Episcopalian rents the house, and receives in lieu of the church rate of 15s. 9d., religious accommodation for himself and his family. A Dissenter renting it would have to pay the 15s. 9d. without receiving anything in return. The amount is small, but the principle involved is not the less oppressive.

A farm of 300 acres is to be sold. The church rate averages £5 yearly, equivalent to £100 capital. If an Episcopalian buy and occupy it, he obtains for that £5 yearly, religious accommodation for his household. If a Dissenter buy and occupy it, he gets no return for the £5 a year; that is to say, the farm is £100 dearer to him than to the Churchman.

Our murmurs we are told are unreasonable, because we buy or hire property subject to the tax. Why that is the very *gravamen* of our grievance. All over the land when we buy or hire property, we are compelled to pay a tax, *not to the nation, but to Episcopalians*; and under this injustice, Nonconformists have been left to suffer from the year 1688 to the present day. . . . The amount in the case of church rates may be small, but the tyranny of the exaction is galling; as Episcopalians would feel if they suffered, instead of inflicting it.

As a citizen, I claim to be placed civilly on a footing of perfect equality with all other subjects, so long as I discharge the duties of citizenship. If a privilege be conferred by the state on my fellow-subjects, which I am by the state debarred from seeking, that is favouritism; and a grievance inflicted on me, unless it can be shewn that I have committed some offence which the state has a right to punish, or failed of some duty which it is the province of the state to reward. Every privilege of every kind given by the state to an Episcopalian as an Episcopalian, is a wrong done to me: and, as every one knows, such privileges are countless.

If the present Prince of Wales, or any future heir to the crown, were, by study of the word of God, to embrace the opinions of Dr. Chalmers, or of the Honourable and Reverend B. W. Noel,[3] he must either violate his conscience, or renounce the throne. None but a member of the establishment is suffered to reign; and so loftily has the establishment, which thus fetters the monarch, reared its head, that it not merely takes its place beside the sovereign, but claims precedence. It is *ego et meus rex* that we still hear, Church and Queen, not Queen and Church. The consequence is, that through all classes of society, from the Prince of Wales down to the stable-boy, the establishment assumes an importance and a right of intermeddling, to which its character gives it no claim; and often does it dare to insinuate a charge of deficient loyalty, against all who repudiate its authority. If the arrangement now existing were reversed, and a law passed that the sovereign should be a congregationalist, how eloquently and vehemently would Episcopalians denounce the violence done to the conscience of the highest person in the realm, and the insult flung in the face of all who are not congregationalists!

The population of England and Wales is about eighteen millions. It is computed that about three millions and a half attended Episcopalian places of worship on the 30th of March, 1851. Make any hypothetical addition you please, even the most extravagant, for absentees. Raise the number to five, or if it be wished, six millions: and still the following startling facts emerge. Five millions sterling, of national property, are year by year lavished on the six millions, in which the remaining twelve millions have no share. If this huge mass of wealth were taken from Episcopalians, and given to the Wesleyans or the Catholics, Dr. Tait would not need a microscope to discover the grievance.

To this enormous partiality must be added numberless chaplaincies; professorships; a thousand fellowships worth, on an average, £200 a year each; public schools; &c., &c; all which are either integral parts of, or appendages to the establishment; and Episcopalians, instead of walking humbly, as becomes men thus subsidized, in the presence of Dissenters who pay their own way, assume that they are the dignified class of society. Exceptions there are, and noble exceptions, and many; but as a rule, Churchmen seem to think that there is something very ennobling in their position: and however strange the fact, it is a fact, that they are as truly a caste in England, as the Brahminical order is in the east; a caste saying to their neighbours 'stand by, for we are better than ye;' a caste employed directly and indirectly in thwarting the success in life of all who will not bow down to their idol. I am never consulted by man or woman on the question of Dissent — and such consultation is no unfrequent occurrence — whithout telling the inquirer first, and most plainly, to count the cost of Nonconformity. The advice is ever, in substance, as follows:

> If you mean to act firmly as a Dissenter, you will assuredly lose caste. You may meet with toleration and condescension, but even that is doubtful, You will certainly find many of the avenues to success in life, closed against you. If you are not prepared to suffer for conscience sake, you had better keep away from the strait gate of Nonconformity.

Dissenters could suggest to Dr. Tait, that he would do wisely to speak of that only which he understands. Many of them could inform him, that they were persecuted for their Nonconformity in childhood; that in later life they have found that they must sacrifice truth, or be shut out from the prizes of the Universities, and from all such pathways as he has climbed: they could assure him that their lives have been happy in a constant course of civil degradation, because they have cheerfully made the sacrifice to Him, who gave himself for them. For themselves they heed not the injustice; but as parents, they utter an indignant protest against the partial and unholy ecclesiastical laws of their country, and the caste which they create. When they look at their children, and hear the bishop, clad in lawn and revelling in an income of ten thousand a year, telling them they have no grievances, they may be forgiven if their patience is exhausted.

Notes

1. *Dr. Tait* : A. C. *Tait (1811–82)*, Archbishop of Canterbury from 1868.

2. *Dr. Wiseman* : Nicholas Wiseman (1802–65), English Cardinal and first Archbishop of Westminster.

3. *Dr. Chalmers . . . B. W. Noel* : Thomas Chalmers (1780–1847) was a pioneer in the founding of the Scottish Free Church. Baptist Wriothesley Noel (1798–1873), son of an English peer, was an Evangelical clergyman who became a Baptist, 1848.

4

The Scientific Approach

'It is the Age of Machinery', Carlyle had declared in 1829, 'in every outward and inward sense of that word', and indeed 'science', of every kind and at every level of meaning, was one of the key words of the period. As the Industrial Revolution showed few signs of abating in the workshop the world, technology increased hand over fist and the cry went up for technical education to meet the emergency (see *Education*).

Until now 'science' had been almost exclusively the preserve of the educated amateur; and, until the science of geology and the Higher Criticism of the Bible in the 1830s and 1840s, the church, far from showing dismay, had encouraged 'natural theology' (see *The Religious Debate*), as the effort to know God through His works.

Now, however, science began to be accepted among the professions. The British Association was founded in 1831, the Royal Institution and the reformed Royal Society flourished, as growing numbers came to regard scientific research as their chief work in life, and called themselves 'scientists'. The old universities, as a result of the 1852 Commission at Oxford (Cambridge in 1856) began to reform the medieval curriculum of classics and mathematics, to include modern subjects, and to recognise the sciences as academic disciplines in themselves. (Cambridge introduced the Natural Science Tripos in 1869.) By 1871 Fellowships were extended to ambitious young scientists whose goal in life was not a curacy in the country, but notable feats of scientific research in the university. Meanwhile, the new universities in the North of England, founded on deliberately Utilitarian lines, specialised from the start in the sciences, numbered internationally famous scientists on their staffs (see *Education*) and confirmed 'science' as a professional and academic discipline.

The movement to reform the universities was supported by the section of society known as Utilitarians, whose philosophy had been developed by Jeremy Bentham early in the century, in the wake of the Enlightenment. Their ideals, which though resisted were enormously influential throughout the century, were based on the theory that takes the ultimate good to be the greatest happiness of the greatest number, and they made usefulness the standard by which every institution should be judged. The most famous of the Utilitarians was J. S. Mill, raised and educated by Bentham, and his father, James Mill, to be the perfect example of Utilitarianism, and the intellectual reformer of the world. And the Utilitarians, of course, promoted the cause of 'science' as useful in the pursuit of happiness.

From the middle of the century, 'science' was the fashionable topic at every level, from the austerely academic to the merely social. 'Such an enormous crowd has run after the fashion of being scientific', remarked an observer in 1851, that 'every district of the town must have its scientific institute, and every suburb its course of lectures', as the public, to show their style, flocked to hear about 'screw-propellers, electric lights, and new manures', and the chemistry of 'a fire, a candle, a lamp, a chimney, a kettle, ashes' (William Johnston, *England As It Is*). More and more 'sciences' emerged as subjects worthy of academic study or the evening lecture, which either survived the craze of the time (like psychology, sociology and political science) or faded as times changed (like phrenology and physiognomy).

Other disciplines, too, took on fresh dimensions as the 'scientific method' was applied. From the early days of the period, for example, theology was an object of scientific inquiry, and history likewise was emerging as a science. History was coming to be recognised as a discipline in itself, governed by laws as open to inquiry and identification as the laws of physical science; and the same scientific methods of inquiry are to be applied even to the study of literature.

4.1   Modern science

From William Johnston, England As It Is, *1851. The writer speaks with irony of the impact of science at popular level.*

That which is *popularly* termed a taste for science in these times, is either the desire to hear the latest news in the scientific world, and a willingness to attend lectures, as one goes to a show or an assembly; or it is the desire to become acquainted with something that may be turned to practical account, for promoting convenience, or for making money. This is what occasions the perpetual bustle of the 'scientific world' in towns. The going to lectures is a fashion, which many people submit to, though it is far from agreeable, just as they do to a thousand other things tedious or unpleasant in themselves, but suffered with patience, or even eagerly followed, because it is the reigning mode.

At the same time it is unquestionably true that in colleges, in observatories, and possibly in many a retired private house, there are profound students searching the heavens or analysing the earth, or wearing out eye and brain in calculations of forces and disturbances — attractions and perturbations: — counting up the almost infinite repetition of minutenesses too delicate for ordinary observation, or weighing the isolated effects of magnitudes and distances so stupendous and overwhelming that the ordinary mind grows dizzy when attempting to contemplate them but for a moment. Of these, some study and die, making no sign, while others write books, which a few read, and which a good many purchase, in order to lay them upon their library tables. I wish to guard against being supposed to believe, or to wish others to believe, that the heights and depths of science are not now explored with the most devoted and persevering care; but I have to speak of what is popularly called science — of that fashion which crowds lecture-rooms, and which deserts the theatres where tragedy and comedy were wont to be performed, in order to frequent the theatres of scientific institutes, where gay bonnets are ranged opposite galvanic batteries, and the natural electric light of ladies' eyes is brought into rivalship with the artifical light of electro-magnetism.

The sciences which 'crowds run to hear', says a writer in a recent number of the *Edinburgh Review*, 'are natural philosophy and chemistry — it would be more just to say that the arts springing out of these sciences are popular, than that the sciences themselves are. The laws regulating the elasticity of steam at different temperatures — the the theory of waves — the idea of polarity — the doctrine of dia-magnetism, and of electro-magnetics, of isomerism, or organic types, and much else, find no favour with such disciples, but screw-propellers, electric lights, and new manures are cordially welcomed. . . . What was the planet Neptune to the utilitarian public, or that public to Neptune? His appearance in the heavens did not lead to any reduction in the window-tax, or to any saving in candles.' This is very well as against the utilitarians, but there are plenty in the scientific world of fashion who affect an interest in 'polarity' and electro-magnetics, and who yawn piteously at the lectures thereon in the intervals between the experiments. The utilitarians, who openly avow that they care for nothing scientific except it can be turned to some use, are respectable in their way, when compared with the danglers and dawdlers who trifle with science as a mode of killing time. If, however, it were merely the wish to be informed on what is interesting in its organization, or exquisite in its action, that led people to lecture-rooms, they might occupy themselves with simpler things than the scientific lecturer generally brings before them. A nettle or a limpet, as the critic of the *Edinburgh* truly says — the meanest weed or the humblest insect — still more a nautilus or a humming-bird, is, after all, at least as curious a thing as gun-cotton or chloroform; and a torpedo or gymnotus is in reality a much more wonderful machine than a voltaic battery.

As it is a prevailing notion that 'liberality' in politics is associated with a due respect for science, while Conservatism, or love of the old ways, is accompanied by a bigoted suspicion of modern proficiency, even in chemistry and geology, I am glad to be able to support my own views of the modern scientific public, by authority, of which the political 'liberality' cannot be questioned. I therefore proceed to quote the *Edinburgh Review*, which I suppose will be accounted *sans reproche* in all circles of genteel Whiggery. As for the Radicals, though they may not like to be laughed at, they will, I hope, have the sturdy candour to acknowledge that *utility* is the chief object of their veneration, and that the new planet is nothing to them if 'the skies looked no brighter for his coming, and if the street lamps are as needful as they were before'. The reviewer assures us that 'intelligent appreciation, childish fear, childish wonder, a feverish spirit of speculation, and a *strong infusion of cupidity*, are all strangely mingled in the popular estimate of what the sciences are destined to effect for the world. The general faith in science as a wonder-worker is at present unlimited; and along with this there is cherished the conviction that every discovery and invention admits of a practical application to the welfare of men. Is a new vegetable product brought to this country from abroad, or a new chemical compound discovered, or a novel physical phenomenon recorded, the question is immediately asked, *cui bono?* What is it good for? Is food or drink to be got out of it? Will it make hats or shoes, or cover umbrellas? Will it kill or heal? Will it drive a steam-engine or make a mill go?' . . .

Such, then, is the 'science' of the crowd in this enlightened age — such the mental superiority of this period of progress! But was it not always so, more or less? No. It has been so these fifty years in a less degree, but not in a greater. In this, as in so many other things, such an enormous crowd has run after the fashion of being scientific, that it has become vulgarised and flattened down into the dullest absurdity. Forty years ago, in the days of Sir Humphry Davy's triumphs, there was doubtless a great deal of scientific affectation in the fashionable world, and carriage company crowded to the Royal Institution, as they do now, to listen to his scarcely less-gifted successor. But in his day the *fashion* stopped with the circle which surrounded him, or not far beyond it; and if May Fair was scientific (on the 'off days' of morning concerts), Finsbury Circus was content to be domestic and commercial, and Hackney enjoyed its evenings with a game of cards or a dance. Not so now. Every district of the town must have its scientific institute, and every suburb its courses of lectures. It is obvious enough that this is up-hill work, and that something more social, concluding with a supper, would be infinitely more to the taste of the company, if that more congenial method of passing the time by good luck happened to be the fashion. But what is *the* fashion must now be followed by the enlightened middle class; and so, while the thing is new, subscriptions are paid and scientific lectureships established in every 'enlightened' neighbourhood. . . .

The greatest triumph of our day in practical science is, I think, the Electric Telegraph. The steamboat and the locomotive engine are of more general, and of more stupendous utility, but their triumph over natural difficulty, their mastery over time and space, their novelty and marvellousness, are all less than that of the Electric Telegraph. Many years ago model boats were made to move through water by wheels at the sides, which owed their motion to clockwork in the interior, and by the same means carriages and puppet-figures were made to move over smooth and level surfaces. The steamboat and the locomotive engine are but the application of the enormous force of steam to effect those motions upon a large scale, and against great resistance, which without steam had been effected upon a small scale, and against a very small resistance. But the electric telegraph, the setting of types as it were, at the distance of hundreds of miles, by means of the electric force carried through continuous wires, is, I believe, as new as it is wonderful. A rapidity in the communication of intelligence is achieved which anticipates time itself. Time is measured by the motion of the earth, but that motion is slowness compared with the motion of the electric fluid. We can announce, from London to the city of Bristol, the demise of the old year and the birth of a new one, while in Bristol the old year has some minutes of existence still left. While Bristol is still spinning round to twelve o'clock, London has not only passed the point, but may have announced it by the lightning telegraph to her western sister, who is a hundred miles behind her. 'Progress' can hardly beat this, let what will happen. In this matter we may rest satisfied that science has done her utmost. The force of nature and of art can no further go.

The utilitarian tendency of scientific inquiry in recent times, and a certain materialistic turn of the general mind, seem to have given a rather undue preponderance to the physical sciences, and indeed to have cast into the shade, so far as popular patronage is concerned, the philosophy of the mind, which at former times gave profound occupation to the most eminent thinkers of our country. In the present time it is only what one can see or handle, or taste or smell, or measure or weigh, that 'philosophers' seem to care for. What they can boil in a retort, or roast in crucible; what they can break in pieces with a hammer, or bray in a mortar, or rend into its primary elements by electrical force, they will industriously attend to, but if you invite them to examine the processes of their own minds, and to consider and classify the powers of perception, reflection, comparison, deduction, and so forth, without which all their tasting, smelling, boiling, burning, weighing, measuring, and all other processes, analytical or synthetical, would be nothing worth — they have neither time or inclination for such inquiries. This, I think, is to be regretted; for though nothing can be more painful than rash speculation concerning the nature and powers of the mind, yet no philosophy can be complete, or can have the

elevation which philosophy ought to have, if the faculties by which
it is apprehended and judged of, be left out of consideration. Upon
this point the late Dr. Thomas Brown, of Edinburgh University,
has said with no less truth than eloquence, that 'In the physics of
the material universe there is indeed much that is truly worthy of
our philosophic admiration, and of the sublimest exertions of
philosophic genius. But even that material world will appear more
admirable to him who contemplates it as it were from the height of
his own mind, and who measures its infinity with the range of his
own limited but aspiring faculties. He is unquestionably the
philosopher most worthy of the name who unites to the most
accurate knowledge of mind the most accurate knowledge of all the
physical objects amid which he is placed; who makes each science
to each reciprocally a source of additional illumination; and who
learns from both the noblest of all the lessons which they can give
— the knowledge and adoration of that Divine Being who has alike
created and adapted to each other, with an order so harmonious,
the universe of matter and the universe of thought.'

4.2   Utilitarianism and the *summum bonum*

From Macmillan's Magazine, *Vol. 8, June 1863. Utilitarianism, or
Benthamism, was an attitude of mind that dominated the century. The
writer, T. E. C. Leslie (1827–82), political economist and moral
philospher, is questioning the views expressed by the most famous
Utilitarian, J. S. Mill, about the nature of morality and happiness.*

The two questions — what is right? and, what are the motives to
do right? — or, what is the foundation of the moral sentiments?
and, what rule should regulate their dictates? — or, again, what is
the *summum bonum*? and what leads men to pursue it? — are now
generally opposed as philosophically distinct. They are not so,
indeed, according to the theory of an innate sense of right and
wrong which assumes that every man's conscience informs him of
his duty. . . . The conclusion to which . . . historical theory would
seem to lead — and it is one to which other considerations also
tend — is, that no complete and final philosophy of life and human
aims has been constructed; that the world abounds in insoluble

problems, and man's ideal of virtue is both historical and progressive; and that the circumstance at which Mr. Mill has expressed a mournful surprise — namely, that 'neither thinkers nor mankind at large seem nearer to being unanimous on the subject of the *summum bonum* than when Socrates asserted the theory of utilitarianism against the popular morality,' is what might have been expected, and could not have been otherwise, from the nature of the subject. Another conclusion to which the considerations referred to lend at least a probability is, that happiness is not the sole nor even the chief constituent of the *summum bonum*, as the utilitarian doctrine asserts. Moral progress may be taken to mean an improvement either in men's knowledge and ideas of duty, or in their dispositions and practice. Taken in either sense, it has been often denied. . . . The absence in the records of very ancient society of anything resembling our standard of right and wrong, and the entirely different direction given to the sentiments of approbation and disapprobation from what we deem just and reasonable, can hardly fail to strike any reader of Homer. An individual, in heroic Greece, was good or bad in reference not to his personal character and conduct, but to his birth and station in society. The chief was estimable because, however cruel, licentious, and treacherous, he possessed the esteemed qualities of rank and power; the common man was base, vile, and bad because the class to which he belonged was despised. . . . The offence of a Red Indian is the offence of his whole tribe and to be visited upon the whole tribe. And, so far from the moral sentiments of mankind having been always and everywhere alike, there are living languages which lack names for the feelings essential to the rudiments even of a low morality. Affection, benevolence, gratitude, justice, and honour, are terms without equivalents in the speech of some savage societies, because they have no existence in their minds. The Englishman is so early taught that he should love his neighbour, that he is ready to think the knowledge of that duty comes to him by intuition. But the African savage thinks that he, too, has intuitive knowledge — but it is of the art of rearing cattle and of making rain; and he cannot believe that God meant him to love anyone but himself. . . . How could the human mind, while carnage was the highest enjoyment and the noblest occupation, conceive or comprehend the moral creed of our time? . . . the people of England were formerly more vindictive and irritable than they are now, and can it be supposed that, in the thirteenth century, any one would have thought of subscribing for the relief of the inhabitants of Lisbon after an earthquake, or to clothe the French prisoners? There is scarcely, again, a page of the history or literature of the seventeenth century, says Lord Macaulay, which does not prove that our ancestors were less humane than their posterity. The code of honour, in the eighteenth century, we may add, commanded a gentleman to commit murder; and drunkenness was then little short of a duty to society.

It has been urged, however, as a decisive proof of the stationary character of moral principles, that 'the only two principles which moralists have ever been able to teach respecting war, are that defensive wars are just, and that offensive wars are unjust'. But it is sufficiently obvious that the words defensive and offensive have no fixed and definite meaning, and may mean one thing in one age, and another thing in another.

The same verbal proposition does not always carry the same import. If progress in both public and private morals can be proved in the past and shown to be probable in the future, can the Utilitarian formula of general happiness be accepted as the final measure of right and wrong, and the sole guide of human conduct? If Mr. Mill has failed to establish this, there is antecedent reason to believe that the theory is essentially defective, and that, if it could have been proved, it would have been proved by the reasoning of so powerful and persuasive an advocate. The common objections to the doctrine must, in fairness, be admitted to be weak. . . . [W]hen it is argued that a piece of furniture, or any other inanimate object, may be useful, yet that no one ascribes to it moral rectitude or virtue, and that it follows, that intention and not utility is the criterion of morality, the Utilitarian fairly replies that things without feeling are not fit objects, however useful, for gratitude or indignation, for reward or punishment, because they cannot feel either, and neither is therefore expedient; because such things tend to do harm as well as good, to hurt or inconvenience as well as to do service; and because no praise or censure bestowed upon senseless matter tends to make the class to which it belongs contribute to the happiness of life. In the Utilitarian estimate intention is of great importance, because of its consequences or tendencies. The Utilitarian blames a small act of malignity, not in proportion only to the actual pain it causes, but to the general mischiefs to which malignity tends. . . . Or take a higher example, 'At the cavalry combat at El Boden, a French officer raised his sword to strike Sir Felton Harvey, of the 14th Light Dragoons; but perceiving that his antagonist had only one arm, he stopped, brought down his sword before Sir Felton in the usual salute, and rode on'. Was this proceeding right or wrong? The first duty of a citizen is to his country, and of an officer to his army. War, too, is not a duel, and the combatants do not measure their swords. Sir Felton Harvey had not lost his head, and the head of an officer is more dangerous to an enemy in battle than his arm. The Frenchman, therefore, ought, it seems, to have cut him down. Yet the Utilitarian would admit that the magnanimous intention alters the character of the act, because it is of supreme importance to human happiness that a spirit should exist among the strong to spare the weak, and that even enemies should show mercy and courtesy to each other . . .

To prove that happiness is the *summum bonum* at which virtue aims, Mr. Mill concedes the necessity of showing that the greatest human happiness results from the employment of the highest faculties of humanity; but of this he gives no other proof than the following: 'Of two pleasures, if there be one to which all, or almost all, who have experience of both give a decided preference, irrespective of any feeling of moral obligation to prefer it, that is the more desirable pleasure. . . . It is better to be a human being dissatisfied than a pig satisfied; better to be Socrates dissatisfied than a fool satisfied. And, if the fool and the pig are of a different opinion, it is because they only know their own side of the question. . . .'

It might be asked, where is the testimony to be found of all those who are competent to judge? and, if they differ, why should their opinions be counted rather than weighed? Or what proof have we that those who have volunteered evidence were competent to testify not only for themselves but for others? The heart knoweth its own bitterness, and a stranger intermeddleth not with its joys. The philosopher has not the experiences of the fool, nor can the fool have the experiences of the philosopher. The unselfish and spiritually minded man may find his greatest happiness in pursuits from which less generous and lofty minds could derive nothing but weariness. . . . There is an illusive semblance of simplicity in the Utilitarian formula. The tendency to produce happiness seems to be an easy test; but it assumes an unreal concord about the constituents of happiness and an unreal homogeneity of human minds in point of sensibility to different pains and pleasures. The things that make life a pleasure or a pain are not the same for the Hindoo, the Englishman, the Chinaman, the Arab, the Italian, the Red Indian, the Frenchman, and the Turk, nor yet for all Englishman, or all Frenchmen. There is a uniformity of character in a tribe of savages, as there is in a flock of sheep or a pack of wolves; but in proportion as society has advanced beyond the simplicity of barbarism, individuality is developed, and diversities of tastes and temperaments baffle the Utilitarian measure. Nor is it possible to weigh bodily and mental pleasures and pains one against the other; no single man can pronounce with certainty about their relative intensity even for himself, far less for all his fellows. And, if it is better to be a sad philosopher than a merry fool, better to be a dissatisfied man than a satisfied pig, it must be so because there is really something better and more to be desired by the elevated soul than happiness, and something worse and more to be shunned than suffering or grief. If the unhappy sage will not change places with the happy brute or idiot, it must be either because he does *not*, as Mr. Mill supposes, 'know both sides of the question', or else because he knows or believes that happiness is not the *summum bonum*.

4.3   Convocation and Dr. Colenso

From Macmillan's Magazine, *Vol. 8, July 1863. Science was invading every area of thought and belief. It seemed to the anxious laity that Bishop Colenso was using it to disprove the Bible. The author is angry at the public response to this man of science. (Colenso was deprived of his bishopric.)*

The Church of England loudly claims to be the keeper of truth and the religious teacher of the nation; and Convocation as loudly claims to be its organ. Let them teach then. There never were more willing pupils than the laity; there never was a time when every educated man was more ready and anxious to hear, in perfect good faith, anything which the clergy have to say. If they would only take a lead, if they would but show the public that they do know their own business, that they have something reasonable to say on the subjects which occupy men's minds, they might make their own terms, for it is idle to conceal the fact that vital questions are at issue. A large proportion of the educated laity entertain grave doubts . . . as to the truth of large and important parts of the Bible. There are sober men, who feel that it is destructive to common honesty to believe in geology and to pretend to believe all the Book of Genesis — who are impatient of the Old Bailey sophistry by which certain writers attempt to explain away the contradictions in the Gospels, and who can come to no other conclusion than that parts of the Bible are true and other parts false, and that no one can tell which is which. Of course such a view is not pleasant, and those who hold it would gladly be shown that it is incorrect. They look, therefore, with natural anxiety, to see what the clergy, as represented by Convocation — the body who claim to be their teachers — have to say on the subject. What have they to say? The matter is pointedly brought before them. One of their own number publishes a book specifically assigning error after error in the Pentateuch; and how do they deal with him? . . . [T]hey have fallen foul of the spirit in which Dr. Colenso writes.[1] The 'general tenor' of his book 'discourages a humble, childlike faith'. Then, though according to his lights, he has tried to bring scholarship, learning, and science to bear upon the Bible, his scholarship is not 'sound', his learning and science are not 'real'; his style must have offended God, and he cannot, they think, have prayed before he wrote his book, and he has brought 'learning and science into disrepute and contempt'. To say all this is ease and safety itself. The general tenor of a book, the 'soundness' of its scholarship, and the 'reality' of its learning and science are matters of opinion, and very charitable persons may possible believe that some of the committee thought that they were telling the truth when they blamed him for 'bringing learning and science into disrepute and contempt'. It required a little more courage to express an opinion on the questions, whether he offended God by writing it, and whether he prayed about it, for these are questions of fact, in which Convocation has no special means of knowledge. All the rest of the report keeps out of harm's way — no one can lay a finger upon it. It all comes to this, that the sacred synod does not like Dr. Colenso's book, and declines to say anything definite on the subject to which it refers. . . . It is very difficult, if not altogether impossible, to believe that some at least of those who condemn Dr. Colenso differ from him radically. . . . Dr. Milman[2] clearly does not. . . . The *History of the Jews* contains a score of passages as strong as anything written by Dr. Colenso; but they are written by a man to whom the public is accustomed — a man who is one of the greatest ornaments of the Church — a man who lives upon terms of personal intimacy with the most distinguished part of English society; and what bishop has taken alarm at his book, or

119

forbidden him to preach in his diocese? Is it honourable, is it English, to treat a Colonial Bishop with every sort of contumely for saying that which a distinguished English Dean is allowed to say with impunity? Dr. Colenso is certainly not equal in a literary point of view to Dr. Milman, but is the Sacred Synod moved by this? Do they sit as writers, or theologians? Or is it really true, after all, that what they lament is, the absence in the Bishop of Natal's work of 'real' science and 'sound' scholarship — that they would like him better if he was an Ewald[3] or a Renan?[4] What a satisfaction it must be to them to know that Dr. Milman's book does inculcate a humble, childlike faith, though he says in so many words that he believes the story of the sun and moon standing still to be 'pure poetry', and though on many occasions he treats the question discussed by the Bishop of Natal as matters which may be decided either way without affecting the interests of Christianity.

It is perfectly useless, as a general rule, to warn any body of men, and especially any body of clergymen, of the consequences of their policy; but a recent memorable precedent might warn the clergy of the present day, if they were capable of being warned, of the probable results of their conduct. . . . There are two consistent and intelligible views in relation to this controversy, and there are no more. A man may either say the Bible is absolutely true, all through, and no man shall doubt or deny a word of it; or he may say the whole is open to criticism like any other book. It is a question of detail, and of specific argument and evidence, whether any particular statement contained in it, however important, is true or not. Of course it is easy to fight against this; but it is the plain result of the whole controversy, and it is better to face it manfully than to wear out one's soul in vain attempts to evade it. The public understand it plainly enough, whether the clergy do or not; and, if the clergy are too timid to take their sides like men, and to act upon their opinions vigorously and openly, they may, and probably will escape a good deal of present obloquy, but they will utterly forfeit the respect of all the intelligent part of the nation.

Notes

1. *Dr. Colenso*: See 'The Clergyman Who Subscribes for Colenso', article 3.5 above, in *The Religious Debate*.

2. *Dr. Milman*: Henry Milman (1791–1868), Dean of St Paul's; historian.

3. *Ewald*: Georg Heinrich August von Ewald (1803–75), German theologian and scholar, Professor of Theology, Tübingen.

4. *Renan*: Ernest Renan (1832–92), French seminarian turned sceptic and philosopher. Wrote *L'Avenir de la Science* and the notorious *La Vie de Jésus*.

4.4 The study of history

From The Cornhill Magazine, *Vol. 4, November 1861. The author, Fitzjames Stephen (1829–94), lawyer and journalist, is defending the right of history to be considered as a science.*

If we wish to see what would be the relation of a science of history to morality, we are not confined to speculation on the subject. Two branches of knowledge relating to human action have been thrown into what may not improperly be called a scientific shape, so that their result on the freedom and morality of the classes of actions to which they relate can be tested by direct observation; and though the study of history cannot be said as yet to have been reduced to the shape of a science, sufficient progress towards such a result has been already made to enable us to form an accurate judgment as to the shape which the future science, if it is ever constructed, may be expected to assume, and the degree of influence which it will exercise.

The alarm excited on the subject is, no doubt, due principally to the general want of distinct notions which prevails even amongst educated people as to the nature and limits of scientific certainty. An attempt was made in the former article to show that, even in the case of the most exact sciences, this certainty is both negative and hypothetical: negative, in leaving out of consideration whatever is not proved to exist; hypothetical, amongst other things, as to the permanence of the conclusions at which it arrives. In applied mathematics, these limitations are not sensibly felt. The scale of the operations to which they relate is so vast, and the principles which they establish are so plain and wide, that they impress the imagination with a notion in reality altogether unfounded, that they form collectively an exhaustive system of eternal unqualified truth. In reality, we never can be sure that our knowledge even on these points is complete, and still less that the truths which we have reached are permanent. All that we can say is, that for all practical purposes we must neglect the possibility that our knowledge is limited, or that its discoveries are transient, because we have no evidence to the contrary. When, however, scientific processes are applied to more complicated subjects, the real nature of scientific certainty makes itself felt; and the fact that science is not a self-existing, overruling power, but a mere classification devised to enable the minds which conceive it to understand the phenomena to which it applies, assumes greater prominence. . . .

If . . . morality and freedom are rather assisted than injured by statistics and political economy, why should they be injured by a science of history, supposing such a science were ever formed? The arguments already advanced show that the apprehension is idle, but such apprehensions arise rather from the imagination and from detached and partial views of particular consequences supposed to be involved in the establishment of such a science rather than from rational conviction. It may . . . be desirable to inquire shortly what a science of history would be like if such a science should ever exist.

In the first place it may be confidently asserted that such a science, when it had attained an authentic form and a recognized position, would be free from the offensive and pedantic phrases by which those who expect do so much to retard its advent. We should hear less than at present of statical and dynamical sociology, the metaphysical stage of thought, the eternal laws which govern human conduct, and other phrases which, generally speaking, are either barbarous adaptations of bad French or incorrect mathematical metaphors. We should not be asked to believe that every crotchet which tickled the insane vanity of a conceited Frenchman was an eternal and self-evident truth, as, for example, that it is an everlasting law of nature that there either is, must, or ought to be, a thing called the Western European Republic, of which the French are the natural presidents . . .

If the science of history were like any other science, and especially any science relating to human affairs, it would consist of a set of maxims lying at such a distance from practical life that their relation to it would hardly be felt. Whoever wishes to realize this, should try to connect in his own mind the rule which lies at the bottom of all mechanics — that the force of gravity varies inversely as the square of the distance — with the different facts which it enables us to explain, the flight of a bullet, the fall of a drop of rain, the effects produced by muscular efforts, and a thousand other matters which to ordinary observation have nothing whatever to do with it. Historical science would, in the same way, have no assignable relation to any particular state of facts. It would form a mere skeleton, giving nothing but hypothetical conclusions, and always leaving unclassified a vast mass of circumstances which the historical philosopher would be able to consider in no other light than that of disturbing causes. . . . The whole subject is at present in an inchoate state; and those who profess to know most about it, employ more energy in boasting of the great results which they are to achieve, than in taking steps to achieve them. Here and there, however, a few observations have been made which contain at any rate a sufficient amount of truth to show what sort of doctrine historical science would establish, and in what sort of relation it would stand to morality. Thus, for example, Mr. Merivale[1] says, 'The annals of the Roman people afford a conspicuous illustration of the natural laws which seem to control the rise and progress of nations. . . . One principle seems to be established by their history. It is the condition of permanent dominion that the conquerors should absorb the conquered gradually into their own body, by extending, as circumstances arise, a share in their own exclusive privileges to the masses from whom they have torn their original independence.' This is a fair specimen of the sort of doctrines of which a science would consist. How can it be said even to tend to fetter the freedom or to injure the morals of politicians? It simply gives a short general inference from a number of the most remarkable passages in the history of Rome . . .

This is certainly not the impression which is conveyed by reading the books of those who, in the present day, proclaim most loudly the approach of the science of history; but this is only because they overstate their case. The 'eternal laws' which they claim to have discovered appear, upon examination, to be no more than maxims generically similar to the one quoted from Mr. Merivale, but thrown into startling shapes, and, generally speaking, smothered in metaphors and rhetoric . . .

It would . . . appear that upon the question whether individuals produce great changes in history, and colour its whole complexion long after their death, those who disbelieve in the possibility of a science of history are right; but to infer from this that there never can be a science of history is altogether wrong. It proves, no doubt, that the professors of such a science will never be able to make specific predictions until they are able not only to predict how many children will be born, and what will be the natural capacity and advantages of each of them, but also to read the thoughts of individuals, and so to predict their actions and the consequences of those actions. But no sane man expects anything of the sort . . .

Thus the only historical science of the future existence of which there is any sort of evidence is a science which will authorize, not absolute, but conditional predictions; and even those conditional predictions will be founded on facts so ill-ascertained, so shifting, and so indefinite that the predictions will be little more than conjectures made on principle, instead of being made at random or from prejudice.

Note

1. *Mr. Merivale*: Charles Merivale (1808 – 93), Dean of Ely. Published *History of the Romans under the Empire*.

4.5   On the scientific study of poetry

From a lecture to the South London Working Men's College, January 1869. Francis Palgrave (1824 – 97), famous as editor of The Golden Treasury, *is lecturing to a Working Men's College on how the 'scientific method' can be applied even to poetry.*

There are two methods of reading poetry, as there are of looking at pictures or listening to music. The one method is that which treats these great arts as mere ministers to our leisure, as things which will, as it were teach themselves, and do all that they can for us without any trouble on our part — nay, as things which we are entitled to throw aside the moment they assume to be anything more than matters of pastime. The other method is that which I wish to describe as the scientific method of studying them. . . . [W]hen the traveller is among the works of man, . . . though he may be struck, as all men are, however ignorant or careless, with the beauty of the cathedral or the grandeur of the castle — yet how small and transient will be his enjoyment and his reward compared to what the traveller gains, who brings adequate knowledge with him, and takes the pains to apply it! Such a one will be aware of the history of the work before him; he will repeople it with the human creatures who once lived and moved there, will see the great man, forgotten perhaps by his descendants, who planned and raised the walls; he will hear the strange, melancholy music of the long vanished days; — in a word, what to the careless eye is a bare skeleton of the present to him will be the living past. Nor does this exhaust his pleasures. Beside the history of the particular monument, the man who travels in this spirit — let me say at once, the man who travels in the spirit without which travelling is only another name for a 'parcels' delivery' — will read a hundred other memorials of human progress in a single building. He will understand why the pillars were disposed in their order, what purpose each buttress has in maintaining the fabric, at what date and under the influence of what feelings the capitals were decorated and the windows filled. Every wall to him will have its handwriting, telling him stories of the thoughts and aims of his fellow-creatures; there will not be so much as the curve of an arch or the cutting of a foundation-stone, that is without that human interest which, of all interests, is the most deep and the most permanent. And, beyond that, he will also know the place which this monument has in the long story of human necessities and human improvement. He will be aware how the style adopted was evolved from those which preceded it by laws as singular and precise as those which we trace in the realm to which the name of Nature is unphilosophically confined; and how, in turn, that style has given way to some other which more accurately corresponded to men's wishes and wants at a later period. That building which, to the uneducated eye, represented perhaps an unintelligible and hence unimpressive mass, or, at best, a simple effect of grandeur or of beauty, to the informed taste will be a fragment of embodied history; a chronicle of human progress. And it would be idle to say that the pleasure which he will thence receive will be twenty times deeper, higher, and more permanent than that of the passer-by: it will be something out of all comparison with it. . . . Substitute the words appropriate to poetry for those which I have used in analysing the pleasure given by . . . the cathedral, and I think you will find that the argument still holds good. He who reads poetry as a pastime, a mere means of making an idle hour idler, or is content with simply asking whether it suits the taste of the moment, without caring to see whether that taste has any rational foundation, will soon see the end of his enjoyment in it. But he who studies it scientifically,

— referring all the elements in a poem to the general laws of the human mind by which it is governed, seeking the cause of every quality and every detail which it presents, and not satisfied till he has put himself in the writer's own place, and as it were, felt the inspiration of the moment with him; he who does this, and not satisfied yet, but desirous to gain the most he possibly can from his study, — trying the particular work before him by the great laws which mark out and limit human faculty, and then comparing it with other works in the same style, — finally is able to weigh truly the value of it; to take the height, and measure the luminous power of the star upon which he is gazing; such a reader will have enjoyed and will continue to enjoy a depth and elevation and purity of pleasure which no one who has enjoyed it will accuse me of exaggerating. And this is the result to which I desire to lead you.

What, then, will be the series of laws, and of facts from which these laws have been deduced, which we require for the scientific study of poetry?

Beginning, as we did in our former examples, with the first or most formal elements, with those which are most closely connected with a poem as a piece of metrical composition, we shall have the general scheme, the general effect; how far the poet has impressed a tone of unity upon his work; how far, without becoming tame or monotonous, he has kept his details subordinate to the whole; how far he has left the impression of grandeur or of beauty predominant when we close the book, and the strain vibrates in our minds like the last chords of the symphony. You see the points which I insist on here, — unity, variety, grandeur, grace; they are those that are essential to a poem as a work of art, and as a work whose object is to give us pleasure. For though it has always been debated how far art is to imitate nature, and probably will be so debated to the end of time, yet there is no question but that it is to be in some way a representation of nature on a smaller scale; that it must show itself bounded by law, that it must satisfy the human sense of completeness — nay, that it must compensate by a greater completeness, a more perfect rounding-off and symmetry, for the limitations under which all human art works, when compared with nature; — in a word, that it must have unity. The charm of variety we all understand; it is, indeed, one of those charms to which, we might be inclined to say, the human mind has an almost undue leaning, were it not so closely connected with the existence of life itself. From unity and variety we pass to beauty, putting it last, and in a certain sense as the most important element in a poem, viewed, as we are now viewing it, as a work of art. For beauty, whether combined with humour or with sublimity, or displayed in its own simple form, is, truly, of the very essence of art. Unless beauty be our final impression, our 'last word', we cannot have that high, durable, and ethereal pleasure which it is the purpose of art to give. I know of no exception to this law; it seems to be one of those instincts or potentialities which are born in us. When we have read a poem, let us try to see whether it fulfills this law of beauty; if it does not, it will be no 'joy for ever' . . . Let me sum up in a few words the ground hitherto traversed. We have, first, examined why the love of poetry is popularly referrred to youth, and why it is, in fact, apt to fade away as men grow up. We tested the object of poetry, and of the other Fine Arts, and argued that it is pleasure; but pleasure of a lofty, lasting, and ethereal kind. Such pleasure, we next noticed, cannot be won easily; we found that, like taste in the true sense, it was really the product and reward of the natural instinct of the mind, when enlarged and enlightened by full know-ledge of the principles, antecedents and processes, under which the Fine Arts are carried on, and which they manifest in their results. This led us to see that poetry, in a word, could only be truly enjoyed, or truly accomplish its purpose, if studied on a method analogous to the sciences. As knowledge is their final cause, and the physical advantage of man their secondary result, so in the Fine Arts the final cause is pleasure, the accompanying result the elevation and purification of the soul. We briefly compared the different modes in which landscape or architecture affect the scien-tific or the non-scientific observer, as analogies to render more clear to the mind, by examples taken from visible and material objects, the similar conditions under which poetry may be regarded. Applying these considerations in detail, we saw that, in poetry, — granting a certain natural and happily common bias towards it, — the main lines of our scientific study would be, first, those more formal or technical laws which govern a poem or a work of art, its unity, its metrical structure, and the like. We then showed that knowledge of the field of poetry in general was needful, in order that we might judge what we read; noticing how those who read without judgment are led aside by false lights, are unbalanced and immod-erate in their pleasure, and finally blunt the mind's edge to the sense of it. We have, in conclusion, to point out those larger laws upon which the whole existence of poetry depends, and thus to bring it (as we did with architecture) into connection with the history and development of the human race . . .

It was as men willing to work that I have preferred to address you; — I should not indeed have cared to address you had you been otherwise. I have, therefore, chosen the more difficult task, endeavouring not to take for granted, or to lay down, by an appeal to sentiment, reasonings capable, as I hope, of more exact and serious proof: wishing, so far as I can, to ground you in the science of the thing; and trusting, perhaps, to the future, for some chance of drawing out in detail what I can now only barely indicate.

4.6   On physiognomy

From The Cornhill Magazine, *Vol. 4, October 1861. Physiognomy, the art of judging character from the face, was a popular amateur science. (Dickens and George Eliot, according to Dallas, both dabbled in it.) The writer, Eneas Sweetland Dallas (1828–79), journalist and author, was a man of wide interests, including science.*

The diversities of physiognomy are infinite. In the whole visible world there is no class of appearances so varied and in their significance so subtle as those of the human form. Fuseli[1] wrote on one occasion: 'Let the twelfth part of an inch be added to or taken from, the space between the nose and the upper lip of the Apollo, and the god is lost.' That is too strong a way of putting it. The god remains in the Greek marbles even when his nose is broken off. It is not in any one feature that he resides, but in all. Let the statement pass, however, as indicating in a rough way what a clever painter and man of genius thought as to the astounding differences of character expressed in evanescent differences of external form. Now, in order to be able to generalize with anything like success all these subtle shades and variations of contour, we require an immense number of accurate observations, and to have them side by side before us, so as to be able to form a comparison. This we have never yet had. Lavater[2] gives a great number of portraits, and he had many more in his collection, but he was always complaining that they were unreliable. In this one the nostril was out of drawing; in that the chin was a falsehood; here the eye was uncertain; there the hand was nothing at all. Especially in the hand have the portrait painters failed, and there is nothing that the physiognomist is so much in want of as a good collection of hands. It is to be hoped that the discovery of the photograph will prove to be the dawn of a new day for him. As the science of chemistry was nothing until a perfect balance was invented, and as the science of physiology was really unknown until the microscope was improved, so it may be that the faithful register of the camera, supplying us with countless numbers of accurate observations, will now render that an actual science which has hitherto been only a possible one. We shall get a great variety of heads, and be able to classify them according to each separate feature, and according to each leading trait of character. Above all, when once the attention of the photographers is called to the want, we shall begin to get hands — hands by themselves, and hands in connection with faces. These are facts which we have only now for the first time the means of getting in sufficient number. The portraits we have had have, for accuracy, not less than for number, been very insufficient. It is not so much portraits that we have had, as engravings of portraits, and engravings after engravings, the representation being thus at third and fourth hand.

Quite as much, however, as the want of adequate collections, and perhaps even more, the false start made by phrenology[3] has retarded the progress of physiognomy. The part usurped the place of the whole, and gave its own bad name to it. Physiognomy we are to understand as embracing the entire form. Every part of the body that has free play indicates more or less clearly the character of the in-dwelling mind, and according to the nature of that character we shall find its most eloquent expression now on the hand, now on the face, and now on the skull. The phrenologists started the theory that the physiognomy of the skull is the most important of all, and that nothing is more easy than to decipher it. They mapped out the head. They assigned a passion to every bump. Every faculty of the mind had its little principality on the brow. The thing was done with incomparable ease. Here was Wit castled high on the head; Music was huddled into a little corner above the eye; Murder lurked behind the ear; Love sought the shady retreat of the back hair; Vanity perched itself on the crown of the head; Lies found places above each ear, where they stood sentry to guard the pass; Poetry, as in duty bound, had its seat not far from Lies; Religion was inclined to both, and overrode Philosophy. It was a strange topography: it was a still stranger psychology. In the most arbitrary manner the human mind was divided into — let us say — thirty different parts; and in the most arbitrary manner the thirty different domiciles. There was no doubt or ambiguity about the system. It was impossible that there could be any mistake; everything was clear, sharp, and defined. The key to all knowledge of the human race had been discovered. Here was the whole mind laid bare to Gall, Spurzheim, and Combe;[4] here is its encampment on our scalps, which it turns into a sort of tented field. The spirit of phrenology is the very opposite of Lavater's. Phrenology makes a pretence of science where there is none at all, affects precision, and leaps to conclusions. The physiognomy of Lavater is modest, expects great things in the future, but abrogates nothing for the present; emphatically disclaims the name of science, and pretends only to collect the bricks from which the house is to be built. Now phrenology, with its precise formulas, and trumpeting of actual, not prospective discoveries, satisfied for many years the public mind. It was a bird in the hand, and worth fifty in the bush. It professed to accomplish nearly all that was possible to physiognomy. Whatever else physiognomy could achieve might be agreeable, but only as a superfluous and ridiculous excess. Two witnesses are supposed to be better than one; but, if one be reliable, what is the use of two? So this narrow, shallow system of phrenology was supposed to be enough, and physiognomy was a useless surplusage. At last phrenology is confessed to be a failure and a mock science. Based on good intentions, these admirable paving-stones have not proved to be of much use for purposes of building. They have only delayed for a little the building of the true temple. The phrenological structure has fallen into ruin, and we now ask ourselves whether it be not possible to rear a more stable fabric on a broader foundation.

Notes

1. *Fuseli*: Henry Fuseli (1741–1825), Swiss artist and art critic.

2. *Lavater*: Joahann Kaspar Lavater (1741–1801), friend of Fuseli, German poet, physiognomist and mystic.

3. *Phrenology*: The study of the shape of the skull, supposed to show a person's mental powers.

4. *Gall, Spurzheim and Combe*: F. J. Gall (1758–1828) a Viennese anatomist, was the founder of phrenology and J. K. Spurzheim (1776–1832) and George Combe (1788–1858) his most influential followers.

5

The 'Woman Question'

Were women Angels in the House, or were they to be classed with criminals, idiots and minors? The question was asked more and more pressingly throughout the period as the 'Woman Question' was debated in law and at home. At the beginning she had little status at all in law, even less if she married than if she remained single, for everything she possessed as a married woman (including her children) became her husband's. She had, of course, no vote in either national or local government, she was debarred from the universities, and the professions were closed to her. Her education, if she were from the middle or upper class, had probably been at the hands of her parents or a governess, for there were very few schools for girls, and almost none of any repute. (See 'An Inquiry into Girls' Fashionable Schools', in *Education*.) If she were from the working class, her education was almost certainly nil.

Stirrings of reform had begun by 1848, with the foundation of Queen's College, Harley Street, devoted primarily, though not exclusively at all, to the training of governesses. (See 'Queen's College, London', in *Education*.) Two of its first students were Dorothea Beale and Frances Mary Buss, the earliest pioneers of girls' education: North London Collegiate School (1850) and Cheltenham Ladies' College (1853) quickly became the models for the wave of girls' schools which followed them. Successive Royal Commissions investigated, and deplored, the state of female education, and as a result the educational endowments of established boys' schools were overhauled and their funds made available to girls as well as boys. Nearly a half, in fact, of the principal girls' schools in England and Wales were founded between 1850 and the end of the 1880s.

International events had their own effect on the 'Woman Question', notably the Crimean War in 1854. Florence Nightingale was at the centre of that stage, and her organisation of nurses in the east was very influential in changing attitudes towards women at work. A grateful nation raised £44,000, which Florence Nightingale used to open the first training school for nurses at St Thomas's Hospital. Led by the forceful Priscilla Sellon, the religious life for women had been tentatively re-established in the Church of England in the 1840s and 1850s, and the sisters, Roman and Anglican, played their part at Scutari. Women doctors, too, were pressing for recognition: the first woman doctor in the world had qualified in the United States in 1849, and had registered in her native England ten years later, to the dismay of the medical profession, which resolutely barred its doors until the late 1870s when it finally yielded to pressure.

Meanwhile Cambridge had admitted women to lectures for the first time in 1869, and Oxford followed in 1878. Women graduates, of course, were unthought of (only the University of London admitted women to degrees on the same terms as men at this time), but shortly there was a body of trained women to staff the new ventures in women's education or take their places in the professions now beginning to open their doors.

Professionally, women advanced much faster towards equality with men than either politically or socially, and by the end of the 1860s women were more and more aware of, and articulate about, the anomaly of their position. One of the great defenders of the rights of women was J. S. Mill, who had been elected to Parliament in 1865 and in 1866 introduced the first Bill for the enfranchisement of women. His plea for female suffrage went unheard by the Commons for more than fifty years; but agitation for social justice for women grew louder. A succession of Matrimonial Causes Acts, beginning in 1857, went some way towards that reform; the Contagious Diseases Acts, which subjected women prostitutes to police and medical registration, were repealed during the 1870s; and the Married Women's Property Acts, which gave women the right to their own earnings, were passed in 1870 and 1882.

Meanwhile the Discussion went on (the term 'feminism' was coined in 1895) as the voices of tradition and the voices of reform were raised in the debate — which is with us still.

5.1   The position of women

From E. P. Hood, The Age and Its Architects, *1850. The writer, a Congregational clergyman, expresses an early, and therefore unexpectedly forceful, view of the deplorable position of women.*

Woman needs the reformer in her social position, as well as her social condition. A great deal of nonsense has been uttered about the rights of woman; but it is yet true that her wrongs are very heavy. The legal position of woman is a most anomalous one, a position altogether at variance with her individuality, with justice, common sense, and Christianity. The law of England does make marriage a legal slavery to the woman. By the law of England, the wife surrenders herself entirely to the will and pleasure of her husband; however sentiment and affection may regard the bond of marriage, evidently, in the eye of the law, it is rather a feudal than a spiritual relationship. The husband may imprison his wife in his house, may strike her so long as he inflicts no severe bodily injury, leave her, and live in adultery with another; yet return, seize on her inheritance, and use it for himself and paramour. We are accustomed to speak of all our courtesy to woman as coming to us from the woods of Germany, with our Saxon fathers; yet from those woods came these ridiculously wicked enactments, which are as much an insult to our nationality as to woman, while they continue in force. There is an unjust inequality in our treatment of woman, unworthy of a free, generous and refined people. Political existence she has none, although she may have property from her father, and live in independence and importance. Widow or spinster, she is no citizen, and as a wife her whole being is merged in the being and existence of her husband. In another aspect the position of woman in society is a false one — an arbitrary conventionalism has contrived to throw round *some* employments the air of feminine propriety. Let woman herself reform it altogether; let mothers and fathers forbear to train their children to the overcrowded and unnatural pursuits of the majority of the daughters of our people, the professions of the engraver, the watchmaker, the artist, are open to them; let the more muscular body, in the name of all honour, betake itself to the more arduous work. Why should not woman be a printer? Why not leave to her more graceful, courteous nature the greater number of our shops and counters?

Give to woman the same chance as man. At present, her lot is indeed a very hard one — the curse is upon her — we have shown our gallantry to her only in words, a few deeds will be acceptable. Scout and scorn the idea that woman should receive an inferior education to man; that her position should be inferior to his; that her individuality should not be so clearly acknowledged, and her opinions held in equal estimation. For it is a word of truth that all depends, or mainly depends, on her; the hope of our land is in the elevation and ennobling of the home affections. And who shall do that work for us? Woman alone can change home, and in doing so, change the man, her husband, who lives there. Whether the girl shall be the wife or not, all the better will it be for her if she receive such an education as shall fit her to be a worthy one; the humblest girl may be educated to become an intelligent companion. Such an education, moral, economical, and prudential, will best shield her from the seducer's arts, will give to her an ideal of excellence fitted to bear her company through life, and enable her, however humble, to meet the toils and trials of life with becoming resolution and virtue.

Reformed, woman will prove the most efficient reformer; when her amazing influence is brought to bear on the side of virtue, and not merely that negative virtue, which scarcely deserves the name, but positive virtue, how rapidly the streams will turn. She may be said almost to hold the manumission of slave and drunkard equally in her power; if she would determine not to wear or use any cotton, purchased by the sweat, and blood, and degradation and slavery of her sisters in America, and as far as possible prevent its entrance to her home, American slavery would be doomed; and if she invariably pushed aside the glass in the parlour and the dining-room, intemperance in England would lose its chief buttress and stronghold. Yes, and she possesses the power of breathing a purity over the whole concerns of life, that may save from desolation many hearts. The world does not need the purity of prudery and cant, but it does need that woman should vindicate purity by shrinking from those stained popinjays, the drunkard and the debauchee. She would rise in her own estimation by refusing the arm, the courtesy, of those men who in the degradation of her sex have insulted her. Her virtue need be neither a boasting, ostentatious exhibition, as little need it be an unfelt, unknown, unobserved thing; she may wear it as good beings wear their smiles, a light so constantly upon the face, as to be rather identified with it than apart from it . . .

This chapter on women was intended to have gone far beyond its present length, and the remarks were prepared upon the psychological character of woman as opposed to man, and on some of the distinguishing characteristics of the education she would confer, especially her power to educate the sense of the infinite, and the moral sense of conscience. But returning to the point from whence we started, what is needed in all works of life is, practical women. There is much said about woman in her sphere and woman out of it. A lady occasionally delivers a lecture, and some good folks are frightened — she is out of her sphere. But few women are really educated for their sphere, in spite of all this fastidiousness. The accomplishments of the boarding-school have little to do with the future of life.

Mothers must reform the education of their daughters, and fit them for happiness. Music is a delightful accomplishment, nay, it is almost necessary as any indispensable of life, and it is a famous tie to keep husbands at home. This is what education indeed should do; for woman should give attractions rather than accomplishments. The last is a heavy material, seldom in request; the former is the secret and source of much sympathy; and, as a loving woman is ever better than a learned one, so must an attractive nature be more useful than one crowded, like a bazaar, with showy accomplishments.

5.2   The rights and wrongs of women

From a paper read before the Social Science Congress, Newcastle, 1870, by F. O. Morris. The piece is typical of much popular response to the 'Woman Question'.

In offering a few remarks on the subject of the rights and wrongs of women, I will first state the reasons put forward by their own chosen champions for thinking it one of their wrongs. I believe their chief wrong, they think — [is], that at present they are debarred from the suffrage, from voting at elections for Members of Parliament . . .

In one . . . pamphlet, . . . the lecture of Professor Newman,[1] at Bristol, . . . the greater part . . . is filled with remarks on the injustice of some of the laws which affect married women and their property. He seems to ask for the franchise that those laws may be altered, and made fair and equitable for both men and women alike. . . . Women should mingle in the crowd at the hustings, to soften the manners of the blue and orange factions.[2]

I heartily agree with any one who contends that any such unjust laws should be altered. They ought to be by men alone, without the votes of women to turn the scale on a division of the House.

It seems to me that those who look — or why do they move in the matter — for the franchise being obtained by women (a much more difficult result to be obtained, and which could only be granted by the House of Commons) would do well rather to move the same House to alter any laws they show to be unjust, the alteration of which they allege to be their object, or at least one of their main objects, in asking for the franchise. It is only asking a less favour or right, rather than a greater, and that of the same parties in both cases, and for the end rather than for the means . . .

Woman is superior and influential only on condition that she is a true woman. Take from her neither her silent action nor her double domestic empire, which includes her household, her children, and in addition to these, the sick and the indigent. Deprive her not of her exquisite sensibility nor her ermine-like delicacy; do not plunge her into the male whirl of outside affairs. She will lose all, even to her grace, even to her beauty! The political woman, the blue-stocking, the woman who has exchanged the family for the public, stands already before us in the road on which we are urged, as a warning and a scarecrow. . . . If woman ought to have the franchise, it seems clear that they ought also to have the right of being elected Members of Parliament. And here innumerable difficulties immediately meet us. Once in Parliament, and the same arguments that brought them there will conduct them to every seat upon the Ministerial Bench, and then to the chair of the Speaker, and the woolsack of the Lord Chancellor himself, the Lady Chancellor, that is to say, herself. There can be no possible denial of this by any one, in fairness. It must thus come in the end to Petticoat Government.

Or even if their ambition were to be satisfied by a mere seat in Parliament, how will the arrangements of the House suit them? How will crowding and crinoline do together in the lobby? How are they to divide when the bell rings for a division? Are they to run helter-skelter to this or that side with the gentleman members?

A wife or a daughter, perhaps, too, going into a different lobby to vote against the wishes of her father, husband, or brother; and if so, causing interminable disputes, and heartburnings at home; or if voting with them, doubling the votes to no purpose.

Then, are they to mingle pell-mell with those of all ranks and all ages, of all character, and of no character, bachelors, and single, old and young, intoxicated and sober? Will they take their cigarettes into the smoking room? How, also, will they make their voices to be heard in a room whose acoustic properties do not suit even those of men? — Nothing, either, I may here say, is more attractive, all the world over, in a woman, than what Shakespeare calls a 'small voice', and nothing more unnatural and unpleasing than a masculine tone . . .

What I say . . . is — that if men have . . . risen, unaided, and in the face of the greatest difficulties, to eminence in various branches of art and science, there is nothing to prevent women doing the same. Not only so, but they have 'appliances and means to boot' to aid them in their studies, if such be their desire. They have opportunities of the highest literary training, the most thorough teaching and intellectual discipline, at St. Mary's College, Brighton; and at Cheltenham, Liverpool, and Manchester etc., there are regular courses of scientific lectures given by persons of eminence for any ladies who may desire to avail themselves of such advantages. I believe, however, that the demand for them is not greater than the supply. If it were otherwise, there is nothing to hinder the like being done in every town in the kingdom for itself and its neighbourhood. Dressing and dancing present much greater attractions to most than Greek or Mathematics: and the Opera-house will be better attended than the Academy.

I fancy most admirers of the young ladies will still prefer hearing them sing some of our touching old English songs and ballads, or perhaps some of Handel's or Mendelssohn's or Beethoven's compositions to hearing their opinion on Newton's Principia, or the undulatory theory of light. 'Home, Sweet Home' will please more than a dissertation on the structure of the heavenly bodies, or the doctrine of gravitation. I repeat, there already have been, and are now, means of educational advancement which women may avail themselves of if they have a real desire for knowledge for its own sake — or for any other sufficient reason — if they would. Libraries are open to them, but I fear more novels are sent for them by fifty to one than books of a severer kind. Booksellers will take a woman's money for any books on his shelf as well as that of a man; and I maintain that there are in the main no teachers like books, which you can take up or lay down, as best suits the power of your mind and your body at the time. What is there to stop the way of a woman to attain the highest excellence that any woman can persuade herself she is capable of attaining to in any one department of art or science or knowledge, whether it be living or dead languages, music, sculpture, drawing, or general literature? . . .

But, as a rule — a general and all but universal rule — women have no taste or turn for pursuits of the kind I have alluded to. Their bias is in another direction, namely, for needlework; and, I think, most happily so. They would rather work their hands than their heads; and sewing will always be more in their way, and to their taste and turn, than science. Walk in front of a row of houses at a watering place on a rainy day, and you may take my word for it that for one lady you will see with a book in her hand, you will see twenty with work of some kind or other. Thus, true to nature, Shakespeare tells us that when Hamlet went to see Ophelia he found her 'sewing in her closet'. To ply the needle is their great delight — it seems an instinct of their nature; and a wise and beneficient one it is, for it is a constant and unfailing source of amusement to them, and its usefulness every one will readily and at once own. Do I impute any blame to them for it? The utter reverse. It is their highest praise! . . .

But further. On every side we hear remarks about the mere physical labour required of Members of Parliament, and statements from themselves to their Constituents of the real actual toil they have to undergo, both by day and night:— Long hours in Committee-rooms, late hours till the morning, speaking, or listening to, or answering speeches, the brain worked and overworked. Women have not the *'robur et aes triplex'*[3] for all this. . . .

But here I wish to remark that I am altogether in favour of every facility being given to women for obtaining employment in any work for which they are fitted by nature, or for which they may be educated; and for the exclusion and extradition by them of men from such accordingly. I think female doctors may most properly attend upon females, especially if females prefer employing them, as I do think they most properly may and should. So, also, in all business and trades in which they can perform the work to be done as well as men; such as watchmaking, chinamaking, painting, and many other departments of art. I rejoiced to hear of the Victoria Printing Office, worked, I believe, entirely by females. If I had my own way I would not allow a single man servant to be employed in a house. They are worse than unnecessary. Men must be had for grooms, gardeners, and other sort of out-door occupation, but I would have none but women within doors.

Whether the minds of women are different from those of men is a question which it is not for me to presume to answer. . . . I may, however, remark that in some respects they do seem to me to be most differently constituted. I have often and often been struck with the incapacity of women to find their way if lost in a strange part of the country; they are utterly at sea, have no conception of the points of the compass, and if they choose a road by the best guess they can make, it is almost certain to be the wrong one. They are utterly without any geographical acumen.

So again, what female writers have there been who have shown any capacity for wit or satire at all to compare with that of men? . . .

If it has been the tyranny of men that has all along kept women in an inferior position, does not that very fact prove that his mental nature is the stronger of the two? At the first they were either equal or unequal — if equal, how came the men to usurp authority over the women? and why did women submit to the consequences of the supposed inequality? If unequal, that is just Q.E.D. . . .

I will not enter into the political part of the question further than to say that I do not think that the advocates of the so-called rights of women will find any ladies at election time who will think the orange colour so becoming to their complexion as the true blue, either the dark blue of Oxford or the light blue of Cambridge.

Notes

1. *Professor Newman:* Francis William Newman (1805–97), brother of John Henry, Professor of Latin at University College, London, and writer (from a sceptical position) on religious matters (e.g. the autobiographical *Phases of Faith*). He was keenly interested in political questions bearing on social problems.

2. *Blue and orange factions:* Blue was the Conservative colour, orange the Liberal.

3. *Robur et aes triplex:* Oak and triple brass. Horace, *Odes*, iii. 9.

5.3 'The Angel in the House'

From Macmillan's Magazine, *Vol. 8, September 1863. A review of Coventry Patmore's famous poem. The writer is the poet Caroline Norton (1808 – 77).*

The'Skeleton in the Cupboard', is a theme heavily dwelt upon. That there is a skeleton in every cupboard — no family without such an appendage, no destiny without such a flaw — is the argument of one of the wittiest and most worldly-wise of our popular prose-writers.[1] But it was reserved for a poet, with a true poet's heart, to oppose to the 'Skeleton in the Cupboard', 'The Angel in the House' — to show that no home, be it ever so humble or ever so lowly, need be without that peaceful presence, and to sing this true and tender 'Psalm of Life' to all who choose to listen — to all who do not wilfully shut their ears to the voice of the charmer, 'charm he never so wisely'.

This task has been accomplished by Mr. Coventry Patmore. The echo of a hundred thousand 'welcomes' to the Princess Alexandra[2] are still vibrating in the hearts of Englishmen. The interest — brother-like, father-like, lover-like — taken by them in the fulfilment of life's best hope, heightened by all the adventitious circumstances that can increase sympathy and surround the picture of happiness with a dazzling halo, is still fresh among us. Crowds run hither and thither on the chance of seeing the Bride of England pass by; groups stand waiting in her path. Her happiness and the happiness of her youthful husband are somehow made part of ours. We triumph in their vision of wedded love. We rejoice that 'the Angel in the House' has come to dwell in the Royal Palace. Yet that part of a royal destiny, which seems to us so superlatively bright, is within the reach of any man who chooses so to school his passions and affections as to make a sane choice in life.

Those who would study the lesson that reads so like a romance, those who would profit by the gentle philosophy of theories which the most simple may put in practice for their own temporal and eternal welfare, cannot do better than make Mr. Coventry Patmore's book the companion of hours spent in the hush of the library, the tedium of the railroad, or the sequestered calm of summer rambles. The stamp of earnest truth is on every page; and the wisdom that permeates through the argument of the story, without one dogmatic sentence to startle or offend, would win the most careless and convert the most scoffing to the true faith of virtuous love. Peace, self-conquest, and the serene joy of religious trust hang like a blessed atmosphere around this poem. It is a book to guide and comfort those who are still midway in the rocking storm of life's uncertain passage, and to lull with the best of harmonies those whose hopes are ended either by fulfilment or disappointment.

In style Mr. Patmore may claim the merit of originality. Undazzled by the Tennysonian radiance, he has pursued a path of his own to the inner recesses of the human heart. In the occasional homely diction, and in the choice of familiar themes, he resembles Crabbe: but he has more skill in rhythmical compassion and a loftier tone of thought.

The framework of his poem, 'The Angel in the House', is simple enough. It is the wooing and winning of a life-companion in the shape of a virtuous wife — such a one as he himself describes in one of his minor poems, in a stanza of perfect beauty:—

'And in the maiden path she trod
　　Fair was the wife foreshown,
A Mary in the House of God,
　　A Martha in her own.'

That such wooing may have, and must have, in the youthful heart, its share of passionate earthliness, is shown in the beautiful lines:—

' "Your name pronounced brings to my heart
　　A feeling like the violet's hearth,
Which it does so much of heaven impart
　　It makes me yearn with tears for death.
The winds that in the garden toss
　　The Guelder-roses give me pain,
Alarm me with the dread of loss,
　　Exhaust me with the dream of gain.
I'm troubled by the clouds that move;
　　Thrill'd by the breath which I respire;
And ever, like a torch, my love,
　　Thus agitated, flames the higher.
All's hard that has not you for goal;
　　I scarce can move my hand to write,

141

For love engages all my soul,
    And leaves the body void of night.
The wings of will spread idly as do
    The bird's that in a vacuum flies;
My breast, asleep with dreams of you,
    Forgets to breathe, and bursts in sighs.
I see no rest this side the grave,
    No rest or hope from you apart;
Your life is in the rose you gave,
    Its perfume suffocates my heart.
There's no refreshment in the breeze;
    The heaven o'erwhelms me with its blue;
I faint beside the dancing seas;
    Winds, skies, and waves are only you.'' '

A fit following to the tender passion of these verses is found in
the proposal:—

'Twice rose, twice died my rambling word;
    The faint and frail Cathedral chimes
Spoke time in music, and we heard
    The chafers rustling in the lines.
Her dress, that touch'd me where I stood,
    The warmth of her confided arm,
Her bosom's gentle neighbourhood,
    Her pleasure in her power to charm;
Her look, her love, her form, her touch,
    The least seem'd most by blissful turn,
Blissful but that it pleased too much,
    And taught the wayward souls to yearn.
It was as if a harp with wires
    Was traversed by the breath I drew;
And, oh, sweet meeting of desires,
    She, answering, own'd that she loved too.'

The familiar sweetness of companionship echoes the foregoing
description:—

'I praised her, but no praise could fill
    The depths of her desire to please,
Though dull to others as a Will
    To them that have no legacies.

The more I praised the more she shone,
 Her eyes incredulously bright,
And all her happy beauty blown
 Beneath the beams of my delight.
Sweet rivalry was thus begot;
 By turns, my speech, in passion's style,
With flatteries the truth o'ershot,
 And she surpass's them with her smile.'

It winds up pleasantly with this compliment to matron charms:—

'For as became the festal time,
 He cheer'd her heart with tender praise,
And speeches wanting only rhyme
 To make them like his gallant lays.
He discommended girlhood, "What
 For sweetness like the ten-years' wife,
Whose customary love is not
 Her passion, or her play, but life!
With beauties so maturely fair,
 Affecting, mild and manifold,
May girlish charms no more compare
 Than apples green with apples gold." '

The disappointment of a rejected suitor was, perhaps, never more simply or touchingly rendered than in the few lines that close Frederick Graham's letter to his mother:—

'My Mother, now my only friend,
Farewell. The school-books which you send
I shall not want, and so return.
Give them away, or sell, or burn.
I'll write from Malta. Would I might
But be your little Child to-night,
And feel your arms about me fold,
Against this loneliness and cold!'

And the vain corroding jealousy in the same heart was never better confessed than later in the volume:—

'And o'er this dream I brood and doat,
And I learn its agonies by rote.

I think, she's near him now, alone,
With wardship and protection none;
Alone, perhaps, in the hindering stress
Of airs that clasp him with her dress,
They wander whispering by the wave;
And haply now, in some sea-cave,
Where the ribb'd sand is rarely trod,
They laugh, they kiss. Oh, God! oh, God!'

A fine warning succeeds against the commonest of all temptations — a marriage from pique:—

'Wed not one woman, oh, my Son,
Because you love another one!
Oft, with a disappointed man,
The first who cares to win him can;
For, after love's heroic strain
Which tired the heart and brought no gain,
He feels consoled, relieved, and eased
To meet with her who can be pleased
To proffer kindness, and compute
His acquiescence for pursuit;
Who troubles not his lonely mood;
Asks naught for love but gratitude;
And, as it were, will let him weep
Himself within her arms to sleep.'

And again at page 65:—

'Many men cannot love; more yet
Cannot love such as they can get.
To wed with one less loved may be
Part of divine expediency.'

The young man marries, however, in spite of these maternal warnings; and the wavering of a mind, which afterwards settles to steadier attachment, is finely given:—

'But sometimes, (how shall I deny!)
There falls, with her thus sitting by,
Dejection, and a chilling shade.
Remember'd pleasure, as they fade,

Salute me, and, in fading, grow,
Like foot-prints in the thawing snow.
I feel oppress'd beyond my force
With foolish envy and remorse.
I love this woman, but I might
Have loved some else with more delight;
And strange it seems of God that he
Should make a vain capacity.'

The yearning of the heart to old days is perfectly described in
another letter to his mother:—

'And then, as if I sweetly dream'd,
I half remember'd how it seem'd
When I, too, was a little child
About the wild wood roving wild.
Pure breezes from the far-off height
Melted the blindness from my sight,
Until, with rapture, grief, and awe,
I saw again as then I saw.
As then I saw, I saw again
The harvest waggon in the lane,
With high-hung tokens of its pride
Left in the elms on either side;
The daisies coming out at dawn
In constellations on the lawn;
The glory of the daffodil;
The three black windmills on the hill,
Whose magic arms, flung willdly by,
Sent magic shadows past the rye.
Within the leafy coppice, lo,
More wealth than miser's dreams could show,
The blackbird's warm and woolly brood,
Five golden beaks agape for food;
The Gipsies, all the summer seen
Native as poppies to the Green;
The winter, with its frosts and thaws
And opulence of hips and haws;
The lovely marvel of the snow;
The Tamar, with its altering show
Of gay ships sailing up and down,
Among the fields and by the Town.

And, dearer far than anything,
Came back the songs you used to sing.'

The gaiety and sprightliness of Lady Clitheroe's letters aptly break the somewhat dreary impression made on the reader by the young sailor's grief and disappointment, and by the death of his simple, loving helpmate, whose dying words may be laid to heart by many who wring impossible promises of faith from those who survive to lament their loss:—

'Oh, should the mournful honeymoon
Of death be over strangely soon.
And life-long resolutions, made
In grievous haste, as quickly fade,
Seeming the truth of grief to mock,
Think, Dearest, 'tis not by the clock
That sorrow goes! A month of tears
Is more than many, many years
Of common time. Shun, if you can
However, any passionate plan.
Grieve with the heart; let not the head
Grieve on, when grief of heart is dead;
For all the powers of life defy
A superstitious constancy.'

And these results of linked companionship, whether for joy or sorrow, are finely contrasted with the fair but barren picture of the resolute maidenhood of Mary Churchill:—

'The world's delight my soul dejects,
Revenging all my disrespects,
Of old, with incapacity
To chime with even its harmless glee,
Which sounds, from fields beyond my range,
Like fairies' music, thin and strange.'

Very fine is the burst against the Pharisaical tutoring (common in these days).

'And if, my Children, you, for hours
Daily, untortur'd in the heart,
Can worship, and time's other part

Give, without rough recoils of sense,
To the claims ingrate of indigence,
Happy are you, and fit to be
Wrought to rare heights of sanctity,
For the humble to grow humbler at.
But if the flying spirit falls flat,
After the modest spell of prayer
That saves the day from sin and care,
And the upward eye a void desires,
And praises are hypocrisies,
And, in the soul, o'erstrain'd for grace,
A godless anguish grows apace;
Do not infer you cannot please
God, or that He his promises
Postpones, but be content to love
No more than He accounts enough.
    At least, leave distant words alone,
Till you are native to your own;
Account them poor enough who want
Any good thing which you can grant;
And fathom well the depths of life
In loves of Husband and of Wife,
Child, Mother, Father; simple keys
To all the Christian mysteries.'

The same just train of thought is continued at page 202, where
the permitted joys of earth are pleaded for:—

    'Be ye not mocked;
Right life is glad as well as just,
And, rooted strong in "This I must,"
It bears aloft the blossom gay
And zephyr-toss'd, of "This I may." '

Till, finally, this sweet picture of tranquil home concludes the
theme:—

    'Here, in this early autumn dawn,
By windows opening on the lawn,
Where sunshine seems asleep, though bright,
And shadows yet are sharp with night;
And, further on, the wealthy wheat

Bends in a golden drowse, how sweet
To sit and cast my careless looks
Around my walls of well-read books,
Wherein is all that stands redeem'd
From time's huge wreck, all men have dream'd
Of truth, and all by poets known
Of feeling, and in weak sort shown,
And, turning to my heart again,
To find I have what makes them vain,
The thanksgiving mind, which wisdom sums
And you—'

It is a sorrowful reflection, at the close of this fine poem, to know that she who inspired it is gone to that world where there is neither marrying nor giving in marriage; but where the hope of future meeting still shines mysterious and starlike from the distance.

Notes

1. *Popular prose writers*: D. W. Jerrold (1803–57)?; R. S. Surtees (1805–64)?
2. *Princess Alexandra*: The Prince of Wales had married the Danish princess, Alexandra, in 1863.

5.4 Criminals, idiots, women, and minors: is the classification sound?

From Fraser's Magazine, *Vol. 78, December 1868. Frances Power Cobbe, (1822– 1904) a philanthropist and reformer in many fields (see* The Religious Debate*), here promotes legislation that led to the Married Women's Property Act of 1872.*

At the end of this paper I have placed the four categories under which persons are now excluded from many civil, and all political rights in England. . . . To a woman herself who is aware that she has never committed a crime; who fondly believes that she is not an idiot; and who is alas! only too sure she is no longer a minor, — there naturally appears some incongruity in placing her, for such important purposes, in an association wherein otherwise she would scarcely be likely to find herself. But the question for men to answer is: Ought Englishwomen of full age, in the present state of affairs, to be considered as having legally attained majority? or ought they permanently to be dealt with, for all civil and political purposes, as minors? . . .

We shall attempt to consider the most striking instance wherein the existing principle presses upon women, and where its injustice appears most distinctly, — namely, in the regulation of the Property of Married Women under the Common Law. We shall endeavour to do this with all possible fairness and equanimity. The acrimony which too often creeps into arguments on this subject is every way needless and mischievous. Of course it is not pleasant to women to be told they are 'physically, morally, and intellectually inferior' to their companions. Nevertheless, they are foolish to be angry with the man who in plain words says straightforwardly that, in his opinion, such is the case. After all, he pays them a better compliment than the fop who professes to adore them as so many wingless angels, and privately values them as so many dolls. . . .

By the Common Law of England a married woman has no legal existence, so far as property is concerned, independently of her husband. The husband and wife are assumed to be one person, and that person is the husband. The wife can make no contract, and can neither sue nor be sued. Whatever she possess of personal property at the time of her marriage, or whatever she may afterwards earn or inherit, belongs to her husband, without control on her part. If she possess real estate, so long as her husband lives he receives and spends the income derived from it; being only forbidden to sell it without her consent. From none of her property is he bound to reserve anything, or make any provision for her maintenance or that of her children . . .

What, in the first place, of the Justice of giving all a woman's property to her husband? The argument is, that the wife gets an ample *quid pro quo*. *Does* she get it under the existing law? That is the simple question . . .

The following story was published many years ago in the *Westminster Review*, as having then recently occurred. . . . A gentleman, of landed estate, in the north of England, became involved in debt, and finally ruined, and reduced to actual want. His wife, a lady of ability and spirit, finding him incapable of any effort for their joint support, opened a little shop for millinery in the country town. Her old friends gave her their custom, and her taste and industry made it a thriving business. For many years she maintained her husband and herself, till at last having realised a small competency, and grown old and feeble, she sold her shop, and retired to spend, as she hoped, in peace with her husband, the remaining years of her life. After a short time, however, the husband died, duly nursed and tended to the last by his wife. When he was dead he was found to have left a will, by which he bequeathed every shilling of his wife's earnings to a mistress he had secretly maintained. Either the wife had originally married without a settlement, or her settlements had not contemplated so singular a fact as her earning a fortune. The husband's will, therefore, was perfectly valid, *and was executed*.

So much for the Justice of the Common Law. What now shall we say to its Expediency? . . .

The great and overwhelming argument against the Expediency of the common law in this matter, is the simple fact that no parent or guardian possessed of means sufficient to evade it by a marriage settlement, ever dreams of permitting his daughter or ward to undergo its (alleged) beneficial action. The parent who neglected to demand such a settlement from a man before he gave him his daughter, would be thought to have failed in the performance of one of his most obvious and imperative duties. Even the law itself in its highest form in the realm (that of the Court of Chancery) always requires settlements for its wards. How then can it be argued that the same rule is generally considered Expedient, yet invariably evaded by all who are able to evade it? . . .

But, as we have said already, there is an argument which has more force in determining legislation about marriage than either considerations of Justice or of Expediency. It is the Sentiment entertained by the majority of men on the subject; the ideal they have formed of wedlock, the poetical vision in their minds of a wife's true relation to her husband. Legislators talk in parliament with a certain conviction that the principles of fairness and policy are the only ones to be referred to *there*. But whenever the subject is freely discussed in private or in a newspaper, there is sure to burst out sooner or later the real feeling. . . . Let us try to fathom this sentiment, for till we understand it we are but fighting our battles in the dark. Is it not this: that a woman's whole life and being, her soul, body, time, property, thought, and care, ought to be given to her husband; that nothing short of such absorption in him and his interests makes her a true wife; . . . Truly I believe this is the feeling at the bottom of nearly all men's hearts, and of the hearts of thousands of women also. There is no use urging that it is a gigantic piece of egotism in a man to desire such a marriage. Perhaps it is natural for him to do so, and perhaps it is natural for a great number of women to give just such absorbed adoring affection. Perhaps it is a tribute to the infinite nature of all love, that for those who know each other best, as a wife knows her husband, there is no limit to human affection. At all events it seems a fact that the typical man (if we may call him so) desires such love, and the typical woman is ready to give it to him. He is impatient at the notion of a marriage in which this conception of absolute absorption of his wife's interests in his own shall not be fulfilled; and, so far as legislation can create such an ideal, he is resolved that it shall do so.

So far all is plain, but the question is this: Supposing such marriages to be the most desirable, do men set the right way about securing them, by making such laws as the Common Law of England? . . .

Truly I am persuaded it is not *thanks* to the Common Law, but in *spite* thereof, that there are so many united and happy homes in England. . . . The existing Common Law is not *just*, because it neither can secure nor actually even attempts to secure for the woman, the equivalent support for whose sake she is forced to relinquish her property.

It is not *expedient*, because while in happy marriages it is superfluous and useless, in unhappy ones it becomes highly injurious . . .

Lastly, it does not tend to fulfil, but to counteract, the *sentiment* regarding the marriage union, to which it aims to add the pressure of force. Real unanimity is not produced between two parties by forbidding one of them to have any voice at all. The hard mechanical contrivance of the law for making husband and wife of one heart and mind is calculated to produce a precisely opposite result. . . .

Justice, Expediency, a truly guided Sentiment, and such experience as is yet unattainable — all these, then, point unanimously to the repeal of the existing Common Law, as it touches the property of married women.

5.5   Female suffrage and married life

From The Contemporary Review, *Vol. 20, 1872. The writer, Julia Wedgwood, a campaigner for justice to women, takes up a topical issue, and challenges some popular misconceptions.*

All large proposals need contemplation from more than one point of view, and many of the strongest arguments for and against such a one as the Enfranchisement of Women are of a kind of which Parliament cannot take cognizance. Of these, the most important concern of the influence which the proposed alteration is likely to have upon marriage . . .

. There is a small body actively hostile to the demand from pure conviction, a large body who regard it with profound indifference, and one almost equally large, and more influential, composed of persons who have nothing that can be called conviction on the subject, who see that it would be more consistent with the fact of a woman occupying the throne that women should have a voice in sending members to Parliament — who are not afraid of the small infusion of female influence which would be added to the electorate while, according to the only plan already proposed to Parliament, men and women vote on the same conditions — but who yet contemplate the proposed change almost with disgust. They do not directly answer any arguments on our side. They feel that their premises are too different from ours for any issue to be joined between us. They look upon the demand as the mere badge of a party, which in its enthusiasm for untried theories ignores unquestionable facts. 'Whatever may be said as to the influence of education and tradition in blinding us to the claims of women', they urge, 'it is undeniable that while the facts of life are what they are, while the mother of a family is for so many years of the prime of life an invalid, the burden of supporting the coming generation *must* rest upon men. No arrangement can open professions to a woman who has a child a year. While nature shuts her off from the work of bread winning, it is vain for any human agency to endeavour to give her a place of which that is the condition, and worse than vain to encourage her to make a demand which could be conceded only as part of a consistent scheme including this impossible condition.'

This line of argument rests wholly on a misconception of what the demand is, not in matters of detail, but in principle. If nature shuts women out from professions, nature will also, as long as the conditions of voting are the same for both sexes, prevent their voting at elections. We do not ask that any steps should be taken to secure a female electorate. We ask simply that a proviso should be withdrawn which secures an exclusively male electorate. We want no bridges built, we merely want a barrier pulled down. We do not say, 'Make the franchise attainable by a particular set of persons who cannot satisfy the test applied hitherto'. We urge only, 'Let it be attainable by all those persons who satisfy the test'. Nay, I am understating our claim. We might say, 'At least, do not make the test cease to operate just where it works most efficaciously'. Surely no one will deny that it is harder for women to earn their living than men — in other words, that their success in doing so is a greater achievement. If it be so, the success of women implies rather more of those qualities, whatever they may be to secure which the property test was imposed, than the success of men does. Is it not, therefore, unreasonable to enfranchise some persons on the ground that they have given a certain evidence of possessing these qualities, and leave unrepresented others, who have given exactly the same evidence of possessing them in a higher degree? And to ask for enfranchisement on other grounds than that this evidence has been given, remember, will not be an expansion of the principle which has been conceded. It will be the admission of another, at variance with it . . .

As men have hitherto monopolized the cultivation of the world, as they have, I should add, a stronger imagination, no woman's picture of a woman has had a chance of competing with theirs. Hence it has come to pass that certain aspects of female life have been put on record with a distinctness and brilliancy which have virtually annulled all the rest, and the average man is rendered even less able to sympathise with a woman than she is with him. Thus it happens that as married people advance in life their standard is apt to be lowered. They have been constantly enlarging the region which by the very fact of their holding it in common is shut off from all moral influence.

They have in so doing cut themselves off from the most elevating joy which we experience in our passage through this world — that sudden generation of power, that sudden enlargement of view, which takes place when two human spirits come into moral contact, and the voice of conscience is echoed by sympathy. This is what marriage might be in every class of life, among the ignorant and hard-working just as much as among the cultivated and leisurely. Our falling short of this ideal has, in addition to all the weakness and imperfection of human nature, this obvious and removable cause, that we have built up an artificial barrier between men and women, so as to make moral sympathy between them impossible.

It is, therefore, in the interests of all we are said to endanger, that we seek to obtain for our sex that educating influence which belongs to political recognition. To make women feel that they belong to a larger whole, that they are connected with the past and the future, and cannot act as mere isolated individuals, must be best even for that particular aspect of their lives, under which alone men are inclined to regard them. It is quite true that the suffrage given to women as holders of property — given, that is, on the only terms which are possible without a return to the false principle of legislating for women as a class apart — would give whatever power it did give to those women who are not men's actual or probable wives. But if it tended in any degree to set before men and women a common ideal — if it awoke in both sides the sense that there was a larger life in which they were sharers, a life not exhausted by their mutual relations — if it made them feel themselves in any degree more capable of judgement of each other, and therefore of a truer sympathy — it would be a step towards a kind of union between average men and women such as is now seen only between the most exceptionally gifted specimens of the race.

It is easy to turn into ridicule the association of such a hope with the demand for female suffrage. There will always be some to whom it will seem gross exaggeration to ascribe much influence to any event which does not change the material conditions of life, who will look upon it as absurd to hope to mould character by large expectations. And yet the course of history and of every-day life shows that hardly any influence is stronger than that of expectation. People become, to a large extent, what their circle takes for granted that they are. Any measure which shall express a national ideal for women, which shall assume that men and women share the great interests of life, must, so far as it has any influence at all, tend ultimately to bind men and women together. And few who ponder over great evils will deny that all will be lightened and some removed when this reunion of interests is once achieved.

It is not mainly, therefore, because we think men incapable of doing justice to women, that we seek for a share in the government of that nation of which we form more than one half. We cannot, indeed, deny that the most generous of human beings must be incapable of doing justice to those who withhold from him their own statement of their case; and we consider that the decisions of average men for average women . . . vary between inconsiderate pampering and inconsiderate hardness — both being exemplified in our police-courts by the damages given to women who want a husband on the one hand, and the light sentences passed on husbands whom their wives would thankfully get rid of on the other. But we seek to be numbered among citizens quite as much from our need of being awakened to higher duties, as from a demand for extended rights. We desire it more for what it would make us than what it would give us. This I conceive to be no exceptional plea, but the true ground on which any demand for the extension of the suffrage should be based. Apart from the educating power of responsibility, apart from the fact that men are ennobled by being made citizens, I doubt if any class could make out for itself a claim of admission to the governing body. It must not, therefore, be treated as a preposterous suggestion (in the true sense of that adjective) that we shall be made fit to deal with political questions by being invited to do so. Our hopes from such aid are no more than are justified by the course of history.

5.6   College education for women

From The Contemporary Review, *Vol. 15, August 1870. The author is Emily Shirreff (1814 – 97), first Mistress of Girton.*

Public opinion is satisfied at length, in this latter part of the nineteenth century of Christianity, that the mental condition of half the human race, — and of that half to which the early training of each fresh generation is inevitably committed, — really is of some national importance; and no matter what other motives may be admitted or rejected, that is enough to make the advocates of female education feel that the difficulties are henceforth a matter of detail. . . .

Of what may be done to remedy the low state of the schools we need not speak here; the subject is too wide for cursory notice: we can only hope that, with the assistance of the Commissioners,[1] a new system may be introduced which shall place effective instruction within reach of all who care to pay for it. But in the meantime some of the other deficiencies pointed out by the reports will perhaps best be met through the courageous effort made lately by opening a college, to give to women opportunities for that more advanced stage of education from which they have hitherto been wholly debarred. . . . In October last the first college for women, claiming a position analogous to that of the colleges in our great universities, was opened, and is now working through its third term.

The name of college has been so indiscriminately used that it does not at first sight convey a definite meaning. Thus for many years in London and elsewhere there have been institutions so called, which, in fact, are only high schools or classes for girls, giving education of a higher order than is afforded by the smaller establishments or by private tuition, but still almost entirely confined to secondary education, terminating, at seventeen or eighteen; for though great efforts have been made in some of them to prolong the period of education, and great advantages have been offered, they have seldom succeeded in retaining their senior pupils. But the college now opened temporarily at Hitchin is a college in the Oxford and Cambridge sense of the term, admitting students at the same age only as those universities, following the Cambridge course of instruction, to extend over the same period, and looking forward to the time when it may be allowed to claim full university privileges. This first bold step in a new direction is also the first step in a course of hitherto unthought-of progress. To this small beginning may we look in time for results which shall change the face of women's education, giving to it that standard and that source of permanent influence it has wanted hitherto, sending out high-class teachers, such as the universities send out for boys, and holding up a ceaseless protest, which will be more and more loudly heard, against that senseless fashion that has closed female education at eighteen. . . .

We have seen that two of the objects most needed are to create such a class of teachers as the universities supply for boys, and to raise the social status of the female teacher. These objects can be secured only by the same means which have secured them for men. There are at present but two liberal professions open to women — medicine and tuition, — and we may consider it fortunate that they both require an unusual amount of attainment. The former has been the conquest of a few determined spirits, whose noble energy will one day be rewarded by the grateful admiration of society; the second is a field naturally opened to women, and in which they might exercise a considerable monopoly; taking the exclusive teaching of girls, — in all higher departments of which the assistance of men is now called in, — and also the entire direction of the very young of both sexes. But high culture will not suffice in this calling: teaching, and still more the power of influencing the young mind, require certain gifts which fortunately are less rare with women than with men; but when we remember that women have been hitherto forced to adopt the profession without consulting their own aptitudes, we cannot wonder at the many failures, and most unjust is the sneer with which they are met. If the various occupations that absorb male mediocrity were abandoned, and men were thrown wholly upon teaching for a livelihood, how would the comparison stand then? . . .

When a boy leaves school, it is only to enter upon another phase of education. Whatever his calling, whether the studies of college, the preparation for a profession, or the mere drudgery of an office, his energies will be strenuously called forth; while the girl at the same age is released from all exertion and exonerated from every useful pursuit. . . . It is . . . the abject idleness into which girls are generally plunged from the time they leave the school-room till they marry, and often long after, till the cares of a family begin to press, that tends more than anything else to place the woman in a position of intellectual inferiority to the man, which the girl did not occupy as compared with the boy. Can we wonder when some of the best years of life are thus wasted, that aims remain low, and views contracted, and that the influence which should be ennobling and purifying social life is helping to foster some of the worst tendencies of the age? . . .

Women have been debarred from high culture, which would have made outward inactivity less irksome, even when not a real boon, as it is to the studious mind; and they have been shut out from employments which would have practically cultivated their faculties and raised their condition; and in this twofold privation we reach the root of the evil, those who would gladly work being debarred from work, and those who have leisure for mental culture debarred from culture. Of late, indeed, there have been some attempts at better things. Women may attend lectures, and even hear an argument now and then specially addressed to themselves, and society wakes up and seems to consider that the female intellect is put by an indulgent public for its trial, somewhat to the amusement of those who happen to bear in mind the fact that the only obstacle to their doing as much before was that there were no lectures to attend! Women only who have studied under the exist- ing circumstances of family life, and of social prejudice, know what the disadvantages are that they have had to struggle with . . .

When we go beyond this to the question that has been so loudly discussed of late, of the expediency for women of entering freely into competition with men in the various callings of public and social life, we come to far more complicated problems which we may well hesitate to deal with. Quite apart from the question of comparative ability, or even the far more decisive one of physical strength, women can never stand on the same ground as men, since the latter may have professions *and* marriage, while marriage *or* professions must be the alternative for women, an alternative which seldom resting freely within their own absolute choice, must always leave a painful element of uncertainty. Nature has placed them at a disadvantage in any struggle, and it is wiser to accept the fact than to begin the song of triumph before they are even armed for the contest. The cost of the experiment might possibly be too great, should it seriously disturb what have hitherto been deemed the natural relations between men and women; should it rouse in the weaker an unsuccessful spirit of rivalry, and deaden in the stronger sex the responsibility for a generous use of strength, which has, after all, been the general rule, however justly we may inveigh against particular laws, and against the oppression exer- cised very often, ignorantly and unconsciously, by men. It might cost too much if it should turn many women who can afford the quiet dignity of home-life to seek the public highways of the world, instead of those secluded paths where their footsteps have been blessed heretofore. Especially may it cost too much if women, in the eagerness of competition, in the visions of ambition, forget that the noblest of human trusts is theirs already, — theirs by right divine. For wide and honourable as we justly consider the field of social exertion, of profitable industry, of scientific research, greater — aye, and nationally more important — than all these is that responsibility for the welfare of each new generation that God has placed in the hands and bound upon the hearts of women.

Note

1. *assistance of the Commissioners*: The Schools Inquiry Commission of

1864, on the education of girls, deplored the standard of girls' education, and the fact that girls were largely excluded from the benefits of traditional educational endowments.

5.7   The practice of medicine by women

From The Fortnightly Review, *Vol. 23, March 1875. The writer is Sophia Jex-Blake (1840–1912), who founded the London School of Medicine for Women in 1874, and established the right of women to practise in 1877. Here she denounces the injustice of the anomaly of the Medical Act of 1858.*

I believe . . . I am correct in stating that there is one instance in this country, and one only, where the law of the land — forcibly wrested indeed from its original purpose — has been made practically to support a stupendous monopoly that certainly could be maintained by no other means, and that only is unsupported by, but absolutely opposed to, that principle of natural fitness which has been already pointed out as the sole legitimate ground of action. It is hardly necessary to say that I refer to the forcible exclusion of women from the legalized practice of medicine, in which they have, from time immemorial, had a recognized and apparently most legitimate share, — an exclusion effected by the means, or rather by the abuse, of the Medical Act of 1858, which certainly was enacted without the slightest intention of producing the results which are now obtained through its agency. To explain the causes which have led to this remarkable effect, and to demonstrate the evils accruing from it, will be the object of the present paper.

Whatever may have been in former times the differences of opinion respecting the principle of free trade, as applied not only to merchandise, but to every kind of art and workmanship, it will at the present moment be almost universally allowed that the State has no right in any way to limit or fetter any private industry, calling, or profession, except for the gravest reasons involving the general welfare of the community as a whole. It is a question which has been very differently decided in different countries, whether considerations of national welfare do justify such legislation respecting the medical profession as shall give to certain of its practitioners a legalized status which it denies to others. In America nothing of the sort has ever been done, and at the present time every practitioner of medicine, however well, or ill, educated, is allowed to compete with all other doctors, on terms of absolute equality, without any State recognition, and exposed (except for manifest malpractice) to no legal penalties. In former days this was the case everywhere, and each medical practitioner could acquire his learning as he liked, and must depend for his success in life solely upon the practical results of his subsequent work. It is, indeed, the opinion of some eminent medical practitioners of the present day, that this after all, is the truest theory, resulting in the most satisfactory practice. . . . In England, as in many other countries, it has been thought desirable to have direct legislation on the subject, and since 1858, a law has existed limiting the authorized practice of medicine to those whose names are entered on the Government Register. It will hardly be contested that such legislation, which gives to one class of medical practitioners so enormous an advantage over all others, could only be justified by considerations of the national welfare; and accordingly it is expressly stated in the preamble to the Medical Act of 1858, that the said Act was enacted solely on the ground that 'it is expedient that persons requiring medical aid should be enabled to distinguish qualified practitioners,' and all its provisions appear intended merely to facilitate such distinction. The *quality* of the medical aid offered, and the possibility of enabling the public to judge of that quality, were manifestly the only points in view. Subsequent events have shown grave cause for regret that the Act did not provide at once for the authoritative and independent examination of all candidates for medical practice, so that such 'quality' might be certified with absolute impartiality. But it was thought at the time sufficient to recognise all the existing examining Boards, nineteen in number, and to consider the licence or diploma of any one of these as entitled to legal registration. . . . The Examining Boards have, however, originated a distinction which, if valid, excludes one half of the community from such compliance with the Act as will entitle to registration; for, with edifying unanimity, they refuse absolutely to admit women to any examination entitling to a registrable licence, diploma, or degree . . .

That the Medical Act does not itself in any way exclude women from its advantages is proved by its wording throughout; and also, still more incontrovertibly, by the fact that two women are at this moment registered under the Act; each of them, however, having obtained this privilege in an exceptional way, which is not now open to other women. One of them obtained registration because she had already a foreign degree, and was in practice in England before 1858.[1] The other was able to obtain an Apothecaries' licence, and in virtue of it to place her name on the register . . .

I have not thought it was necessary to enumerate the reasons which make it desirable that there should be medical women, nor the benefits which I believe will accrue to the community when it is at least optional for every sick woman to consult a qualified physician of her own sex, rather than of the other. To go at all fully into this phase of the subject would demand far more time and space than I have at my command; and it is perhaps better to leave the question to rest on the broad principles of equity which apply to both sexes and to all classes alike. The natural laws of supply and demand may well be trusted here as elsewhere; and if women doctors do not meet a real need, they will simply die out of themselves. At present it is certain that a definite amount of demand for their services does exist, or sixteen thousand women would hardly petition Parliament on the subject; and seeing that 'an injustice is not small because it concerns a small number,' I hold that if a single woman desires to consult a physician of her own sex, and if one other woman desires to qualify herself to be that physician, no third person whatever has a right to interfere with the accomplishment of such legitimate desires. To quote the memorable words of the late Mrs. Mill,[2] 'We deny the right of any portion of the species to decide for another portion, or any individual for another individual, what is, and what is not, their "proper sphere". The proper sphere for all human beings is the largest and highest which they are able to attain to. What this is, cannot be ascertained without complete liberty of choice.'

Notes

1. *in practice in England before 1858*: Elizabeth Blackwell, who had qualified in the US in 1849, and became the first woman doctor to be registered when she returned to England.
2. *Mrs. Mill*: Harriet Taylor (1807–58), noted feminist, author of 'The Enfranchisement of Women', later wife of J. S. Mill.

5.8   Male and female morality

From a paper read by Josephine Butler (1828 – 1906) in Croydon in 1871.
The writer was a great campaigner for social reform, fighting particularly on
behalf of prostitutes and for the repeal of the Contagious Diseases Acts.

The legislation which we have opposed deals, as you know, with
the evil of prostitution; but how does it deal with it? It attempts to
facilitate the practice of sin; — to make a soul-destroying vice
comfortable with health, good order, and public comfort. I need
not tell you that vice can never be regulated so as to be compatible
with the health and welfare of the people; but the *attempt* to regulate
vice in this manner is so impious, that, if continued, I expect it will
sooner or later draw down the judgments of heaven upon our
country, as they have been drawn down upon France.[1] For
recollect that this attempt is founded on a belief which I must call a
blasphemy against God and against human nature — a belief that
purity is impossible or unhealthful, and that man cannot be any
other than the slave of sin. Now, it is the great evil of prostitution
against which our future must be, in a large measure, directed;
and before we can fairly attack this evil we find it absolutely
needful to get rid of the Acts[2] whose repeal we seek. . . .

Now nothing is more manifest than that the temporal and
spiritual welfare of this nation is hindered and turned into the
opposite mainly by the same causes, which must be boldly entitled
the lusts of the flesh — not all equally base or hateful; but this it is
that lies at the root of our threatening national decay. The most
familiar to us of these, particularly among the humbler classes, is
the lust of intoxicating drink, which even when it does not induce
flagrant drunkenness, pauperises, and keeps families on the edge
of want, . . . More terrible still, and closely connected with this
vice, is the great curse of prostitution: and here it is not the poorer
classes who are the most guilty. Immorality among the poor, bad
as it is, is a less deadly poison in society than the profligacy of the
upper classes. There are men among us, thousands of them, who
have had every advantage of birth, education, and fortune, yet
who can only be truly described as 'lewd fellows of the baser sort;'
of the baser sort undoubtedly, although the boasted 'best blood' of
the aristocracy may flow in their veins . . .

It is stated, very truly, in the paper which was circulated here,

. . . that 'it is an awful and astounding fact that a very large and influential portion of English society has made up its mind to accept prostitution with all its train of moral horrors, as a necessary and inevitable portion of Christian civilisation'. Now the legislation which we have been opposing for two years is but an embodiment of this hopeless heathenish fatalism which has taken possession of a portion of society — mainly of the upper classes; for in the course of our agitation we have found that the mass of the humbler classes, and especially the working men, do *not* hold this hopeless and impure doctrine. They reject with horror the idea of prostitution being a necessity.

These Acts, and all legislative measures which deal with prostitution, have up to this time been devised and set on foot by men alone, without the aid of women. Nay, not only have women been debarred from attempting to deal in any large sense with this evil, but they have been systematically drilled into silence on this topic. Men have demanded of them an affectation at least of ignorance on the subject, albeit it is one which more intimately and terribly concerns the whole of womankind than any other. Can the soul of my sister be defiled and my own soul not be the worse for it? It cannot . . .

We shall never have faith and courage enough in Parliament to attack this monster evil in its sources until the convictions of women as well as of men are represented there, until we admit all the light which women — not wise indeed in their own wisdom, but enlightened from a holy and unerring source — are able to contribute to the dispersion of the darkness; for in order to achieve the solution of this chief mystery of iniquity, above all others, the united wisdom and strength of man and of woman is required.

Many think that silent intercession to God, and the exercise of a quiet influence on their own nearest male relatives, are the limit of the means which a *woman* can use. But a time has come when we require more than this. We must have a holy league, a national league of men and women banded together to make war against this evil from every side, patiently, valiantly to fight it at all points at once. Unless we make common cause in an open, a recognised, and a determined manner, our country will go down before the tide of evil . . .

A gentleman once said to me, expressing the generally accepted opinion, 'I own that a profligate man is a disagreeable thing, but it is obvious to all that a vicious woman is an infinitely more degraded being'. I replied to him, 'I beg your pardon, sir; you see it so from your point of view; but I am a woman, and I must say that, although a vicious woman is a dreadful thing, to my mind a profligate man is an infinitely more degraded being'. He was quite astonished at my expression of what I truly felt and feel. Probably the revulsion is greater in most minds against sinners of the opposite sex, and women are therefore the more deeply guilty ever to have allowed men to cherish the theory that they (women) do not look with displeasure on vice in men. It will be our duty henceforward, fellow-women, to require, sternly *to require* of men that they be pure, to demand it of them as they have hitherto demanded it of us. The history of human life is encouraging, inasmuch as it shows that men are not generally slow to come up to the mark of what the women around them require, whether it be in folly or in goodness. See then what a responsibility rests on us!

Notes

1. *judgements . . . drawn down upon France*: The defeat of France by Bismarck's Germany in 1870.

2. *the Acts whose repeal we seek*: The Contagious Diseases Acts required that prostitutes be registered with the police and with doctors. Any woman could be apprehended on these grounds.

6

Education

In its urgent call for technical education in 1868, 'for the English almost a new question', *Macmillan*'s had added tartly, 'Education of any kind can hardly be called their *forte*', and Matthew Arnold had denounced English middle-class education as the worst in Europe. At the beginning of the period education at every level was in a state of torpor. It was largely in the hands of the church, of one denomination or another, and, as far as popular education went, religious rivalry was often stronger than educational principle. So schooling for the Anglican poor was provided by the National Society, Dissenters founded a similar society of their own, and both preferred to see children not educated at all than educated by their rivals. Some unsystematic adult education was offered in the Mechanics' Institute, begun in 1823 in the light of Benthamite thinking (see *The Scientific Approach*), and viewed by the church with deep distrust. From the 1830s the state had shown a half-hearted interest in national education, but the Education Act of 1870 was the first decisive step taken to make primary education the responsibility of the government, and it took successive Acts to make elementary schooling free and compulsory for all.

Secondary education in the 1830s was a privilege enjoyed by few boys and still fewer girls. For boys it was offered in either the old endowed grammar schools, or in one of the great public schools identified by the Royal Commission in 1864. But with the reform and expansion of the professions — the church, the army, the administration, the civil service — and the development of the colonial Empire, the clamour went up for an educated middle class (see *The Gentleman*). A handful of great headmasters set new standards for the public schools (Arnold of Rugby, Butler of

Shrewsbury, Thring of Uppingham), old foundations were reformed, and dozens of new schools (like Malvern, Clifton, Wellington, Cheltenham and Marlborough) were founded in the middle years of the century.

'Higher education' had been represented for centuries by the universities of Oxford and Cambridge, both traditional fortresses of the Established Church, and by 1830 long overdue for reform. All but Anglicans, of course, were excluded from the universities, and fellowships for most of the clerical dons were merely a stage on the way to a country benefice. The curriculum had barely changed since the times of Archbishop Laud in the seventeenth century — the new knowledge of the sciences and technology simply did not exist for the university. The Royal Commission at Oxford in 1852 demonstrated that the university's only function seemed to be elementary teaching. Newman, in the same year, had firmly excluded research as a concern of the university, whose function was 'the diffusion and extension of knowledge rather than the advancement'.

One result of the Commission was the beginnings of reform in the curriculum: both universities broadened their curriculum to include a wide variety of modern subjects, especially natural science. (Oxford, for instance, established schools for Law, History and Natural Science in 1853, and schools for Theology and Oriental Studies followed hard upon. Cambridge introduced the Natural Science Tripos in 1869.) First Oxford and then Cambridge were thrown open to undergraduates of any religion, and in 1871 both universities made all degrees, and all university posts, open to men of any persuasion or none: able young Dissenters and ambitious scholars with agnostic views were free to enjoy the privileges of the reformed university. Moreover the new Fellows, embarking on a professional career in teaching and learning, included such novel personnel as chemists, engineers and physicists.

Men, but not, of course, women: anything but elementary education for girls was scarcely thought of until the middle of the century. The establishment of Queen's College, with the training of governnesses in mind, was in 1848, and marked a significant if very gradual change in national thinking. Two of its students, Miss Buss and Miss Beale, started, or re-founded, famous schools for girls with North London Collegiate (1850) and Cheltenham Ladies' College (1853). (See *The 'Woman Question'*.) The old universities made concessions towards higher education for women when women were admitted to lectures in the late 1860s and the 1870s, though they were not, of course, permitted to take degrees for many years.

Meanwhile, even before the first cracks had appeared in university defences in the 1850s, new universities had been established in Lampeter (1822) and Durham (1832). The University of London, where the method of instruction was systematically different, was founded in 1836 specifically to educate the middle classes excluded from the older places. At the other end of the period came the foundation of the Victoria University, in 1880, with its centres in Manchester, Liverpool and Leeds, undenominational in charter, scientific in bias; and polytechnics, founded on continental models, made their appearance in the 1880s. To these, and to successive new universities, women were admitted almost from the beginning (though Lampeter, ever the *laudator temporis acti*, delayed admitting women until 1965!).

6.1   The manufacturing poor — education

From Fraser's Magazine, *Vol. 39, January 1849. The writer sketches some of the problems confronting the reformers of popular education, particularly in industrial areas.*

Of all the subjects which have been discussed of late years, none has occupied more general attention than that of education among the poor. As to the character it ought to assume, the means whereby it is to be supported, and the nature of the subjects it should embrace, perhaps no question has given rise to greater diversity of sentiment; as to its political importance and personal advantages, there is no point on which men are so universally agreed. The minister of state has at length discovered that all his measures must be futile, unless the mind of the great human mass be enlightened to distinguish truth, to acknowledge justice, and to obey law. The minister of the gospel understands that the awakening of mind and expansion of heart here below is that only springtime process whereby these faculties can be prepared for their full development in a future existence. . . . The manufacturer perceives how dangerous it is for the mighty body of a people to awake to the consciousness of a giant's power without the intellect of a child to regulate and direct it . . .

Let us, then, first of all, draw the reader's attention to the condition of the manufacturing poor in its bearing upon education. And here, remember, we are not speaking of an agricultural population, nor of the order of shopkeepers in towns, but of that class among which education is especially needed, and from which the absence of it is especially to be dreaded — the lowest portion of the operative poor.

National schools[1]

We need not inform the reader, if connected in any measure with a manufacturing district, that at nine years of age children are admitted into a cotton factory as 'short-timers'; that, so long as they work the limited period, they are sent to school one-half of each day, Saturday excepted; and that at the age of thirteen they are admitted to employment for the full number of the factory hours. Now, in a purely manufacturing district, it may be asserted, without fear of contradiction, that of those who enter a mill as operatives nineteen out of twenty commence as 'short-timers'. These are, for the most part, sent to the National school for the daily instruction of three hours, which the law enforces. Whether the arrangement be a good one may be questioned; but this, at least, is certain, that in many districts the National schools would be very thinly attended without these short-timers . . .

We may now be permitted to offer a few remarks on the means which may be taken for the improvement of our National schools. This has been the great problem of late years. The subject has been so far divested of its incumbrances, that the propriety of educating the poor is all but universally admitted . . .

The great wants at present existing in our schools are — a better and cheaper class of school-books, a better trained order of masters, and their number increased three-fold. Large demands, we admit, and unattainable, we believe, all at once! But how approximate nearest to these ends, with the least outrage in the employment of means? Three modes of proceding are open to our choice: we may either leave the education of the poor entirely dependent on Voluntary exertions; or we may adopt some Government plan of general and promiscuous instruction; or we may engraft on our existing systems certain aids and adjuncts from Government, without any material interference with the present management of our schools.

Upon the effect of unaided voluntary exertions there can hardly be two opinions seriously entertained. The 'cheerful givers' are already sufficiently taxed; even now they shrug up their shoulders at the term 'voluntary' . . .

Again, if any comprehensive scheme of education were to be imposed upon the country by the Government, what prospect is there of its being effectual? . . . The Romanists are a very numerous body in the manufacturing towns. Would they join in carrying out the plan? Would they associate with Churchmen, Wesleyans, Independents, Presbyterians, Unitarians, Baptists, Ranters — not to mention the infinite subdivisions of these sects — in the education of their children? . . . In the working of such a comprehensive scheme, simplicity and uniformity are indispensable requirements; every loophole ought to be stopped which could give an opening for the 'letting out' of the waters of strife. But what can be discovered in this notable project but the elements of confusion, the seeds of dissension, and the unsettling of the principles of all religious faith? . . .

It remains, therefore, that the only feasible plan for the improvement of education among the poor is to engraft fresh shoots into the present system. . . .

The Government[2] has, without question, acted with the best judgement in their late *Minutes of the Committee of Council on Education*. The measure is but a small one indeed: it will hardly be felt in many districts more sensibly than a hornet on the hide of a rhinoceros; but it is in the right direction, and, if followed up by the present and successive Governments, must lead to the best practical results.

Infant schools

The National schools of our manufacturing districts, we have observed, are for the education of children varying from six or seven to thirteen years of age. But education must begin before six, and continue after thirteen, if it is to be effectual. Other schools, therefore, are required, that the mellow ground of the infant heart may be prepared for the seed, and that the blade as it springs up may not wither and die from want of cultivation and care.

The Infant school is intended to be a feeder for the National. In a populous district the one ought never to be found without the other. The establishment of Infant schools has been opposed and scouted by many, and is so still by some, like almost every other benevolent and useful institution at its commencement . . .

But is it possible to convey instruction to infants who have only just escaped from their mothers' arms? Without any question it is. From Aristotle to Locke, from Locke to Lord Brougham, from Lord Brougham to the first intelligent nurse you meet in the streets, it has been a maxim, deduced from experience and supported by common sense, that education must commence with the earliest dawn of the faculties. Education, remember, not so much in the exercise of the mental powers, as in the training of the infant feelings to a sense of right and wrong. Look upon the matter, too, not only in the light of the good the children acquire but of the evil they avoid. Take the school we have inspected; where would the scholars have been had they not been there? Rolling about in the street channels, or sunk in filth at their homes. On the other hand, within these walls they are taught the duties of cleanliness, neatness, order, and submission. They are instructed in the rudiments of secular learning; they become attached to their school; they are made to comprehend the simplest truths of revelation; they become impressed with a sense of obedience and duty; and their minds and feelings receive a tone of decency and propriety, which in some, we trust never be effaced through life.

Sunday schools[3]

But, after thirteen years of age, what means of instruction are within the reach of the manufacturing poor? We point to our Sunday schools, not so much as promoting the secular department of education as imparting scriptural knowledge and implanting religious truth. . . . In the present condition of education, Sunday schools are, beyond all question, the most successful, if not the only real, instruments of diffusing a religious tone of feeling among the younger members of our flocks. This may be a startling assertion to some; but it is so, simply from their being unacquainted with the nature of such institutions in populous districts . . .

The difficulties that meet a clergyman in the management of a large Sunday school are doubtless very great. He has many conflicting agencies to guide, and direct, and control: he has hostile feelings to reconcile; he has debts and duns to contend with. . . . But our province is rather to consider the phenomena they exhibit, and the effects they produce; and, from our own personal experience, we can affirm that, however arduous may be the task of conducting them, they afford ample encouragement to zealous exertion in this field of Christian labour . . .

Night schools[4]

It was one argument in favour of the Ten-hours' Factory-bill,[5] that the leisure gained by the operative might be employed in useful pursuits. The argument was the philanthropist's, the labour is the clergyman's. And yet we do not think he will shrink from the duty. We have ourselves tried the Night-school system and found it fully remunerative for the time occupied by it. . . . On the whole, we are assured that Night schools for writing, arithmetic, grammar, spelling, sewing, and knitting — established with judgment and system, adapted to the particular wants of the locality, and personally superintended by the clergyman — will prove valuable auxiliaries to the Sunday and Day schools, and be a means of converting the benevolent measure of the legislature into a source of intellectual as well as physical enjoyment to the poor.

Notes

1. *National schools:* Founded at the beginning of the century by the Church of England for 'the education of the poor in the Principles of the Established Church'.

2. *The Government:* Government control of education was wholly nominal. The first grant of public money for education (a mere £20,000) was paid to the National Society and its Nonconformist equivalent, the British and Foreign Society, in 1833, and school inspectors were appointed in 1839. The administration was in the hands of a Special Committee of the Privy Council.

3. *Sunday schools:* Started by Robert Raikes, of Gloucester, in 1780.

4. *Night schools:* One that was to become famous was founded by George Birkbeck in 1829.

5. *The Ten-hours' Factory-bill:* John Fielden, a notable Yorkshire factory owner and reformer, and Lord Ashley, later the Earl of Shaftesbury, had finally, in 1847, persuaded Parliament to accept a Bill limiting hours of work to ten hours a day for women and young people.

6.2   Thoughts of an outsider: public schools

From the Cornhill Magazine, *Vol. 27, 1873. Leslie Stephen (1832 – 1904), Eton and Cambridge, comments wryly on the myth of the Victorian public school, then in its heyday.*

An English public school, we are often told, is a miniature world;

and certainly, the world is in many respects a big public school. The training it gives is of the rough and ready order, with plenty of hard blows and little allowance for sentiment. . . . It may be . . . that the recent edifying discussions upon our great schools have revived in outsiders certain old-fashioned reflections not quite in accordance with the orthodox opinions of to-day. Few things are more astonishing to such observers than that mysterious sanctity which broods over such places as Eton and Winchester. To touch a single twig of the hallowed birch is regarded as a kind of sacrilege. . . . There is a special magic about the old schools. They have a double measure of that strange enchantment which is more or less common to all ancient corporations. Any one who has touched, as it were, the mere hem of their garments, who has the most shadowy and distant claim to a share in their prestige, is affected by the spell. The connection is sometimes grotesque enough, and may remind one of the claim set up by somebody to a great man's acquaintance because the hero — was it the Duke of Wellington? — had once damned him for getting in his way. To have been flogged, in accordance with traditions handed down from hoar antiquity, and embodied in a special local jargon, is to have gone through a sacred initiatory rite. From the moment that the accolade has been laid — not upon your shoulders — you are a member of a sort of strange order of chivalry. No oaths have been taken, and no formal obligations imposed, but you are bound for the rest of your life to stand up against all comers in defence of the thrice-noble body to which you belong. It is in vain that you will try to shake off the impression. Let anybody who has been a public schoolboy try to state the fact simply and unostentatiously to the dearest friend of his bosom who has been brought up at an academy. He may, if he happens to be a pattern of all the Christian virtues, succeed in conveying the information in a manner not actually offensive. He may speak condescendingly rather than boastfully. But no effort of imagination will divest him of a share of conscious superiority. His friend, he may admit, is 'one of God's creatures,' but he is not, and cannot be his equal. To have been flogged by Dr. Keate or Dr. Arnold was to receive an indelible hall-mark, stamping the sufferer for ever as genuine metal. . . . [And yet] the little victims imbibe unconsciously the peculiar code of morality which justifies their sufferings. They sympathise more with their tyrants than with themselves. The rough discipline forms their minds as much as it affects their bodies. They are as much convinced as any of their rulers, that a

boy who can't row or play cricket is unworthy to cumber the earth;
he is an anomalous creature, existing only on sufferance, and his
humiliation is a marked feature in the general arrangements of
Providence. The domestic affections too are mere nuisances which
ought to be studiously suppressed; they are a kind of thorn in the
flesh, which, for mysterious purposes, is permitted to tempt the
childish nature into occasional ebullitions of sentiment; but to
allow their existence to be manifest to others is a distinct act of
indecency, if not of immorality. The weakly, sensitive child perse-
cutes himself, even when his persecutors are absent; or, at best,
skulks into corners to indulge in feelings for which he is half
persuaded that he ought to blush like a criminal. All this, as every
public school man will declare, is a silly exaggeration, or at least
refers to a past generation. The last statement may be freely
admitted. No abuse, so far as I have been able to observe, ever
exists except in the past tense. But certainly it is not a mere fancy
picture. There used at a certain period — not so far removed as to
be beyond the memory of persons still living, and indeed still
writing — to be a good many such pariahs as I have described,
poor little fragments of humanity, convicted by school opinion of
being physically weak and morally sensitive, kicked contemp-
tuously aside, when not actively bullied, and heartily ashamed of
themselves for their undeniable atrocity. With what deep envy
they regarded their robuster companions, and what a surprising
revelation it was to them when they discovered at the university
that a youth might be tolerated, and even popular, without physical prowess, is still engraved pretty deeply on some memories. A
public school in those old days might be Paradise to the Tom
Browns, but it was purgatory to the luckless lads marked out for
brutality by the thinness of their skins . . .

Having once adopted the theory that our public schools are perfect, there is of course no lack of arguments in their favour. Like so
many other of our admirable institutions, they appear to be absurd
a priori, and *a posteriori* turn out to be inimitable. Nobody could
have guessed that an ideal education would be provided by
bringing together a few hundred lads and requesting them to
govern themselves. Experience, however, proves triumphantly
that, barring a little brutality, and a good deal of gross ignorance,
and some snobbishness, and a rather low standard of morality
upon certain points, and much excessive devotion to athletic
sports, the typical schoolboy is as noble an animal as could be
desired. The proofs of the proposition are numerous; as, in the

first place, boys from private schools are notoriously worse; secondly, people are ready to pay very high prices to acquire for their sons this inestimable privilege; and thirdly, the greatest Englishmen have been educated at such places and, of course, owe their greatness to their education. This last argument indeed, verges upon the audacious. It is one of those daring commonplaces which bring down the applause of an audience; but which, when retailed by men of standing and ability tempt one to despair of the perfectibility of human reason. People can still repeat without blushing the poor old platitude about the battle of Waterloo having been won in the playing-fields. Of how many muddles and disasters were the seeds sown, one would like to know, in the same historic ground? Perhaps the argument about our system is even more astonishing. Put into a formal proof it would seem to involve the assumptions, first, that English statesmen are the best of all statesmen; and secondly, that they owe their greatness to their schools. Passing over the first, which, after all, can hardly be regarded as a self-evident proposition, how is the second assumption established? Why should the surpassing merits of our immutable breed of statesmen be ascribed to our schools more than to any one of fifty other causes? Why should we not say with equal plausibility that their virtues and talent are due to our inimitable constitution, to our happy mixture of monarch, aristocracy, and democracy, to our established church, to our land laws, to our religious creed, to our fortunate mixture of races, to our climate, to Oliver Cromwell, or to William of blessed memory, to the fact that we inhabit an island, to our foxhunting and horseracing, to freedom of the press, or trial by jury, or — for that seems to be the most convenient formula for explaining things in general — to the Gulf stream? What is there after all which requires any explanation? The governing classes in England prefer certain schools; and the schools which they prefer are attended by the governing classes. The son of a peer is sent to Eton as he afterwards goes into Parliament and is appointed to office by a certain natural fitness of things; and the public school has no more right to claim all his virtues than any other of the luxuries in which he has indulged . . .

[But] to condemn public schools is indeed further from my intention than to praise them. An humble outsider cannot profess to form any trustworthy opinion on such matters. Infinite collation of bluebooks and study of inspectors' reports, and balancings of the opinions of foreign observers would be necessary for such a task. I am merely uttering a feeble protest when I am called upon to bow the knee before a popular idol of the day. Let us assume, and the opinion seems to be the most probable one that public schools, as at present conducted, are free from many gross faults by which they were once stained, and that they succeed in providing a very fair education for ingenuous youth. So far as private observation enables one to judge, they produce what ladies call without any suspicion of irony, very nice young men. They are, as a rule, very well dressed and have the manner of gentlemen. They of course display a stupendous ignorance; the average lad of eighteen who comes up to the Universities from our great places of education shows a negation of all useful knowledge, which is, in its way, a really impressive phenomenon. His knowledge of literature is confined not to English authors, or to modern English authors, but to the trashiest kind of modern English authors; he is not merely ignorant of science, but ignorant that such a thing exists; and his classical training, which doubtless deserves all that is said of it if he belongs to the select few, amounts, if he belongs to the promiscuous many, simply to a blind faculty for guessing at the English equivalent of common Greek and Latin words. Of course there is not much in this, for ignorance of this kind is characteristic of the young male of the species in general, and not to the public school lad in particular. Moreover, it is said by sanguine people that matters are improving and intellectual training rising by degrees to be valued as at least a useful supplement to the athletic. And, in a more positive sense, such a boy has generally more attractive qualities. His moral standard is not always of the purest and most delicate kind; indeed it may be said that the fine bloom of innocence has not unfrequently been robbed off by the rude contact of his fellows. But still that mysterious corporate spirit, whatever be its origin, has done something for him. He has a profound conviction that he ought to be a gentleman; and though the precise meaning of that word be a little indefinite, it includes much that we would be sorry to lose. The ideal may not be the loftiest conceivable; but after all the cant and the false sentimentality has been dispersed, he still is an animal of whom one finds it difficult not to be rather proud. Standing in the Eton playing-fields, one would perhaps rather not talk about the battle of Waterloo, and ask too curiously whether the training would be equally adapted to produce the heroes of some future Gravelotte or Sedan.[1] But one cannot resist the spirit of the place. There is a certain fine stoicism, a sturdy, tough-fibred sense of manly duty, which seems to pervade the atmosphere and, with all its sacred absurdities, one feels that lads brought up under such influences have a chance of carrying on the old tradition with fair credit to themselves and their country. After all, the old maxim holds true that one virtue lies at the base of all others; call it force, energy, vitality, or manliness, or whatever you please, it has perhaps a better chance at a public school than at most places. Perhaps the explanation is not very flattering. One thinks sometimes that all educational systems are so bad, that the system must be best which educates least; and public schools may claim great excellence on that showing. Whatever weakness they may have, they have not the positive defect of unduly cramping boyish energy and spirit, and the absence of the defect is a high merit.

Note

1. *Gravelotte or Sedan*: Battles of the Franco-Prussian War. Gravelotte was an indecisive encounter in August 1870; Sedan was the final battle (2 September 1870) which resulted in the total humiliation of France.

6.3   An inquiry into the state of girls' fashionable schools

From Fraser's Magazine, *Vol. 31, June 1845. An indictment of the current deplorable level of female education.*

Before we throw out any hints on the subject of the present inquiry, we must request our readers to bear in mind, that we assume as facts the extension of womanly duties, and the necessity of more active exertion than has hitherto been required from the sex. . . . We need only point to our machinery and our distant colonies, to the eager rush made in every profession and calling of life, to be assured that the leisure of 'merry Englonde' is fast growing into 'all work, and no play'. Women will share in the social revolution: indeed, by every token we may know that, for the future, the bulk of English women, married and single, must bear their part in the *work* of life. With those, therefore, whose views of womanhood do not range beyond the vista of society, we have nothing in common; but of those who believe that woman is capable of being more than a toy or a slave we would ask, 'Have the means of improvement kept pace with the growing demands on the powers of women?' 'Is their education suited to their extended responsibilities?' Surely, the means as yet provided are ill suited to attain the end; for, if women are henceforth to be members of a commonwealth, girls should be trained to a sense of high moral responsibility and self-dependence. Now what is the broad mark on the ordinary means of providing instruction — to wit, *schools*? Fine ladyism. Mistress, teacher, pupil, household, all bear the same impress. . . . [I]t is to be doubted whether parents who really reflect seriously on their own responsibility, and on the duties of their daughters as beings who have work to do for this world and the next, would send them to the mere fashionable school. . . . Half the houses set apart for schools are not fit for the purpose; very few would be suitably airy and roomy: a garden or playground is necessary, if girls are to be kept in health; for exercise is but slightly beneficial unless taken with pleasure; and what recreation can there be in the formal walks along highroads, in a long line of two-and-two? In many of the gaudiest establishments, the food provided is very insufficient in quantity, and bad in quality. . . . Health is too often cruelly sacrificed, either through culpable neglect or ignorance, or for the sake of gaining a few more wares for the marriage-market.

We come now to that part of the matter which relates to the *over-working* of growing girls in the acquisition of tawdry accomplishments; and the fact must be known through the length and breadth of the land, since in every house drooping girls are to be seen, spiritless victims of *ennui* (the effect of a reaction after the killing excitement of school), with languid faces, and often misshapen forms. And all for what? Not for knowledge, nor for an intellectual growth, which is to make up for the stunting of bodily power, for, with few exceptions, the modes of teaching which prevail in reference to women are fitted to act upon the surface alone, to accomplish the one end of attracting attention. If health were sacrificed in order to attain self-knowledge, and sources of interest which would lift the possessor above the chances of events, and make to her a world within the world, her own, beyond the touch of accident, the price would be paid for an equivalent: but health is not our own, we may not consciously barter it for the rarest gifts of mind and heart. What shall be said, then, to those who suffer their daughters to fritter it away in the pursuit of bubbles that shall

177

break as they are breathed on? What to those who, undertaking to guide the young, destroy in them the very sap of life for the sake of a few petty acquirements, that will never solace one hour of weariness, or fit them for one practical duty of life? Woman was ordained to be the *help-meet* of man; but this high calling is utterly overlooked in the present system of female instruction. . . . Women learn nothing thoroughly; in their education the *reason of things* is altogether left out, they are taught by rote instead of rule. Their memories are quickened, their imaginations excited, their passions stimulated; but their understandings are left to slumber. What more common speech from female lips than this, 'I know what I mean myself, but I cannot explain it to you?' So that the woman who can clearly convey her reasons, or patiently follow those of another, is looked upon as an exception to her sex. But this is an error. Women are capable of being taught the three parts of a sentence in common with men; and men who have been only partially taught take one-sided views and state their notions after the fashion of all unlearned folks. But we will admit, for argument's sake (still insisting that until the experiment of sound female instruction be tried the assumed inferiority cannot be proved), that a woman's natural defect lies in her logical faculty — her thinking power; for what is education but to supply deficiency and counteract bad tendencies? and how does the ordinary system answer these purposes? Who, for instance, was ever told at a parsing class the derivations of the parts of speech? . . . [W]hat do most lady musicians know of any of the laws of harmony, whereby seven sounds may be wrought into liquid maze or solemn fugue? As they learn Lindley Murray[1] 'by heart' and call it grammar, so they learn the art of playing 'by ear' and finger-craft, and think it music. Yet music and grammar might be in a woman's education what logic and mathematics are to a man. The one would teach her to *think* and the other to *combine* and *adapt*, thus bearing on the very weakest points in her mind. . . .

Every one who reflects on the present smattering which is given to women as knowledge, and on the whole system of her education *at home* often as well as at school, but eminently so in the latter, must see that it is calculated to produce the very converse.

Note

1. Lindley Murray: *English Grammar* by Lindley Murray (1795), a very popular Victorian textbook.

6.4   The University of London and middle-class education

From The National Review, *Vol. 5, July 1857. The University of London, incorporated in 1836, was proposing to grant degrees by examination alone, and without the necessity of residence. The writer protests that to do this would be a contradiction of all that a university represents.*

Hitherto a London degree in Arts, like all other degrees in Arts which have commanded general respect in this country, has denoted that the holder has not only passed an university education, but has had a university training. He must have spent a long time in a college of the university. It is now proposed to grant that degree on examination alone, without a university training. We propose to show how vital the difference is, how much a right estimate of it has to do with any true conception of middle-class education, and how peculiarly it behoves the University of London to attend to the true interest of the middle classes in the matter. College education for the Middle Classes is the part of their subject which the authors of the pamphlet on Middle-Class Education have ignored. They take a lofty Oxford view of well-to-do society, as divided into those who are to go at once from school to business, and those who are either rich and distinguished or devoted to professions, whose members take conventional rank with the rich and distinguished, — to which latter class alone they seem to consider university education appropriate.

This mode of thinking must pass away. There is no necessary connection between liberal culture and ambition. There is necessarily a strong connection between liberal culture and the power to discharge with efficiency the functions of a governing citizen in peace and war. The ambitious classes no longer monopolise government; more and more power is passing into the hands of those who begin life as thrifty acquirers, and reach political influence through the natural tendencies of a successful mercantile career; more and more of our members of Parliament, more and more of our magistrates, are taken from a class which has not, as a general rule, enjoyed the advantages of college ·education. This ought not to continue. There is such an increased and increasing diffusion of every kind of information among all classes, that it is a painful anomaly that the training which would turn that information into a great source of available power should be confined to so few. The effect is very obvious. The middle-class men have power; but they cannot work by their own instruments, or get credit of carrying into effect the principles which they espouse. Middle-class ideas are committed to men of another class to work out, and their originators lose alike the honours and the discipline of a first-rate position. They do not see the bearings of particular views on the general world of thought — they are often insensible to the very existence of a general world of thought — and it is therefore next to impossible to go through to the bottom of a subject in arguing with them. It is necessary to begin by *teaching* them that the human mind has found it possible to run in other tracks besides the tramroad to which they are accustomed, and that a variety of considerations *must* be understood and respectfully entertained to which they are utter strangers. Culture is needed. The curate whose son is to be a curate after him, manages that he shall have it; and we must dismiss as unreasonable the notion that the son of the prosperous manufacturer or merchant, who is to tread in his father's steps, cannot have it. It is sufficient to say, that if society is reorganising itself on such a basis that a particular class is rapidly becoming sovereign, that class must succeed to the education as well as to the powers and the duties of those who held the sovereignty before it. . . . The beginnings must be slow; for it will not be till we see business-men who have themselves been at college sending their sons to tread in their own steps, that rapid advances can be hoped for.

The University of London was established as the means of supplying the highest culture to the middle-classes, and putting an end to the monopoly of university honours enjoyed by the Established Church. . . . It is probable that Oxford and Cambridge will continue to be hardly fitted for producing the class of educated men of business to whom we have referred, or for educating the Dissenting clergy. The *genius loci*, the social habits, the tone of society, the small ecclesiastical assumptions, which belong to them, are alien to the feelings of those of our middle class who have no wish to change their station or pursuits. The University of London was founded expressly for that class; and, with time and patience, we believe that they would largely avail themselves of it. Even now it is the university of the Dissenting clergy; and this alone shows that it is no failure. . . .

But let it be well understood that, whatever a degree implies, its possession ought to mark that the graduate is not self-educated or home-educated, and that the very office of a university is to encourage, to regulate, to distinguish, and to dignify, that training which colleges alone can supply. The liberal culture of an accomplished citizen is not that which the solitary student achieves for himself, or which the pet prodigy of the domestic system receives from the tutor or the parent. It is to be obtained by frequenting seats of learning in early manhood, and a degree in Arts is the recognised evidence that its possessor has done so. A university which neither teaches itself, nor has any organic connection with an educational system, ought to change its name. To promote and reward the formation, and regulate the aims, of academical institutions of the highest class, and to give the stamp of public honour to seats of learning, whatever their character, religious or secular, is the characteristic function of the University of London.

6.5   Universities of England — Oxford

From The Edinburgh Review, *Vol. 53, June 1831. The author, Sir William Hamilton, philosopher and metaphysician, and professor at Edinburgh, attacks Oxford primarily on the grounds of its administration and its system of Fellowships. (The article was still topical when reprinted in 1852.)*

This is the age of reform. Next in importance to our religious and political establishments, are the foundations for public education; and having now seriously engaged in a reform of 'the constitution, the envy of surrounding nations,' the time cannot be distant for a reform in the schools and universities which have hardly avoided their contempt. . . . The vices of the present system have been observed, and frequently discussed; but as it has never been shown in what manner these vices were generated, so it has never been perceived how easily their removal might be enforced. It is generally believed that, however imperfect in itself, the actual mechanism of education organized in these seminaries, is a time-honoured and essential part of their being, established upon statute, endowed by the national legislature with exclusive privileges, and inviolable as a vested right. We shall prove, on the contrary, that it is new as it is expedient — not only accidental to the University, but radically subversive of its constitution, —

without legal sanction, nay, in violation of positive law, — arrogating the privileges exclusively conceded to another system, which it has superseded, — and so far from being defensible by those it profits, as a right, that it is a flagrant usurpation obtained through perjury, and only tolerated from neglect.

Oxford and Cambridge, as establishments for education, consist of two parts, of the *Universities proper*, and of the *Colleges*. The former, original and essential, is founded, controlled, and privileged by public authority, for the advantage of the state. The latter, accessory and contingent, are created, regulated, and endowed by private munificence, for the interest of certain favoured individuals. Time was when the Colleges did not exist, and the University was there; and were the Colleges again abolished, the University would remain entire. The former founded solely for education, exists only as it accomplishes the end of its institution: the latter, founded principally for aliment and habitation, would still exist, were all education abandoned within their walls. The University, as a national establishment, is necessarily open to the lieges in general; the Colleges, as private institutions, might universally do as some have actually done — close their gates upon all, except their foundation members . . .

In the original constitution of Oxford, as in that of all the older universities of the Parisian model, the basis of instruction was not confided to a special body of privileged professors. The University was governed, the University was taught, by graduates at large. Professor, Master, Doctor, were originally synonymous. Every graduate had an equal right of teaching publicly in the University the subjects competent to his faculty, and to the rank of his degree. . . . With the qualities of this system, as organized in Oxford, we have at present no concern. We may, however, observe, that if not perfect, it was perfectible; and at the date of its establishment, there were few universities in Europe which could boast of an organization of its public instructors more complete, and none perhaps in which that organization was so easily susceptible of so high an improvement.

In the system *de facto* all is changed. The University is in abeyance. . . . In none of the faculties is it supposed that the professors any longer furnish the instruction necessary for a degree. Some chairs are even nominally extinct where an endowment has not perpetuated the sinecure; and the others betray, in general, their existence only through the Calendar. If the silence of the schools be occasionally broken by a formal lecture, or if on some popular subjects (fees being now permitted) a short course be usually delivered; attendance on these is not more required or expected, than attendance in the music-room. For every degree in every faculty above Bachelor of Arts, standing on the books is allowed to count for residence in the University, and attendance on the public courses; and though, under these circumstances, examinations be more imperatively necessary, a real examination only exists for the elementary degree, of which residence is also a condition.

It is thus not even pretended that Oxford now supplies more than the preliminary of an academical education. Even this is not afforded by the University, but abandoned to the Colleges and Halls; and the Academy of Oxford is therefore not one public University, but merely a collection of private schools. The University, in fact, exists only in semblance, for the behoof of the unauthorized seminars by which it has been replaced, and which have contrived, under covert of its name, to slip into possession of its public privileges.

But as academical education was usurped by the tutors from the professors — so all tutorial education was usurped by the *fellows* from the other graduates. The fellows exclusively teach all that Oxford now deems necessary to be taught; and as every tutor is singly vicarious of the whole ancient body of professors . . . the present capacity of the University to effect the purposes of its establishment must, consequently, be determined by the capacity of each fellow-tutor to compass the encyclopaedia of academical instruction. If Oxford accomplishes the objects of a University even in its lowest faculty, every fellow-tutor is a second 'Universal Doctor'. . . . But while thus resting her success on the *extraordinary* ability of her teachers, we shall see that she makes no provision even for their *ordinary* competence.

As the fellowships were not founded for the purposes of teaching, so the qualifications that constitute a fellow are not those that constitute an instructor. The Colleges owe their establishment to the capricious bounty of individuals, and the fellow rarely owes his eligibility to merit alone, but in the immense majority of cases to fortuitous circumstances. The fellowships in Oxford are, with few exceptions, limited to founder's kin — to founder's kin, born in particular counties, or educated at particular schools — to the scholars of certain schools, without restriction, or narrowed by some additional circumstances of age or locality of birth — to the natives of certain dioceses, archdeaconries, islands, counties, towns, parishes or manors, under every variety of arbitrary condition. In some cases, the candidate must be a graduate of a certain standing, in others he must not; in some he must be in orders, perhaps priest's, in others he is only bound to enter the church within a definite time. In some cases the fellow may freely choose his profession; in general he is limited to theology, and in a few instances must proceed in law or medicine. The nomination is sometimes committed to an individual, sometimes to a body of men, and those either within or without the College and University; but in general it belongs to the fellows. The elective power is rarely, however, deposited in worthy hands; and even when circumstances permit any liberty of choice, desert has too seldom a chance in competition with favour. With one unimportant exception, the fellowships are perpetual; but they are vacated by marriage, and by acceptance of a living in the church above a limited amount. They vary greatly in emolument in different Colleges; and in the same Colleges the difference is often considerable between those on different foundations, and on the same foundations between the senior and the junior fellowships. Some do not even afford the necessaries of life; others are more than competent to its superfluities. Residence is *now* universally dispensed with; though in some cases certain advantages are only to be enjoyed on the spot. In the church, the Colleges possess considerable patronage; the livings as they fall vacant are at the option of the fellows in the order of seniority; and the advantage of a fellowship depends often less on the amount of salary which it immediately affords, than on the value of the preferment to which it may ultimately lead.

But while, as a body, the fellows can thus hardly be supposed to rise above the average amount of intelligence and acquirement; so, of the fellows, it is not those best competent to its discharge who are generally found engaged in the business of tuition.

In the first place, there is no power of adequate selection, were there even sufficient materials from which to choose. The head, himself, of the same leaven with the fellows, cannot be presumed greatly to transcend their level; and he is peculiarly exposed to the influence of that party spirit by which collegial bodies are so frequently distracted. Were his approbation of tutors, therefore, free, we could have no security for the wisdom and impartiality of his choice. But in point of fact he can only legally refuse his sanction on the odious grounds of ignorance, vice or irreligion. The tutors are thus virtually self-appointed.

But in the second place, a fellow constitutes himself a tutor, not because he suits the office, but because the office is convenient to him. The standard of tutorial capacity and of tutorial performance is in Oxford too low to frighten even the diffident or lazy. The advantages of the situation in point either of profit or reputation, are not sufficient to tempt ambitious talent; and distinguished ability is sure soon to be withdrawn from the vocation — if marriage does not precipitate a retreat. The fellow who in general undertakes the office, and continues the longest to discharge it, is a clerical expectant whose hopes are bounded by a College living; and who, until the wheel of promotion has moved round, is content to relieve the tedium of a leisure life by the interest of an occupation and to improve his income by its emoluments. Thus it is that tuition is not solemnly engaged in as important, arduous, responsible, and permanent occupation; but lightly viewed and undertaken as a matter of convenience, a business by the by, a state of transition, a stepping-stone to something else.

But in the third place, were the tutors not the creatures of accident, did merit exclusively determine their appointment, and did the situation tempt the services of the highest talent, still it would be impossible to find a complement of able men equal in number to the cloud of tutors whom Oxford actually employs.

This general demonstration of what the fellow-tutors of Oxford must be, is more than confirmed by a view of what they actually are. It is not contended that the system excludes men of merit, but that merit is in general the accident, not the principle, of their appointment. We might, therefore, always expect, on the common doctrine of probabilities, that among the multitude of college tutors, there should be a few known to the world for ability and erudition. But we assert, without fear of contradiction, that, on the average, there is to be found among those to whom Oxford confides the business of education, an infinitely smaller proportion of men of literary reputation, than among the actual instructors of any other University in the world.

6.6   Queen's College, London

From Fraser's Magazine, *Vol. 40, July 1849. The writer explains the principles of this new experiment in higher education.*

True it is and undeniable, that better and cheaper means of education are required for this particular class of women than for others;
most true, that we are inundated with ill-educated, under-bred,
weak-minded, inefficient teachers, who take up the profession of
instruction merely because they can turn to nothing else for a
livelihood. . . .

It appears from Mr. Maurice's[1] introductory lecture that such
was in fact the object first contemplated in founding the Queen's
College . . . [But] to educate a separate class of women as teachers
of other women is a mistake, and could not succeed . . . [and] Mr.
Maurice points out the reasons which induced the founders of
Queen's College to depart from their original plan, and to take up
the cause of female education in a far larger and more generous
spirit.

Before entering on some details respecting the working and progress of Queen's College . . . we are inclined to look back for a
moment to the means which, up to this time, have met the demand
for the better education of women of all classes. We no longer hear
that demand responded to by vulgar sneers about 'making pies
and puddings', and wifely cares and nursery duties . . . as if there
were not thousands and thousands of women in the world who,
alas for them, have no pies or puddings to make or eat, no
husbands to obey or to love, no children to nurse! As if it had not
become most necessary to educate a woman so that she may be
strengthened not only to exercise these blessings and duties, but,
what is far more difficult to the womanly nature, to exist without
them! Still there are objects and objections to the idea of female
colleges; objections no longer, perhaps, taking the form of grave
treatises or cruel sneers, but of elegant poetical satire and gay
complimentary allusion to the number of distinguished, highly-
endowed women, who now adorn society. 'Educate the women!'
exclaimed an accomplished and excellent man in our hearing, and,
with marked surprise; — 'Where is the necessity? A college for
ladies! nonsense! women are admirably educated. I see none but
well-educated women around me!' in the tone of a man who, when
told of those who hunger for bread, should reply, 'What bread!
nonsense! Hunger! there is no such thing! I see a good dinner
before me every day!' . . . Happy man! representing a large and
influential class, whose notions so formed are intelligible, and
whose prejudices so accounted for are pardonable; who know not
that, beyond the refined and cultivated circle with which they are
conversant, are found, not only the women who toil in fields, and

the women who labour at the washtub, and the women whose very existence it is a part of the law of elegant social life to ignore altogether; but also . . . who are seeking in vain for the means of feeding the soul, hungry and thirsty after intellectual food, — whose worst want is not the want of bread, but of a sphere of usefulness proportioned to their energy of spirit and their warm and ready sympathies, — asking where they may learn, not only the best means of teaching and controlling others, but the best means of informing and occupying, controlling and managing, their own active minds and wandering affections . . .

When men refer, some with pride and some with wonder, to the great number of women now distinguished for their attainments, they forget that such women either belong to the highest classes, or are the *self-educated* women of the class immediately below them. In these days, when the principles of a sound physical and mental education are beginning to be understood, though they are far from being generally diffused and acted on, the young women of our aristocracy reap many of the benefits of such better knowledge . . .

And yet, with all these advantages, there are certain grave disadvantages to be taken into account. We should say, that in the young women of this class education is too exclusive, too anxiously overdone. . . . We create an artificial atmosphere round them: they are treated as if the common knowledge and experience of our humanity were too coarse for them, as if they were 'too bright and good for human nature's daily food'. A young girl of high rank is acquainted with but two orders of society, — her own, and the poorest, lowest of all, on whom she is taught to expend her charity and to employ her beneficence. . . . If we were a duchess . . . we should gladly seize the opportunity of sending a daughter for a few hours once or twice a week to such an institution as Queen's College. But for certain prejudices, and scruples, and fears, — the greatest fear being the fear of ridicule, — we believe many mothers of high rank would gladly do so . . .

Having seen what a careful and expensive education can do for women, let us see the next best thing, — what they can do for themselves. . . . We know instances of self-educated women who are admirable, charming; who are distinguished for the extent of their reading and their acquirements of all kinds, but who cannot apply their powers and accomplishments to any specific objects in actual life: for instance, they make very inefficient teachers, whether as mothers or governesses. For such women the attendance on the classes at Queen's College, — taught by eminent men whose minds have gone through a course of training obliging them to reconsider and rearrange the knowledge they have acquired in a desultory and disjointed manner, — is especially useful.

From the women who by their position can command every means of improvement, and those who, through original power and resolute will, surmount the narrow limits of circumstance, turn we to the daughters of merchants, manufacturers, and professional men, those who form the upper and lower middle classes, — in this country how large and how important a part of our community! In these classes parents who can afford it have governesses, resident or daily teachers; where the family is large this is considered the cheapest and best expedient. Where the parents live in towns, or where from domestic circumstances a governess cannot be employed, the next expedient is a boarding school . . .

It was to meet the wants of this large class that the plan of the college in Harley Street was altered and enlarged.

Note

1. *Mr. Maurice's introductory lecture*: F. D. Maurice (1805 – 72), founder and principal of the Working Men's College, helped to found Queen's College. The staff of the college included such notables as Charles Kingsley (English Literature), T. H. Hall (Mathematics) and Sterndale Bennett (Harmony).

6.7   Technical education a national want

From Macmillan's Magazine, *Vol. 18, April 1868. The years following the Great Exhibition of 1851 saw rapid technological advances throughout Europe: J. Scott Russell (1808 – 82), engineer and naval architect, warns that English supremacy in the field is threatened.*

Technical education is for the English people almost a new question; education of any kind can hardly be called their *forte*. . . . [I]t is beginning to be felt vaguely, rather as an apprehension than a conviction, that a Government may have some sort of moral if not political responsibility for the intellectual and technical condition in which it keeps the people it governs, or in which it leaves them when it ceases to govern . . .

Many causes, political and other, have served to raise these questions in public interest; but mainly the Universal Exhibition at Paris has served to give them definite form and expression . . .

Extraordinary pains have moreover been taken, on this occasion, to gather the lesson and moral of the Exhibition for the benefit of the British people. . . . A second series of reports, of a . . . more strictly technical nature, was elicited by the Commissioners of Schools, who had ascertained that many of the reports on the French Exhibition appeared to throw the blame of certain cases of inferiority on the lower technical education of the British people, and the Commission issued a series of inquiries of which they then published the report . . .

Taking up first the 'Report relative to Technical Education by the School Inquiry Commission of 2nd July, 1867', we find the Commissioners issuing a request for information to some eminent jurors and others and the truth of certain 'evidence considered to be afforded by the International Exhibition at Paris, of the inferior rate of progress in manufacturing and mechanical industry in England compared with that made in other European countries'; and they add, 'it has been stated to us that this alleged inferiority is due in a great measure to the want of technical education'. . . .

Dr Lyon Playfair[1] gives as the result of his own inquiry as a juror, and of those of other jurors, 'A singular accordance of opinion prevailed that our country had shown little inventiveness, and made little progress in the peaceful arts of industry, since 1862. Out of ninety classes there are scarely a dozen in which a preeminence is unhesitatingly awarded to us. The one cause upon which there was most unanimity of conviction is that France, Prussia, Austria, Belgium, and Switzerland possess good systems of industrial education for the masters and managers of manufactories and workshops, and that England possesses none'.

Professor Tyndall says — 'I have long entertained the opinion that, in virtue of the better education provided by Continental nations, England must one day, and that no distant one, find herself outstripped by those nations, both in the arts of peace and war.'

Mr Huth writes '. . . I found that it is the want of industrial education in this country which prevents our manufacturers from making the progress which other nations are making. I found both masters and foremen of other countries much more scientifically educated than our own. The workmen of other countries have a far superior education to ours, many of whom have none whatever. Their productions show clearly that there is not a machine working a machine, but that brains sit at the loom, and intelligence stands at the spinning-wheel.'

Mr M'Connell says — 'In the class for which I was juror for England I made a very careful examination and comparison of our locomotive engines, carriages, railway machinery, apparatus, and materials, with those exhibited by France, Germany, and Belgium. I am firmly convinced that our former superiority, either in material or workmanship, no longer exists. Unless we adopt a system of technical education for our workmen in this country, we shall soon not even hold our own in cheapness. It appears to me Government should take the matter in hand. There should be mining schools in South Wales, Staffordshire, and Durham; and machinery and engine schools in Manchester, Glasgow, &c.' . . .

Mr Mundella — '. . . Some of the sons of our poorest workmen in Saxony are receiving a technical education at the Polytechnic schools such as the sons of our manufacturers cannot hope to obtain. I am of opinion that the English workman is gradually losing the race, through the superior intelligence which foreign Governments are carefully developing in their artisans. The education of Germany is the result of a national organization which compels every parent to send his children to school, and afterwards affords the opportunity of acquiring such technical knowledge as may be useful in the department of industry to which they are destined' . . .

What do our technical workers think of their own skill, intelligence, taste, judgment, knowledge, culture, refinement? What do they think of their education, of their school-training, and apprenticeship? What do they think of the opportunities provided for the matured workman who wishes to study, to copy, to increase his stores of science, and rise to higher grades of skill? What do they think are the duties of Government to him and his fellows? Do they think foreign Governments wiser in their care for their working people than ours? Do they think the systematic education of their people to be waste of pains or wise foresight? In short, do they find in the institutions of any other country any social amelioration which they would wish to introduce into our own?

On all these points, and a great many more, we have the evidence of eighty-eight witnesses, all workmen, most of them, evidently, superior workmen, and who are entitled by their acquirements to be termed at least self-educated men. . . .

Mr Lucraft, the chairmaker, says — 'Seeing some lads at work with the men in the carvers' shop, I went to the bench of one about fourteen. He was carving a chairback of a medieval form, from a working drawing. I expressed my surprise that one so young was found capable of carving so well, and was informed that boys at school are specially prepared for the trade they fancy: so that a boy about to be apprenticed to learn carving is instructed in ornamental drawing, modelling, and designing.' 'Further I am bound to repeat that in the race we are nowhere. Without the least doubt or hesitation, yet with the most profound regret, I say that our defeat is as ignominious, and I fear as disastrous, as it is possible to conceive. We have not only made no progress since 1862, but it seems to me we have retrograded. . . . The fault is less our own than our rulers', who have denied us education, or who have at least given us nothing to fit us for our destination in life, but have left us groping in the dark, for ever feebly attempting to overtake lost opportunities. . . . We have been groping our way in ignorant and bigoted security, and quarrelling in which way education should be given, or denying it altogether, while other nations have been getting before us . . .'

Mr Winstanley says — 'I should like to see a number of institutions.— they might be called colleges, or any other name. I would have them fitted up with a number of workshops for different trades, and one large room, to be used as a lecture-room, and for periodical exhibitions. I would have lectures delivered twice a week by the best professors upon different branches of art-manufactures. There should be a well-stocked library and reading-room, all on art-manufacture. There should be schools attached for drawing and modelling. Why I propose workshops is, because working men in large towns have a great difficulty in finding convenience to do anything for themselves by way of improvement . . .'

Mr Whiteing, in his special report, says on this subject — 'The notion of the functions of Government entertained in this country would not be tolerated for a moment across the Channel, and it may be doubted whether our dislike to what is called special legislation — to legislation, that is to say, which proposes as a direct aim the improvement of the social condition of our people — has not its weak as well as its strong side. . . . The Technical education of French workmen is of two kinds — elementary and advanced. In the first, the child, having been early destined to a particular trade, is placed in an institution, where he serves a kind of preliminary apprenticeship to that trade, and where primary instruction goes hand in hand with the special training requisite to give him a more enlarged knowledge of his business. . . . Humboldt, many years ago, foresaw . . . 'That the time was not far distant when science and manipulative skill must be wedded together; that national wealth, and the increasing prosperity of nations, must be based on an enlightened employment of natural products and forces'. . . . Peel saw this, and uttered the memorable words: 'If we are inferior in skill, knowledge, and intelligence to the manufacturers of other countries the increased facilities of intercourse will result in transferring the demand from us to others.' And England's noblest Prince foresaw in International Exhibitions (which he was the first to inaugurate) the coming activity in things industrial, and, in order to provide for the coming competition, he inaugurated ere his lamented death a system of industrial education . . .

In conclusion, we will state our deep conviction, that the working men of England expect and demand of their Government the design, organization, and execution of systematic technical education; and there is urgent need for it to bestir itself, for other nations have already five-and-twenty years start of us, and have produced one or two generations of educated workmen. . . . To-morrow, then, let us undertake with all energy our neglected task: the urgency is twofold — one half of our youth, let us say, has received elementary but no technical education: for that half let us at once organize technical schools in every small town, technical colleges in every large town, and a technical university in the metropolis. The other half of the rising generation has received no education at all, and for them let us at once organize elementary education, even if compulsory.

Note

1. *Dr. Lyon Playfair*: Chemist, MP, administrator. See 'Report on the Civil Service' in *Politics and Administration*, evidence submitted to the Playfair Report, 1875.

7

Leisure and the Arts

Victorian leisure, represented as the grim 'Victorian Sunday' of countless reminiscences, autobiographies and novels, has become a by-word for the negative side of Victorianism. Thoughtful contemporary commentators took the joyless Sunday as an image of a sick society so obsessed with materialism and its short-term rewards that it was oblivious of the true objects of life — 'happiness, refinement, education, health, civilisation itself'. By 1834 the forty holidays held to honour the saints had all been abolished, and the number of statutory holidays reduced to four; and it remained at that number after the Bank Holidays Act of 1871 until the re-institution of May Day in 1977, to honour organised labour.

And yet in spite of this unpromising context the arts prospered. Pre-eminent among literary forms in the period is, of course, the novel: the story of its progress — from its largely apologetic and defensive beginnings before 1840, to its establishment as the most serious and significant of all art forms, the organ of advanced thinking fifty years later — is one of the most interesting evolutionary processes of the period. And its intellectual prestige came late and via a chequered career: even at the end of the century it was still open to the disparagement of critics who saw it as 'the diversion of an idle hour' rather than as 'the vehicle of all thought for which a large audience is required' (*Contemporary Review*). 'The novel will never be able to assume a position of equal importance with the drama', however, declared a critic in 1874 (referring, perhaps, only to the structure of the two forms).

The theatre was still barely recovering from the depths to which it had sunk in the pre-Victorian years, and its real renaissance belongs to the 1880s and the names of H. A. Jones, A. W. Pinero, and the arrival of Ibsenism, and then Bernard Shaw. For most of the mid-Victorian period the theatre, only recently released from the Licensing Act (1843), which broke the monopoly held for a century by Covent Garden and Drury Lane, was not frequented by polite society: it offered only scenic spectacle and 'all the crimes that make life hideous — robbery, murder, suicide', to which 'the lower order rush in mobs, and in shirt-sleeves' (William Eddie, *The Theatre: Its Pernicious Tendency*, 1853). Gone even were the days of the great actor-managers, for whom the play was of scant importance next to the central part it offered to them.

English art, however, was in a very notable stage of its development. In 1843 the young John Ruskin, scarcely more than an undergraduate, had published the first volume of *Modern Painters*, a passionate defence of Turner which did much to bring the public to a sympathetic understanding of the elderly landscape painter. Then at the end of the decade he made the acquaintance of a group who, for some years, called themselves the Pre-Raphaelite Brotherhood, whose theories of painting revolutionalised and dominated art for the rest of the century. The Brotherhood (a very literary movement) had split up by 1855, but the individual members — the painters Rossetti, Holman Hunt, Millais and Collinson — pursued their separate, and very different, careers with great success. Meanwhile their early popularity was assured when Ruskin espoused their cause, and in 1851 wrote a notable series of letters to *The Times*, influential pamphlets, and then his annual *Academy Notes* (1855–9). The individual members of the Brotherhood had secured a redoubtable champion, and they and their successors were the unquestioned arbiters of English art from then on.

It seemed to some that the whole calling of the artist was threatened when in 1839 came the invention of photography, 'Art's youngest and fairest child' (*Photographic News*, 1857), discovered almost simultaneously by Daguerre in Paris and Henry Fox Talbot at Lacock, Wiltshire. The potentialities of this newest piece of technology were quickly recognised, and the photographer soon threatened to supplant at least the portrait painter. Among amateurs, photography became the hobby of millions, probably the most famous of whom is Lewis Carroll, whose enthusiasm was almost obsessive.

7.1   Sundays and festivals

From a lecture delivered by Frederic Harrison (1831 – 1923), a well-known Positivist, in 1867. The writer denounces 'public opinion' and the 'work ethic', and urges the English to learn the art of relaxation from their own past, and from their neighbours in Europe.

At no date in English history, in no country throughout Europe, perhaps at no age in the annals of mankind, has the spirit of national holidays presented an aspect less impressive than they do now with us. In other ages of our history, in other countries now, the observance of the great public festivals, national or religious, enters largely into the life of the nation, forms no mean part of the people's happiness, purifies and harmonizes men's daily mode of life, diffuses a sense of common enjoyment and social unity, fills the most thoughtless with some dim sentiment of the ideal and the venerable. We may scan the various peoples of the Continent, the successive pages of history, and everywhere we find the public festivals forming bright tranquil islands amidst the troubled sea of their existence, we see the people always at their best in these festivals; then if at no other moment discords abate, or if they are not entirely abated, certainly their festivals themselves cause no fresh ground of discord; on the contrary, in every country and age the churches or religious bodies, where any such have power, and, whether they have power or not, everywhere the whole social forces combine to give these festivals a character and a system of their own, to make them at once dear and beneficient to the people; make them, and make them felt, to be great engines of civilisation which every order of men alike may love, promote, and sustain.

Dare any man say this of England of to-day? Holidays and Sundays we have, but how unlike this picture! The few and rare secular festivals of the year come round, and what are they but breathing moments between days of exhaustion? How dreary, joyless, stiff they are for the most part. Past almost before we know they are come, past whilst we are thinking how to use them, past in spasmodic efforts to enjoy them, or in the aimless sauntering of lassitude. How little of art, cultivation, morality and intellect surrounds them. How little of public celebration, of social movement within them. How little are we then like a nation whose soul rejoices naturally and rationally. They come when we are too much exhausted to rise up to them, too rarely for us to know how best to use them, with too little public organisation and form to give them a national shape and meaning . . .

A barbaric potentate may call on his slaves to fall down and worship at the sound of the sackbut or dulcimer, but neither governments nor churches can make national festivals by edict. We ask them not to make fresh regulations, but to leave us free; yet, if authorities can do so little by force, combined public opinion and its recognised guides can do everything in this matter. To make holiday, a people must be free — but they must use freedom freely to combine. However much we are disposed to repudiate official interference, however much we are disposed to leave to individual liberty, a public festival is something which involves social co-operation as its essence. A man may take his rest by himself as a weary animal may lie down to sleep. But no man can keep a festival, no man can make public holiday by himself. It is a contradiction in terms. Nor can a multitude together do this without more. They must be actuated by a common spirit. It must be something instinctive and habitual. It is like language — something essentially social. Mere individualism in will and thought is its death. Like language itself, no holiday or festival time in the world can be joyous, or elevating, or harmonious, unless it grows out of the harmony of great common purposes and sympathies. . . . Men fail to smile happily when they are burdened with care and doubt, and so too do nations.

Let us turn to the example of foreign countries. Far be it from me to defend or approve everything which is done abroad in this matter. Folly, vice, and idleness are plants which thrive in very various soils. But, take them as a whole, I will maintain, in spite of all that is said, that the Sundays and the Holidays of Foreign nations make an Englishman blush for his own land. In the first place the religious origin and character of these festivals has more of good and less of evil in it than it has with us. Enough of that religious origin and character survives to make these festivals far more frequent, more respected, more universal and social than they are with us. That religious influence has never been distorted so as to make them hypocritical forms and soul-depressing engines of bigotry. These festivals still do much to cheer and beautify the life of the labourer. They are so observed as to give him all possible means of rational enjoyment, they still offer him the boon of some artistic education, or of some public display or time-honored

custom. The State, where it interferes at all, does what it can to
make these occasion minister to the happiness and improvement of
the people. Society combines to make them real national holidays,
the bright spots in the poor man's life.

I recall to mind a Sunday in a rural village in France, such as I
have often witnessed. Early betimes there is the Church Service,
low mass and high mass, chants and benedictions, and all that
appertains to the rites of their belief, — a service perhaps not very
rational and not very practical — but still it is a Church Service,
with no high-backed pews, with no grades and places for each rank
and class, and especially a church with no Squire, — a service
which they seem to care as much for as people in this country care
for Church Services, and which I believe does them just as much
good as Church Services do here. And let me say once for all, far
be it from me to decry the sincere practice of any faith, or withhold
respect and goodwill from any man who holds honestly to the creed
that he has lived by, be he Protestant or Catholic, Churchman or
Dissenter, Mohammedan or Hebrew, so that he keep charity and
earnestness and sympathy within his heart. Far be it from me to
suggest that men are approaching civilisation as they are quitting
religion. On the contrary I hold that festivals are better observed
on the Continent, mainly because the better influences of religion
survive there most. I believe in a word that there is more real
religious observance and that of a higher kind throughout the body
of the people amongst those nations who keep the Sabbath holy in
the spirit of joyfulness, than with those who keep it in the spirit of
gloom.

These French villagers, of whom I was speaking, will in the forenoon attend their churches just as much and more than our own.
Thenceforward it is a day of festival. In their own humble way it is
a day for domestic gathering and social relaxation. Those families
that can will manage to meet and are not afraid of any mode of
natural exhilaration; a rude attempt at a piece of acting or recita-
tion, a dance or a song, or, it may be, a homely game of active
sport. . . . It recalls what once was common here till the Demon of
Overwork and of pharisaical religion almost drove it from our
country, — though not I trust for ever.

Turn even to the French capital, about which such dreadful
things are reported. Far be it from me to justify all that goes on
there whether on week days or Sundays, on holidays or on working
days, but there is much even there that we might imitate with
profit. In the forenoon there is just as much church going as there

is in London, and I have no doubt to quite as much profit. But beyond this the day is one of public recognised holiday. All the museums, public galleries, exhibitions of all kinds are open and are filled. The galleries of the Louvre, that vast and marvellous collection of pictures, statues, drawings, and works of art, an entire art education in itself, is crowded from morning till night. . . . Or it may be there is a review of a regatta on the Seine, or a fête in one of the suburbs or neighbouring parks, and the military bands are all playing in the public grounds, the concert rooms are all open and all filled, and, horror of horrors, the theatres are crowded to the ceiling, some of them not very desirable on any day, though I never knew that they were worse on Sundays than on any other day. Here again, I am far from saying that it is a very high type of public holiday, but at least it is a scene of quiet relaxation without the sottishness, vulgarity, and vacancy which we know so well, and whatever the State does in it at all, it does what it can to minister that which shall give a rational and elevating shape to the enjoyment of the day, and does not, as with us, do nothing except rigidly withold it . . .

But there was a state of society, remote indeed from ours, but peaceful and civilised and Christian, like ours. In the great days of the middle ages — great with all their faults — the Church ordered the holidays and festivals of men. In no spirit of bigotry, in no sectarian, in no class spirit. The public holidays were days of public recreation. They were the days of public education. The churches were not mere places of worship, and the clergy were not mere priests. The church or cathedral itself was a museum of art. It supplied the music, the painting, the sculpture, the drama of the people. The priesthood were the moralists, the men of science, the schoolmasters, the artists, the poets of the people. The saints' days and festivals were not mere days of idleness; they had their national character, their artistic, their dramatic, their social character as well. They were days on which men rested from their work, but rested only to cultivate the tastes which gild and chasten life, to revive the memory of great deeds and great men, to recognise the majesty of social harmony.

Here, then, whether we turn to foreign lands at the present day, or to distant ages of history, we see that there is a something about these festivals with which we have little to compare. Those days of old are gone, never to return; those habits of foreign nations are not our habits. We cannot imitate the customs of other days and other climates; but why have we not the same spirit in our own way? In all these pictures there is a common notion. In all the holiday means a national celebration, the cultivation of the beautiful, some dramatic representation of the public activity. Why have we lost or forgotten the very idea of a holiday in this sense? Is it certain that we do not need it; that we have no need to rejoice together as a people; no need to cultivate the beautiful and the grand; no need of anything that we cannot get with our own selves or at our own homes? We have as much need of it as men ever had, but it will not come because we need it.

Is not one cause of this the grinding, pitiless, endless overwork which oppresses our nation like a spell? What malignant power has condemned us all to toil in the same treadmill of labour from the cradle to the grave? What is the use of being rich, of being strong, of being ingenious, unless we have leisure to know what life is? Life is the activity of the human powers as a whole; our powers of enjoyment, of sympathy, of benevolence, of art and poetry, our powers of veneration and emotion. Why are these for ever crushed by infinite toil, beating always fiercely, yet drearily, like the cranks of some vast machine? We hear continually, not from the poor and the miserable alone, but from the well-to-do, the rich, and the cultivated, a cry rising up from amongst them like that weird burden of the poet's song, — 'Work, work, work!'. We all work too much; too many days, too many hours each day, too hard each hour. As the Roman said, for the sake of a livelihood we are throwing away the very objects of life. We sacrifice at once the future, the past and the present; happiness, refinement, education, health, civilization itself. There never was a period of the world's history — there is no country in the world now — where the rests are so few, and the toil so severe, as here in England of this nineteenth century. Merry England, too, this was once, when work was relieved by its due rest, and rest was ennobled by social celebrations and by cultivated enjoyments, before our holidays became too few to be of use; too narrow and flat to stimulate the sympathies and the imagination. When holidays were constant and truly national, Englishmen were famous for the love of public merry-makings, for public contests in feats of skill and strength, when the yeomen met to practise the bow, and the young to dance round the maypole; the mysteries and miracle plays, and allegories and processions delighted the public eye, and poetry, and songs, and tales. When labour, by common consent, is reduced, we shall produce much less, and shall be much more careful what we produce, and what we do with our productions. Till then we may

look in vain for real holiday enjoyments any more than we expect
them from the overdriven beast in his stall.

7.2   Pictures and picture-criticism

From The National Review, *Vol. 3, 1856. The author, probably George
Richmond (1809–96), the popular portrait painter, reflects with satisfaction on the current state of English art.*

It is true that all evil has its counterpoise. As thunderstorms clear
the air, and wars quicken the stagnation and rub off the rust of
peace, so the present strife in art has its hopefulness as a sign, and
its usefulness as an agent. It shows that there is life both in our
painters and our critics of painting, and it quickens for work the
pencils of the one and the pens of the other. We never remember a
time in which painters of established reputation strove more
energetically to justify their fame, in which aspirants for distinction in painting laboured more studiously to win it, or in which
worthy efforts in art were more worthily estimated — of course,
out of the daily newspapers. But among the innovators whose work
has awakened the present strife, the critic preceded the craftsman.
Mr. Ruskin's pen was Pre-Raphaelite before the pencils of
Rossetti, Hunt, and Millais. These young men invented the
name; but Mr. Ruskin might have been their guide to the aims it
symbolises, their encourager to the effort it describes. . . .

We have no means of knowing how far the early practice of
these remarkable young painters was prompted by Mr. Ruskin's
first volume. . . . In it he tells our young artists that 'they should
go to nature in all singleness of heart, and walk with her
laboriously and trustingly, having no other thought but how best
to penetrate her meaning; rejecting nothing, selecting nothing,
and scorning nothing'.

Now Mr. Ruskin assuredly was not the first teacher of art who
had sent the young artist 'to nature'. That had been the universal
direction of all the lecturers on painting since the foundation of the
Academy. But the direction in their mouths had been coupled with
stringent cautions. To 'select nothing' was the very last precept
that would have been ventured on from an academic chair. When

the academic professor sent his students to nature, he took care to insist on their first coming to him for spectacles through which to look at her. Selection and combination were urged to the full as much as study of nature. And if the student of our own day, when told to 'study nature', turned from the precepts of his teacher to his practice, he found himself in presence of a huge contradiction. Constable stood alone in the Academy as the sturdy champion of English landscape — neither gilt by the sun of Claude nor embrowned by the twilight of Gaspar Poussin;[1] and Constable's pictures hung unsold on the walls of his painting-room. Turner was beyond students' comprehension: the reverent wondered, the irreverent scoffed, before his mysterious canvases. Wilson[2] was more Italian than English; Gainsborough was English all over; but both were of the past; and the student, at the outset of his career, is always mainly amenable to contemporary influences.

Mr. Ruskin was the first authoritative writer on art who sent the student to the teaching of nature — *pure et simple.* . . .

One great contrast between Academy-lectures and Mr. Ruskin's books could not fail to strike the thoughtful student. His professor talked to him about art, its great masters, their works, and the laws of their working; Mr. Ruskin about nature, its mighty manifestations, their modes, and the causes of them. The former sent him to the gallery and painting-room; the other to the plains, the mountains, the forests, and the sea. The art of the one seemed to divide dominion with nature; the art of the other was sternly called to account as nature's servant and sworn interpreter. In proportion as God's work is vaster and grander than man's, it exercises at once repulsion and attraction on those within the sphere of its influence. It repels by manysidedness and mystery: it attracts by grandeur and completeness. Whatever introduces law into its mighty maze, and furnishes a clue to its inner meaning, increases this attractive power, and diminishes that repulsive force. Mr. Ruskin has, for some fourteen years past, aimed at this with a zeal that has been vouchsafed to few, a knowledge rarely equalled, an eloquence seldom surpassed, and an industry that has never faltered. He has shown the soul underlying the ribs of death in the laws that regulate the delicate curvatures of the primal granite, the great heart that pulses in the ebbing and flowing of the sea, the love that clothes the meadows with delight, the unity that gives beauty to man and beast, to forest tree and wayside weed. In one word, he has preached God in the physical world, and proclaimed, with a voice of power, that all which we worship in art and love in nature is typical of God's attributes — His infinity, His comprehensiveness, His permanence, justice, energy, and law.

It is either wonder or pity that such a gospel has found believers — urged as it has been with all the authoritative force of conviction, and all the seductive graces of style — contrasted, moreover, with such chaff and husks as academics have ever set before their learners? Is it any wonder if these disciples have been among the most capable and thoughtful of those who listened to the preacher? But Mr. Ruskin's teaching is pre-eminently the teaching of scholars. His art-criticism — in so far as it deals with particular schools, masters, and pictures — is the least part of it. His power has been that of a guide to nature. Once introduced to that school — with such a key to the language of its text-books and such discipline of mind and eye as his writings can give — Mr. Ruskin hands over the student to the great volume of the outward world, and bids him read reverently therein, and copy faithfully and submissively from the living emblazonments of its fair and various pages.

Notes

1. *Claude . . . Gaspar Poussin:* Seventeenth-century French landscape painters. Gaspard Duget adopted the name of his more famous brother-in-law and teacher, Nicolas Poussin.
2. *Wilson:* Richard Wilson (1713–82), Welsh landscape painter who paved the way for Constable and Turner. He was more Welsh than either English or Italian.

7.3 A petition to novel-writers

From Wilkie Collins, My Miscellanies, *1863. The writer, an immensely popular novelist himself, is commenting ironically on what he sees as the double standards of the reading public.*

I hope nobody will be alarmed if I confess that I am about to disclose the existence of a Disreputable Society, in one of the most respectable counties in England. I dare not be more particular as to the locality, and I cannot possibly mention the members by name. But I have no objection to admit that I am perpetual Secretary, that my wife is President, that my daughters are Council, and that my nieces form the Society. Our object is to waste our time, misemploy our intellects, and ruin our morals — or, in other words, to enjoy the prohibited luxury of novel-reading.

It is a settled opinion of mine that the dull people in this country, are the people who, privately as well as publicly, govern the nation. By dull people, I mean people of all degrees of rank and education, who never want to be amused. I don't know how long it is since these dreary members of the population first hit on the cunning idea of calling themselves Respectable; but I do know that, ever since that time, this great nation has been afraid of them — afraid in religious, in political, and in social matters. . . .

The dull people decided years and years ago, as every one knows, that novel-writing was the lowest species of literary exertion, and that novel-reading was a dangerous luxury and an utter waste of time. They gave, and still give, reasons for this opinion, which are very satisfactory to persons born without Fancy or Imagination, and which are utterly inconclusive to everyone else. But, with reason or without it, the dull people have succeeded in affixing to our novels the stigma of being a species of contra-band goods. Look, for example, at the Prospectus of any librarian. The principal part of his trade of book-lending consists in the dis-tributing of novels; and he is uniformly ashamed to own that simple fact. Sometimes, he is afraid to print the word Novel at all in his lists, and smuggles in his contraband fiction under the head of Miscellaneous Literature. Sometimes, after freely offering all histories, all biographies, all voyages, all travels, he owns self-reproachfully to the fact of having novels too, but deprecatingly adds — Only the best! As if no other branch of the great tree of literature ever produced tasteless and worthless fruit! In all cases, he puts novels last on his public list of the books he distributes, though they stand first on his private list of the books he gains by. Why is he guilty of all these sins against candour? Because he is afraid of the dull people.

Look again — and this brings me to the subject of these lines — at our Book Clubs. How paramount are the dull people there! How they hug to their rigid bosoms Voyages and Travels! How they turn their intolerant backs on novels! How resolutely they get together, in a packed body, on the committee, and impose their joyless laws on the yielding victims of the club, who secretly want to be amused! Our book club was an example of the unresisted despotism of their rule. We began with a law that novels should be occasionally admitted; and the dull people abrogated it before we had been in existence a twelvemonth. I smuggled in the last morsel of fiction that our starving stomachs were allowed to consume, and produced a hurricane of virtuous indignation at the next meeting of the committee.

All the dull people of both sexes attended that meeting. One dull gentleman said the author was a pantheist, and quoted some florid ecstacies on the subject of scenery and flowers in support of the opinion. Nobody seemed to know exactly what a pantheist was, but everybody cried 'hear, hear,' — which did just as well for the purpose. Another dull gentleman said the book was painful because there was a death-bed scene in it. A third reviled it for morbid revelling in the subject of crime, because a shot from the pistol of a handsome highwayman dispatched the villain of the story. But the great effect of the day was produced by a lady, the mother of a large family which began with a daughter of eighteen years, and ended with a boy of eight months. This lady's objection affected the heroine of the novel, — a respectable married woman, perpetually plunged in virtuous suffering, but an improper character for young persons to read about, because the poor thing had two accouchements — only two! — in the course of three volumes. 'How can I suffer my daughters to read such a book as that?' cried our prolific subscriber indignantly. A tumult of applause followed. A chorus of speeches succeeded, full of fierce references to 'our national morality' and 'the purity of our hearths and homes'. A resolution was passed excluding all novels for the future; and then, at last, the dull people held their tongues, and sat down with a thump in their chairs, and glared contentedly on each other in stolid controversial triumph.

From that time forth (histories and biographies being comparatively scarce articles), we were fed by the dull people on nothing but Voyages and Travels. Every man (or woman) who had voyaged and travelled to no purpose, who had made no striking observations of any kind, who had nothing whatever to say, and who said it at great length in large type on thick paper, with accompaniment of frowsy lithographic illustrations, was introduced weekly to our hearths and homes as the most valuable guide, philosopher, and friend whom our rulers could possibly send us. All the subscribers submitted; all partook the national dread of the dull people, with the exception of myself and the members of my family enumerated at the beginning of these pages. We resolutely abandoned the club; got a box-full of novels for ourselves, once a month, from London; lost caste with our respectable friends in consequence; and became, for the future, throughout the length and breadth of our neighbourhood, the Disreputable Society to which I have already alluded. If the dull people of our district were told to-morrow that my wife, daughters, and nieces had all eloped in different directions, leaving just one point of the compass open as a runaway outlet for me and the cook, I feel firmly persuaded that not one of them would be inclined to discredit the report. 'This is what comes of novel-reading!' they would say — and would return, with renewed zest, to their Voyages and Travels, their accouchements in real life, their canting 'national morality', and their blustering 'purity of our hearths and homes'.

7.4   A word about our theatres

From Theodore Martin, Essays on the Drama *(1874, privately printed). The writer gives a gloomy view of the state of contemporary theatre.*

Time was when the visitor to town was pretty sure, if his evening hung heavily on his hands, that he had but to go to the Haymarket, or one or other of the great theatres, to have his *ennui* dispelled. We will not speak of the great artists who were there to minister to his delight. Time has done its work with them, and if they have left no successors, we must be content to wait until a fresh constellation of actors equally gifted shall appear. Grant genius comes in no regular succession. We may lament its absence; to complain of it would be absurd. But it was not only the presence of unquestionable genius which in those days illuminated our theatres. They were under the guidance of men who had a pride in the national drama, and upheld it with a vigorous hand. The actors might not all be good, but they all looked up to certain standards in their art, and worked to the full measure of their ability, to make the representation as complete as possible. . . . A London audience in those days was not to be trifled with. Forward incapacity found no mercy at the hands of the pit. Pretentious weakness was certain of detection. Actors and audience thus acted and reacted upon each other. A high standard of aspiration in the one, and of judgment in the other, produced the finest development of histrionic art which England has ever seen . . .

How entirely we have lost this is but too well known. . . . The present degradation of our theatres, like all great changes, is owing doubtless to a variety of concurrent circumstances. . . . The altered habits of society, the increase of cheap books, the late hours of dining, the great distances from the theatres to which it is now the fashion for all classes to remove, have all combined in some measure towards the same result. Not a little, too, of the change may be owing to the tendency to individual and domestic isolation, which is one of the least healthy of our social symptoms. All these causes, by withdrawing from our theatres the better part of the audience, and leaving them almost exclusively to the idle and the frivolous, have aided in bringing down the character of the performances to a level suited to those who are their chief support. At the same time, it is from no want of public encouragement that our drama has declined. Never was more money spent upon theatres than now. There are in London some seven-and-twenty of them, all more or less flourishing; and the crowds, on all occasions where a sufficient attraction is presented, demonstrate very clearly that the blame lies with the managers and actors themselves, more than with the public, if theatres have degenerated so far that people of intelligence and culture can no longer count upon them as the means of a delightful and instructive recreation, but are in fact driven away from them by the wretched style of entertainment, and the incompetence and careless conceit of the performers.

Let any one, for example, who has undergone the penance — and it is no slight one — of going to see the burlesques, which, either alone or as introduction to pantomimes, are now filling the West-end theatres, ask himself if they are exhibitions which he can with propriety take any woman or child to witness. The sickening vulgarity of the jokes, the slang allusions, the use of words and phrases unknown in the vocabulary of ladies and gentlemen, the ridicule of associations which are all but sacred, the outrageous caricatures of grave passions, the exhibition of crowds of girls in costumes only suitable for the *poses plastiques* of Leicester Square, above all, the way in which young actresses are made to say and do things which must destroy every shred of modesty and feminine grace in them, make these burlesques pernicious alike to performers and audience. When, too, as we generally find, they are based upon some drama or poem that is hallowed by every association with which genius and art can invest it, the contempt and disgust which they provoke in all educated men inevitably recoil upon the theatre where they are presented. How should it be otherwise? If the stage has a purpose at all, it is to elevate, not to debase; to lift the real towards the ideal, not to drag down the ideal into the very mire of a sordid reality. It is meant to educate, not to pervert; and if the character of the audience declines where such fare is presented, who can be surprised? . . .

Among the influences from which the drama has suffered of late years, none, we believe, have operated so strongly as the resort to splendour of spectacle as the great source of attraction. The question, how far scenic illustration and care in costume may be carried, is one of vital consequence to the drama, and to which, in these times, so little reflection is given that in dealing with it we are forced to call attention to the merest truisms in criticism, and to ask our readers to consider for a moment what the drama really is.

The higher drama, then, is poetry in action; the lower drama is a delineation of life in its every-day aspects, under certain conditions of emotion or excitement, which raise it above the level of commonplace. In both cases what we have to deal with are human beings, in their various moods and humours, — human sufferings, sorrows, perplexities, joys, or eccentricities. Men and women are the primary objects of interest. So true is it that landscapes, architecture, furniture, and dresses are the mere adjuncts, that the finest dramas in the world, those of Shakespeare, were produced for a stage where the scenic appointments were of the most meagre kind. To make these picturesque and to keep them from offending by incongruity or unsightliness, is the first consideration. If they can also be made beautiful, without obtruding too much on the attention, then, it seems to us, every object is gained. The moment they go beyond this point, the moment we are made to think more of the scenery, dresses, groupings, and processions, than of the actors and the development of the human interest, the fundamental law of the drama is violated and the play degenerates into the spectacle.

7.5   The present state of photography

From The National Review, *Vol. 8, April 1859. In the face of the new craze for photography the writer, Herbert Story-Maskelyne, is minimising this threat of technology to traditional art.*

It is no rare phrase that characterises the exciting age on which our lives are thrown as the age of the electric telegraph and of photography. These two of its most startling productions are naturally selected by the popular mind as representing in an emphatic and characteristic manner the rapid growth of a stupendous offspring from a seed of human knowledge so small that our fathers remember the day when it was hardly visible . . .

On the relations of photography to art there is room for much discussion, and probably also for controversy. Photography has driven into the limbo of the unemployed a class of miniature-portrait painters, and they, like the ostlers and innkeepers of the old 'roads', who occasionally revenged themselves upon the railways by becoming *employés* upon them, have in many instances joined the motley ranks of photography itself. But that the true artist will not throw down his brush and retreat before the advance of photography into his domain, is evident enough. The utter powerlessness of the chemical pencil of the sun to give the true relations of intensity of colour, the absence from the photograph of that ideal element which is the soul of art, leaves the relation of the photograph to the picture at best only as that of a useful auxiliary to a great result. Even were it possible for the photographist to surmount the former of these difficulties and to depict not only in correct relative intensity of light and shade but even in actual colour the truth of nature, of which at present there is not the faintest hope, must not the photograph still stand towards the artist's great work as the truest prose description to the imagery of the poem?

The artist need not fear the encroachment of the photographist. He may take the results of the camera, — he has already done so, — and by careful scrutiny of nature thus depicted on a flat surface in such marvellous detail he may learn a new reverence for the patient elaboration of particulars which need not mar his whole, and he may thereby feel that if he never can attain he can yet approach that infinite delicacy of finish which marks the photograph, and that in

that approach he is being truer even to the poetry of art than if he
were to live in that scorn of detail and emulation of 'broad effect'
alone, which was born of the consciousness of the limit placed to
human action in the production of minutiae, but has never charac-
terised any really great school of art in any age. M. Le Gray may
startle by the instantaneous production of a sea piece, crisped with
laughing waves, fringed with the froth and foam of breakers, and
overhung with skies of magical reality. But these pictures only
startle — the artist feels all their want of true soft harmony, in fact
their want of truth; and the public express the same consciousness
of their false contrasts by asking if they are indeed moonlight
views, or if the heavy clouds are really thunder-clouds. M. Baldus
and the Bissons have it all their own way in their colossal views of
the new Louvre and the new Tuilleries, or of other vast buildings
in Paris and elsewhere. But what artist would select such huge
masses of masonry alone for the subjects of a picture? To convert
them into a picture, he must make them into the background of
some living scene, with humanity stamped upon it; or must throw
round them the garb of beauty — some tinted gauzy atmosphere
won from a setting sun, caught in those transient moments when
nature is, as it were, her own poet; or rather when the exuberance
of her beauties can overflow and deck in a foreign grace scenes not
else beautiful, and so make even such to appeal to the seat of poetic
and artistic sympathy, the human heart. De la Motte, and Fenton,
and Bedford, and a few others, may strive, and may now and then
succeed in catching some happy effect in their camera; but it is
where the camera is pointed to some expressly lovely scene at some
happy moment; and is it not also due in no small degree — in fact
entirely, in so far as such a result is not accidental — to the artistic
feeling in the mind of the photographist himself, who knows how
to choose and when to take his view? But in fragments of foreground, in those small bits of detail in which the artist has to
subordinate his genius to mechanical and patient labour, the
photographist is his best colleague; and it is in the careful study of
such photographs that he will feel that art has nothing to fear, but
much to learn, from her mechanical associate, photography.

The invention of the stereoscope has given a remarkable
stimulus to photography. Without photography the stereoscope
would have been but a curious apparatus confined to the lecture-
room or the drawer of philosophic toys; with photography it has
become an article of furniture in every household.

The two images, separately seen by the two eyes, but united into

one in the region where optical phenomena pass into the percep-
tions of the sense, must needs be different. The stereoscope represents such two images, and by an ingenious contrivance brings
each before that eye that might have seen it in nature. . . . It is
where the angle is correctly taken, and the stereoscopic influence
confined to a foreground and to near objects, that the spell of a
solid reality investing the objects looked at is complete; and this
pretty philosophic toy becomes the instrument of a beautiful
illusion, and possesses a charm of that rare kind that may truly be
called a new one.

7.6   A sportsman's apology

From Macmillan's Magazine, *Vol. 21, February 1870. The writer,
T. H. Ward (better known as the husband of the novelist, Mrs Humphry
Ward) outlines a familiar argument against fox-hunting.*

In the October number of the *Fortnightly Review* Mr. Freeman[1] the
historian, in an article of great length, great learning, and great
ability, attacked the morality of field sports. In December Mr.
Trollope replied; then Miss Helen Taylor[2] came to Mr.
Freeman's rescue with an exceedingly neat rejoinder. And all this
time the daily and weekly papers had letter after letter, article after
article, on the subject — the balance of argument, of eloquence, of
repartee being (it must be owned) in favour of the assailants.
Meanwhile a letter from Leicestershire says: 'We turn out thirty
"pinks" every morning. *Melton was never so full.*'
  Our object is not to plunge into a controversy which is already
too bulky — not to do more than merely glance at the points which
Mr. Freeman raises, and to which Melton has given its practical
answer. There is another question that occurs to impartial people;
a question that perhaps logically ought to take precedence of this
probing the morality of sport — a 'previous' question as to its
nature. Mr. Freeman brought up a train of siege-guns, a little
elephantine in their carriage perhaps, but very effective, and
demolished everything, from the amphitheatre to the hunting-
stable; Mr. Trollope, as fond of fox-hunting as of literature, and
nettled by the charge that intelligent fox-hunters are silent because

they know their pet pleasure to be indefensible, sent back a talkative and rather feminine answer; Miss Taylor, on the other hand, was quite masculine in the logic of her reply. That is to say, she showed a trained reasoner's aptitude for the use of logical weapons, fixing on at least a brace of fallacies, and then pinning her opponent with a dilemma.

'Fox-hunting is natural,' says Mr. Trollope; 'trout hunt minnows, cats hunt mice; it is refined, gentlemanly, moral, because English gentlemen practise it.' We imagine that intelligent fox-hunters will wish their advocate had acquiesced in Mr. Freeman's fling at his kindred and at least kept silence from such puerilities as these — puerilities which hardly required so serious an exposure as Miss Taylor's. Her dilemma is clever, but scarcely conclusive. 'Either the same pleasure — of air, exercise, scenery, &c. — which is apt from fox-hunting can be got in other forms of out-door amusement, or else the real pleasure lies in the excitement of the chase. In other words, fox-hunting either inflicts unnecessary pain on an animal, *or* else the pleasure actually consists in the con-templation, conscious or semi-conscious, of pain, whether the pain of terror, or the pain of death.' The last alternative we need hardly consider; nor need we, with Lord Winchelsea, appeal to the fox himself, and ask him whether he does not prefer his present life, with its brilliant episodes and really heroical dangers, to the fate that would be his if fox-hunting were abolished — proscription as the sneaking foe to hen-roost and game-preserves? The real defence of field-sports lies in the rebutting the other horn of Miss Taylor's dilemma. First, the pain is not unnecessary, because without the fox, without his endless shifts of animal cunning, the ever-varying phases of the chase, phases whose highest attraction lies in their variety, would not be there in anything like the same degree. Secondly, as a clever champion has said, the infliction of the pain is justifiable, because it is inseparable from an exercise which con-tributes to human health; as justifiable, for instance, as the infliction of death upon a sheep or a turkey — pain that is inseparable from another exercise that contributes to human health. We do not see an escape from Mr. Cracroft's argument, that a man who thinks it right to *enjoy* roast turkey — an act which necessarily implies pain and death on the turkey's part — cannot logically think it wrong to enjoy fox-hunting. To those who answer that life requires food, and does not require fox-hunting, we can only answer that it is not proved that life require *animal* food, and that it *does* require the digestion to be in good order.

Here we may leave the question of the morality of sport to be fought out by those whom it concerns. The world cannot help being edified almost as much as it is amused. Only, in the interest of humanity and the horses, we may express our joy that things are as they are with the two principal combatants — that Mr. Freeman is not a fox-hunter, and that Mr. Trollope is. If literary style is any index to character, how Mr. Freeman would have ridden if he had chanced to take to horsemanship in his youth! How he would have crashed through hedges, dashed through ditches, and wielded his hunting-whip as heavily as he now wields his pen! Mr. Trollope, on the other hand, must let his blows fall upon his own top-boots, or, at best, upon the flap of the saddle.

Possibly, as is so often the case with English institutions, the fact that sport is beginning to be seriously discussed is the signal for its fall. Possibly in a few score years it may have become a problem for moral archaeologists, and 'tally-ho' may only live in the pages of some historian of old enthusiasms. But as yet there is time to look at field-sports in themselves — to touch upon that previous question of which we spoke, their nature; saying no more about their morality, nor dwelling only, or even mainly, upon that branch of sport which has till now been the chief object of attack. None of these writers have yet asked what sport is, what are its elements, how the existence of sport and sportsmen is accounted for. None of them have cared to suggest in any detail what it is that fills 'refined gentlemen', as Mr. Trollope calls them, 'gentlemen otherwise refined', as Mr. Freeman would prefer, with an eagerness that grows as September approaches, or as the 'southerly winds' of autumn proclaim the hunting season. None of them has endeavoured to find a reason why civilized men in the nineteenth century should be well satisfied to spend day after day in the laborious pursuit of animals, of which some are useless, some only useful because they add something to the dinner-table. The fact of course is that in this case, as in a hundred others, civilization has refined a necessity into a luxury, a mode of life into a mode of enjoyment.

Notes

1. Mr. Freeman: E. A. Freeman (1823–92), Professor of Modern History at Oxford.
2. Miss Helen Taylor: Stepdaughter of J. S. Mill.

Further Reading

General

Houghton, W. E., *The Victorian Frame of Mind, 1830–1870* (Yale University Press, Newhaven, 1957).

Best, G., *Mid-Victorian Britain, 1815–1875* (Weidenfeld and Nicholson, London, 1971).

Davidoff, L. and Hall, C., *Family Fortunes. Men and Women of the English Middle Class, 1750–1850* (Hutchinson, London, 1987).

Politics and Administration

Hamer, D. A., *The Politics of Electoral Pressure: A Study of the History of Victorian Reform Agitations* (Harvester, Brighton, 1977).

Hyam, R., *Britain's Imperial Century, 1815–1914: A Study of Empire and Expansion* (Batsford, London, 1976).

Callini, S., Winch, D., Burrow, J., *That Noble Science of Politics: A Study in Nineteenth Century Intellectual History* (Cambridge University Press, Cambridge, 1983).

MacDonagh, O., *Early Victorian Government, 1830–1870* (Weidenfeld and Nicholson, London, 1977).

The Gentleman

Franklin, J., *The Gentleman's Country House and Its Plan, 1835–1914* (Routledge and Kegan Paul, London, 1981).

Girouard, M., *The Return to Camelot, Chivalry and the English Gentleman* (Yale, New Haven, 1981).

Mason, P., *The English Gentleman: The Rise and Fall of an Ideal* (Deutsch, London, 1982).

Smith, D., *Conflict and Compromise: Class Formation in English Society, 1830–1914* (Routledge, London, 1982).

The Religious Debate

Bebbington, D. A., *The Nonconformist Conscience: Chapel and Politics, 1870–1914* (Allen and Unwin, London, 1982).

Chadwick, O., *The Victorian Church*, 2 Vols. (A. and C. Black, London, 1966, 1970).

Gillespie, C. G., *Genesis and Geology* (Harvard University Press, 1951).

Ospovat, D. *The Development of Darwin's Theory: Natural History, Natural Theology and Natural Selection, 1838–1859* (Cambridge University Press, Cambridge, 1981).

Symondson, A. (ed.), *The Victorian Crisis of Faith* (S.P.C.K., London, 1970).

The Scientific Approach

Basalla, G., Coleman, W., Kargon, R. (eds.), *Victorian Science* (Anchor Books, Doubleday and Co., New York, 1970).

Cosslett, T., *The Scientific Movement and Victorian Literature* (Harvester, Brighton, 1982).

Cosslett, T. (ed.), *Science and Religion in the Nineteenth Century* (Cambridge University Press, Cambridge, 1984).

Heyck, T. W., *The Transformation of the Intellectual Life in Victorian England* (Croom Helm, London, 1982).

Guistino de, D., *Conquest of Mind: Phrenology and Victorian Social Thought* (1975).

Paradis, J. and Postlewaite, T. (eds.), *Victorian Science and Victorian Values: Literary Perspectives* (New York Academy of Sciences, New York, 1982).

Sutton, A. (ed.), *A Victorian World of Science* (Hilger, Bristol, 1986).

The 'Woman Question'

Foster, M., *Significant Sisters, the Grassroots of Active Feminism, 1839–1939* (Oxford University Press, Oxford, 1984).

Helsinger, E. and Sheets, R. (eds.), *The Woman Question: Society and Literature in Britain and America, 1837–1883*. Vol. 1 *Defining Voices*; Vol. 2 *Social Issues*; Vol. 3 *Literary Issues* (Garland, London, 1983).

Harrison, B., *Separate Spheres: The Opposition to Women's Suffrage in Britain* (Croom Helm, London, 1978).

Vicinus, M. (ed.), *Suffer and Be Still: Women in the Victorian Age* (Methuen, London, 1972).

Vicinus, M. (ed.), *A Widening Sphere: Changing Roles of Victorian Women* (Methuen, London, 1977).

Hollis, P., *Women in Public: The Women's Movement 1850–1900* (Allen and Unwin, London, 1979).

Education

Engel, A. J., *From Clergyman to Don: The Rise of The Academic Profession in Nineteenth Century England* (Clarendon Press, Oxford, 1983).

Kamm, J., *How Different from Us: Miss Buss and Miss Beale* (J. Lane, London, 1958).

Kamm, J., *Hope Deferred: Girls' Education in English History* (Methuen, London, 1965).

Rothblatt, S., *The Revolution of the Dons: Cambridge and Society in Victorian England* (Faber, London, 1968).

Honey, J., *Tom Brown's Universe: The Development of the Victorian Public School* (Millington, 1978).

Leisure and the Arts

Baker, M., *The Rise of the Victorian Actor* (Croom Helm, London, 1978).

Gernscheim, H., *Lewis Carroll, Photographer* (Max Parrish and Co., London, 1949).

Hunt, J. D., *The Pre-Raphaelite Imagination, 1848–1900* (Routledge and Kegan Paul, London, 1968).

Itzkowitz, D., *Peculiar Privilege: A Social History of English Foxhunting, 1853–1885* (Harvester, Brighton, 1977).

Sheridan, P., *Penny Theatres of Victorian London* (Dobson, Durham, 1981).

Walton, J. and Walvin, J. (eds.), *Leisure in Britain, 1780–1939* (Manchester University Press, Manchester, 1983).

Wigly, J., *The Rise and Fall of the Victorian Sunday* (Manchester University Press, Manchester, 1980).

Index

see also Cambridge, London,
  Manchester, Oxford, etc.
upper class 31 – 3, 41, 50 – 1
Utilitarianism 7, 11 – 15, 17 – 19,
  52, 108 – 18

Vernon, J. R. 3, 57 – 61
Victoria Printing Office 138
Victoria University 167
Vienna, Congress of 2, 49n

Wales 67, 190
Wales, Prince of 106
Walpole, Sir Robert 62
Ward, T. H. 18, 210 – 12
Wedgwood, Josiah 51
Wedgwood, Julia 152 – 5
Wellington, Duke of 24, 55 – 6,
  77, 172
West Africa 47 – 9
Westminster Review 14, 15,
  149 – 50
Whewell, William 91
whigs 34, 111

see also Liberal party
William III 174
Wilson, Richard 201
Wiseman, Nicholas 104
woman question 5, 14 – 17,
  131 – 64, 166
  education 16, 131 – 2, 152,
    155 – 8, 166 – 7, 176 – 8,
    185 – 8
  female suffrage 15, 131 – 2,
    136 – 8, 152 – 5
  married women's property 16,
    132, 134, 136, 148 – 51
  see also schools, professions
work, attitudes to 17, 195 – 200
working class 18, 30 – 3, 35,
  167 – 71, 195 – 200
  see also proletariat
Wren, Sir Christopher 68

Yarmouth 37
Yonge, Charlotte M. 15
  Monthly Packet 14 – 15
Young, G. M. 1